GUARDIANS OF THE GALAXY

COSMIC AVENGERS

WRITER: BRIAN MICHAEL BENDIS
ARTISTS: STEVE McNIVEN AND SARA PICHELLI
WITH MICHAEL AVON OEMING, MING DOYLE
& MICHAEL DEL MUNDO
INKERS: JOHN DELL, STEVE McNIVEN
& SARA PICHELLI

LETTERS: VIRTUAL CALLIGRAPHY'S CORY PETIT
& JOE CARAMAGNA
COLOURS: JUSTIN PONSOR, JAVIER RODRIGUEZ
& RAIN BEREDO

ASSISTANT EDITOR: ELLIE PYLE
EDITORS: STEPHEN WACKER & SANA AMANAT
EDITOR IN CHIEF: AXEL ALONSO
CHIEF CREATIVE OFFICER: JOE QUESADA

COVER: STEVE McNIVEN, JOHN DELL & JUSTIN PONSOR

marvel.com
© 2013 MARVEL

TM & © 2013 Marvel & Subs. Licensed by Marvel Characters B.V. through Panini S.p.A., Italy. All Rights Reserved. First printing 2013. Published by Panini Publishing, a division of Panini UK Limited. Mike Riddell, Managing Director. Alan O'Keefe, Managing Editor. Mark Irvine, Production Manager. Marco M. Lupoi, Publishing Director Europe. Brady Webb, Reprint Editor. Samuel Taylor, Junior Editor. Angela Gray, Designer. Office of publication: Brockbourne House, 77 Mount Ephraim, Tunbridge Wells, Kent TN4 8BS. This publication may not be sold, except by authorised dealers, and is sold subject to the condition that it shall not be sold or distributed with any part of its cover or markings removed, nor in a mutilated condition. Printed in Italy by SIZ. ISBN: 978-1-84653-542-0. Do you have any comments or queries about this graphic novel? Email us at graphicnovels@panini. co.uk. Join our Facebook group at Panini/Marvel Graphic Novels.

FSC
www.fsc.org
MIX
Paper from
responsible sources
FSC® C005613

MARVEL GRAPHIC NOVEL

GUARDIANS OF THE GALAXY #0.1

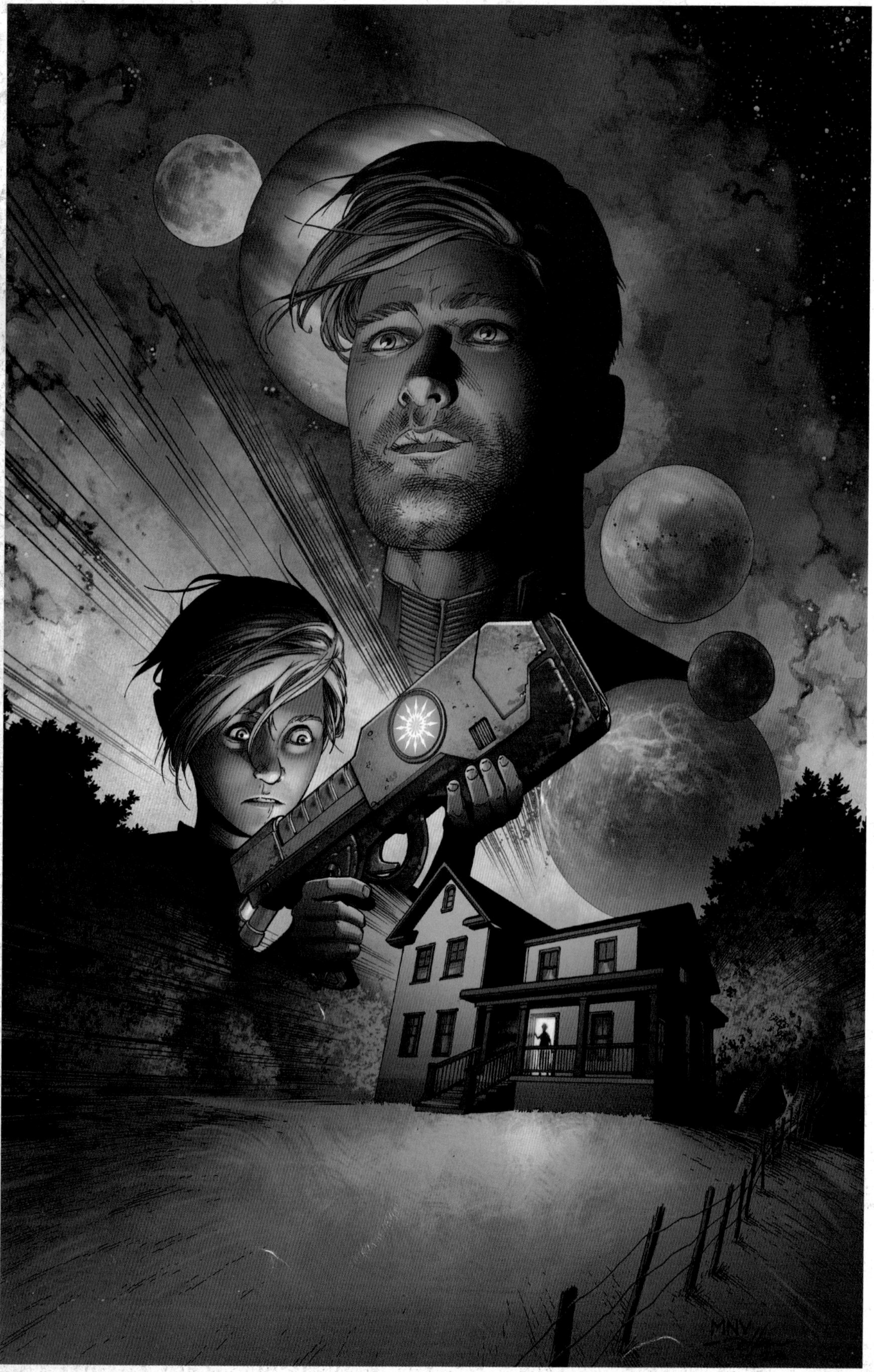

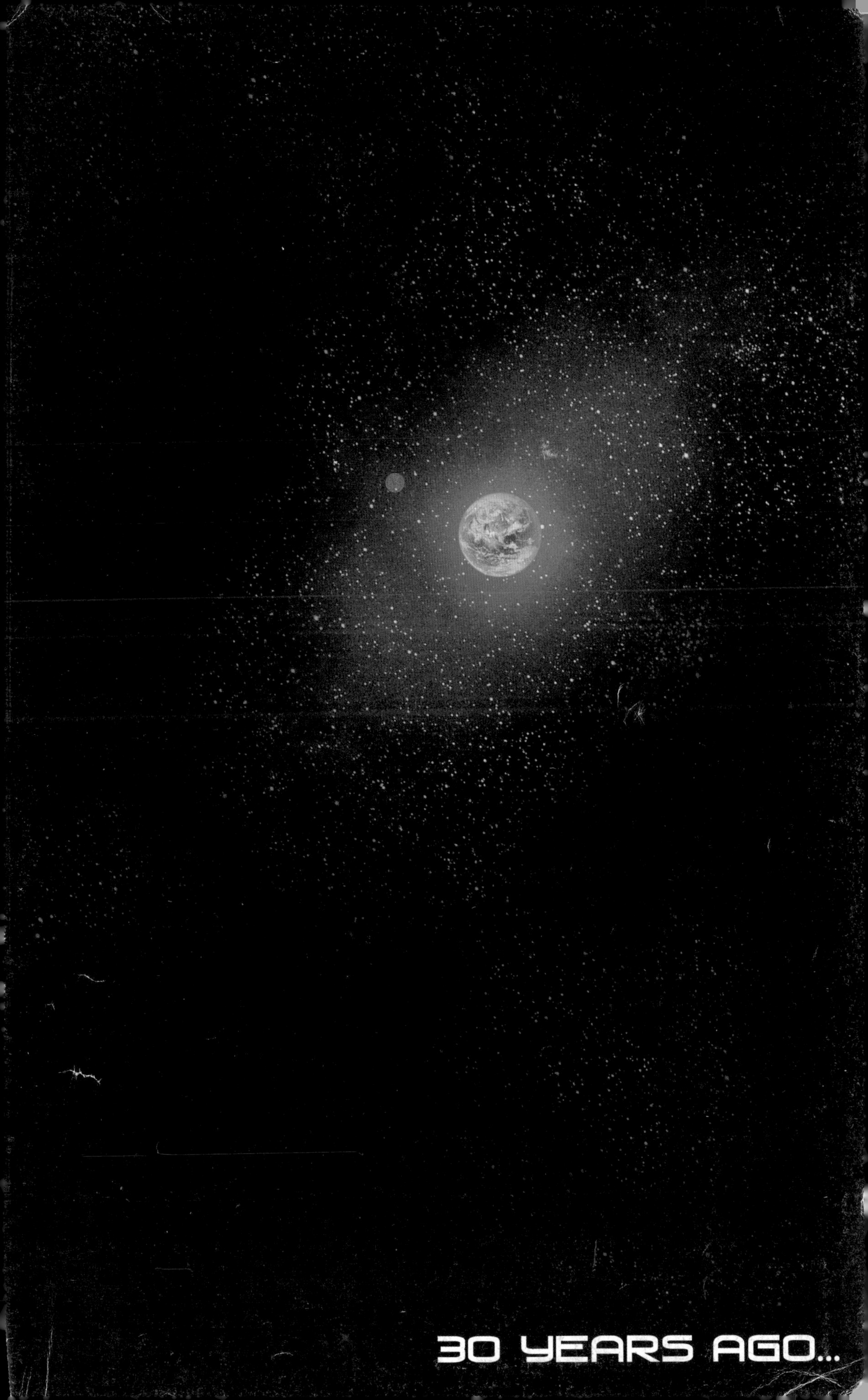
30 YEARS AGO...

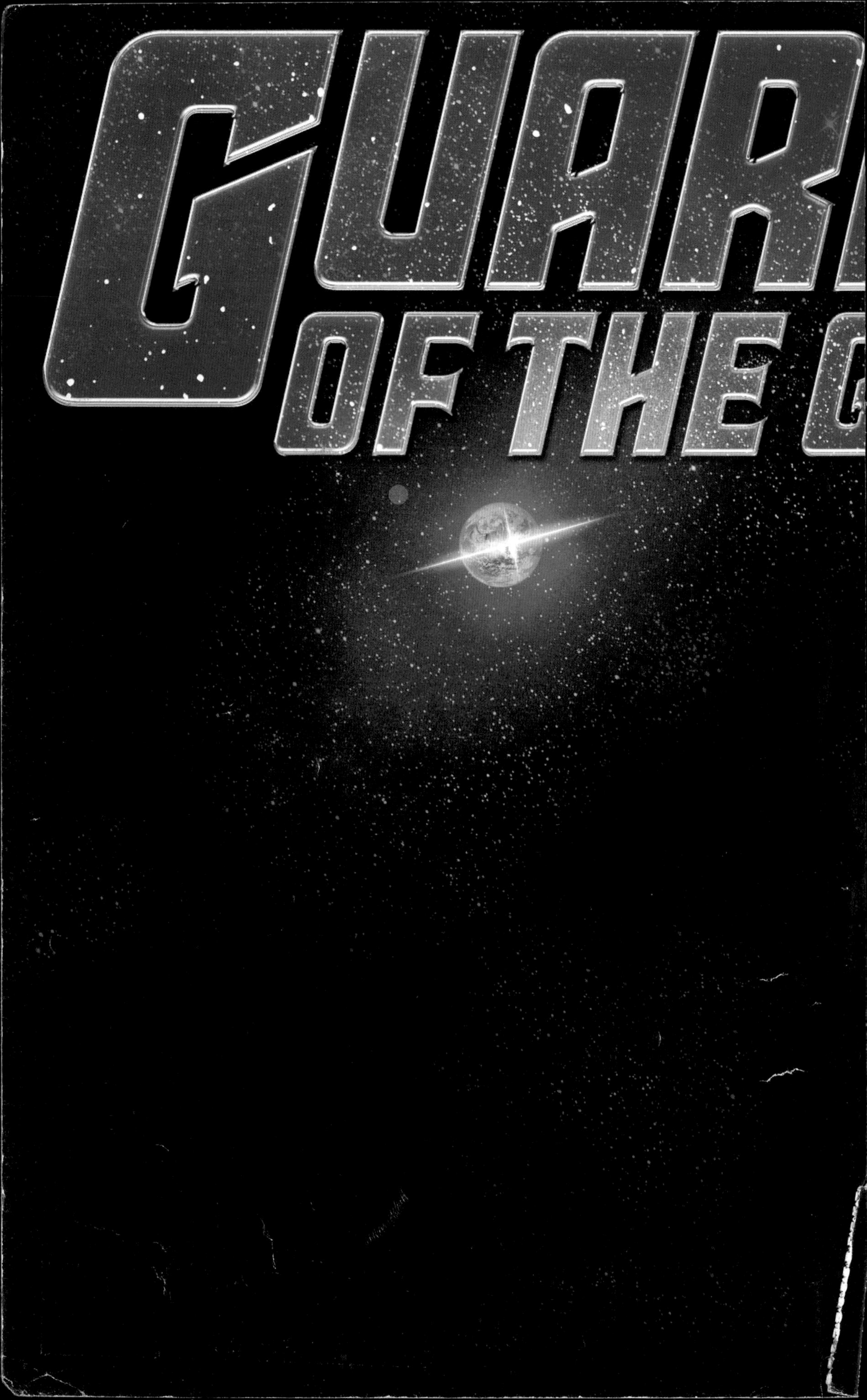
GUAR
OF THE G

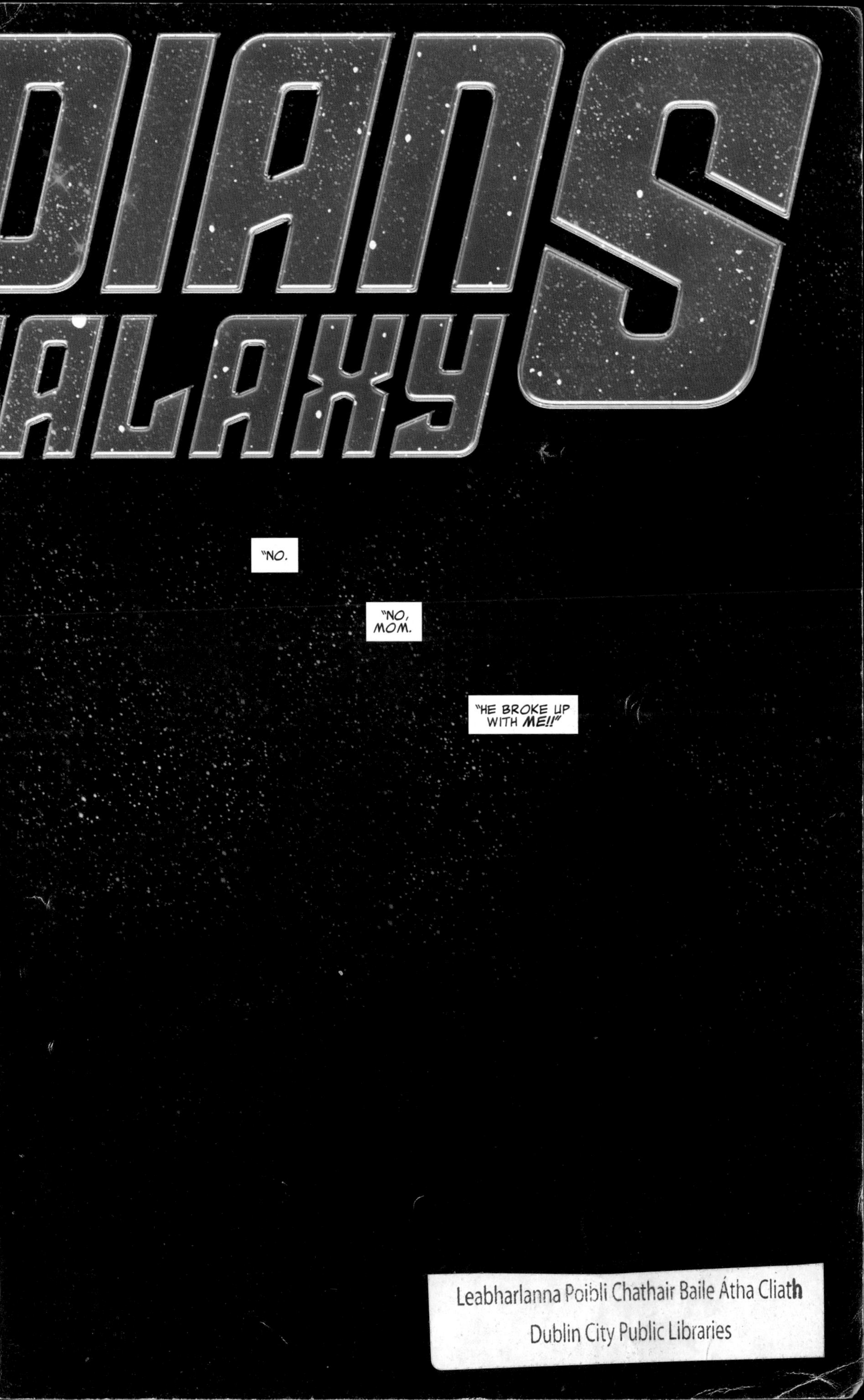
"NO.
"NO, MOM.
"HE BROKE UP WITH ME!!"

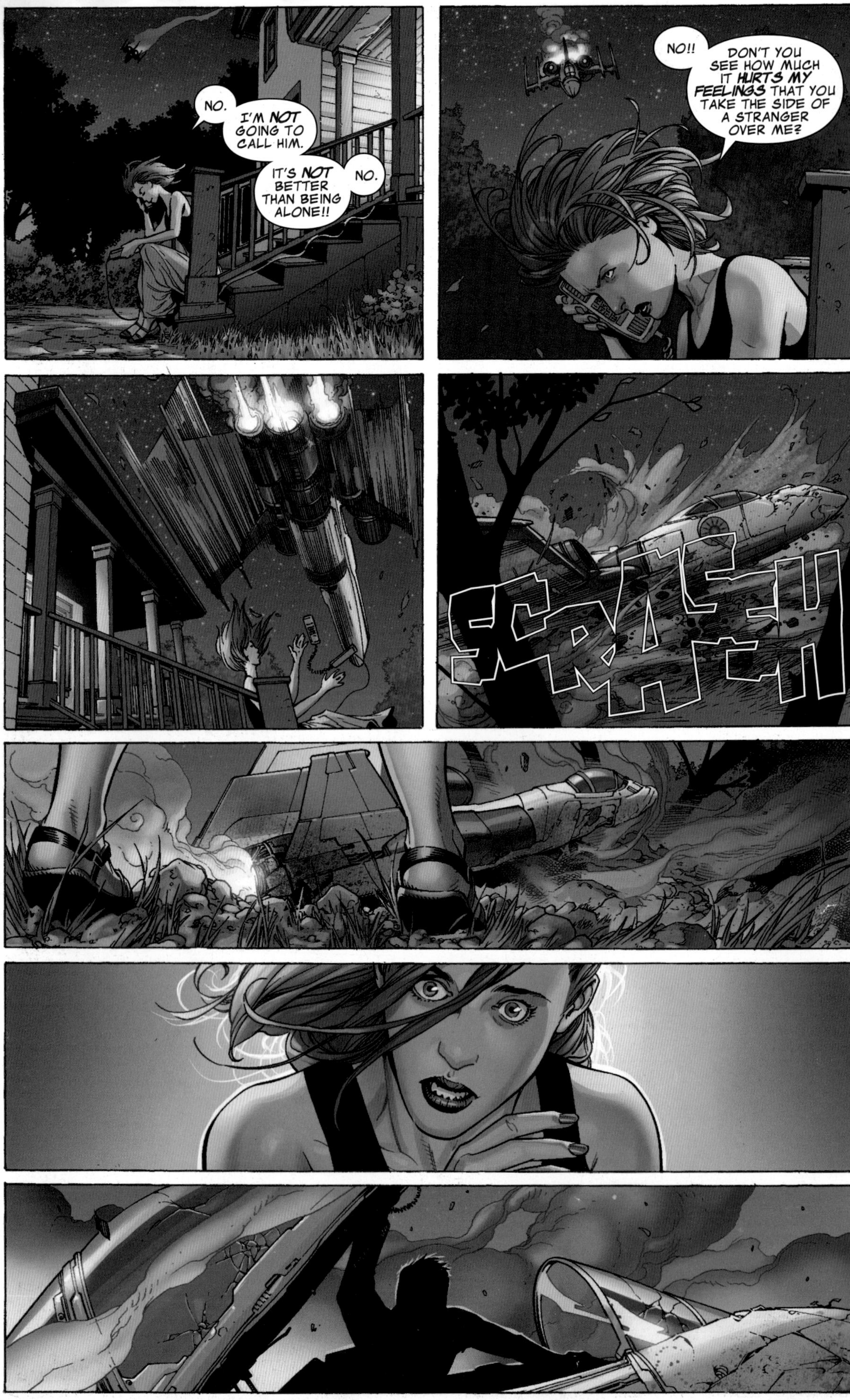
NO.
I'M NOT GOING TO CALL HIM.
IT'S NOT BETTER THAN BEING ALONE!!
NO.
NO!!
DON'T YOU SEE HOW MUCH IT HURTS MY FEELINGS THAT YOU TAKE THE SIDE OF A STRANGER OVER ME?

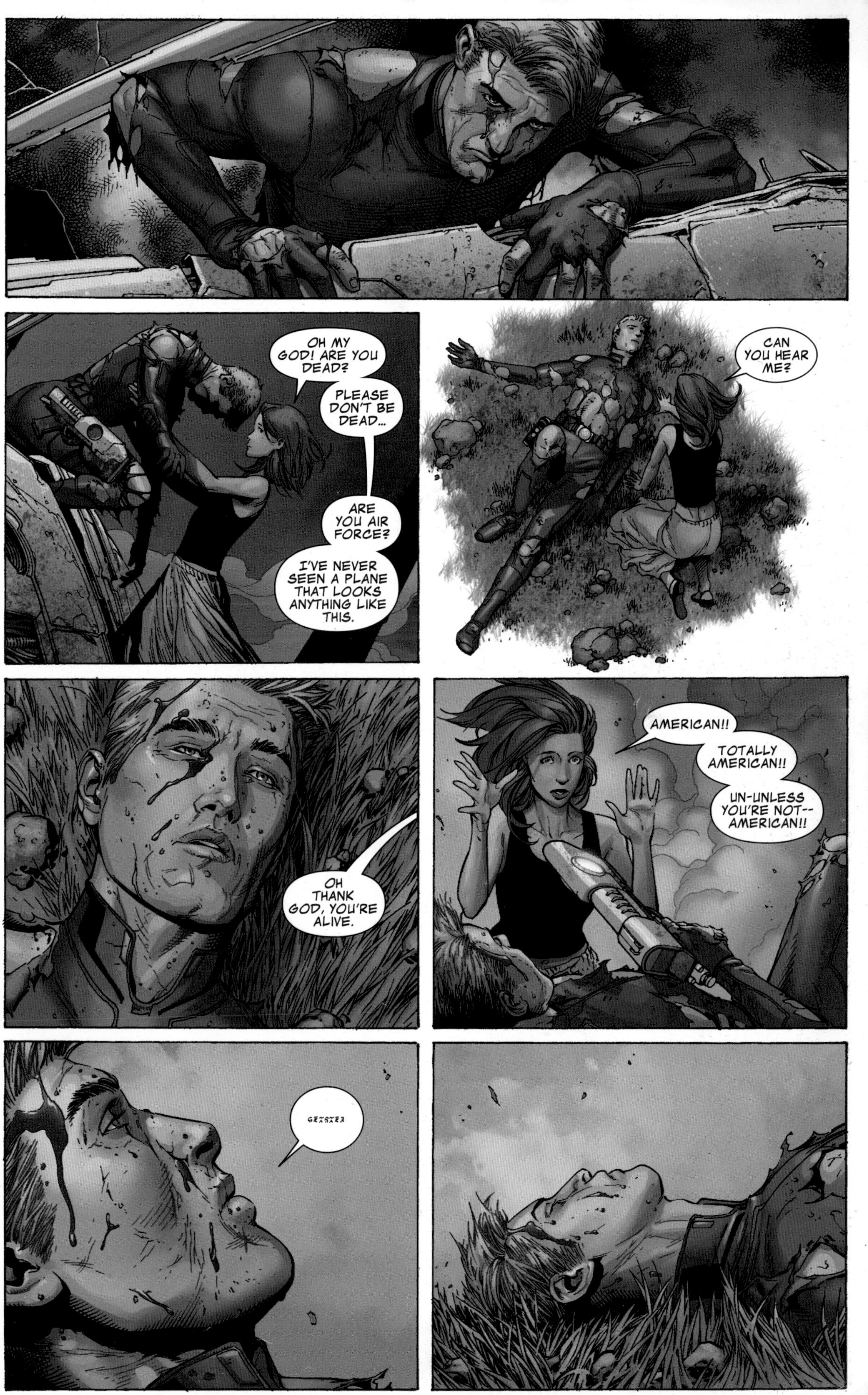
OH MY GOD! ARE YOU DEAD?
PLEASE DON'T BE DEAD...
ARE YOU AIR FORCE?
I'VE NEVER SEEN A PLANE THAT LOOKS ANYTHING LIKE THIS.
CAN YOU HEAR ME?
OH THANK GOD, YOU'RE ALIVE.
AMERICAN!!
TOTALLY AMERICAN!!
UN-UNLESS YOU'RE NOT--AMERICAN!!

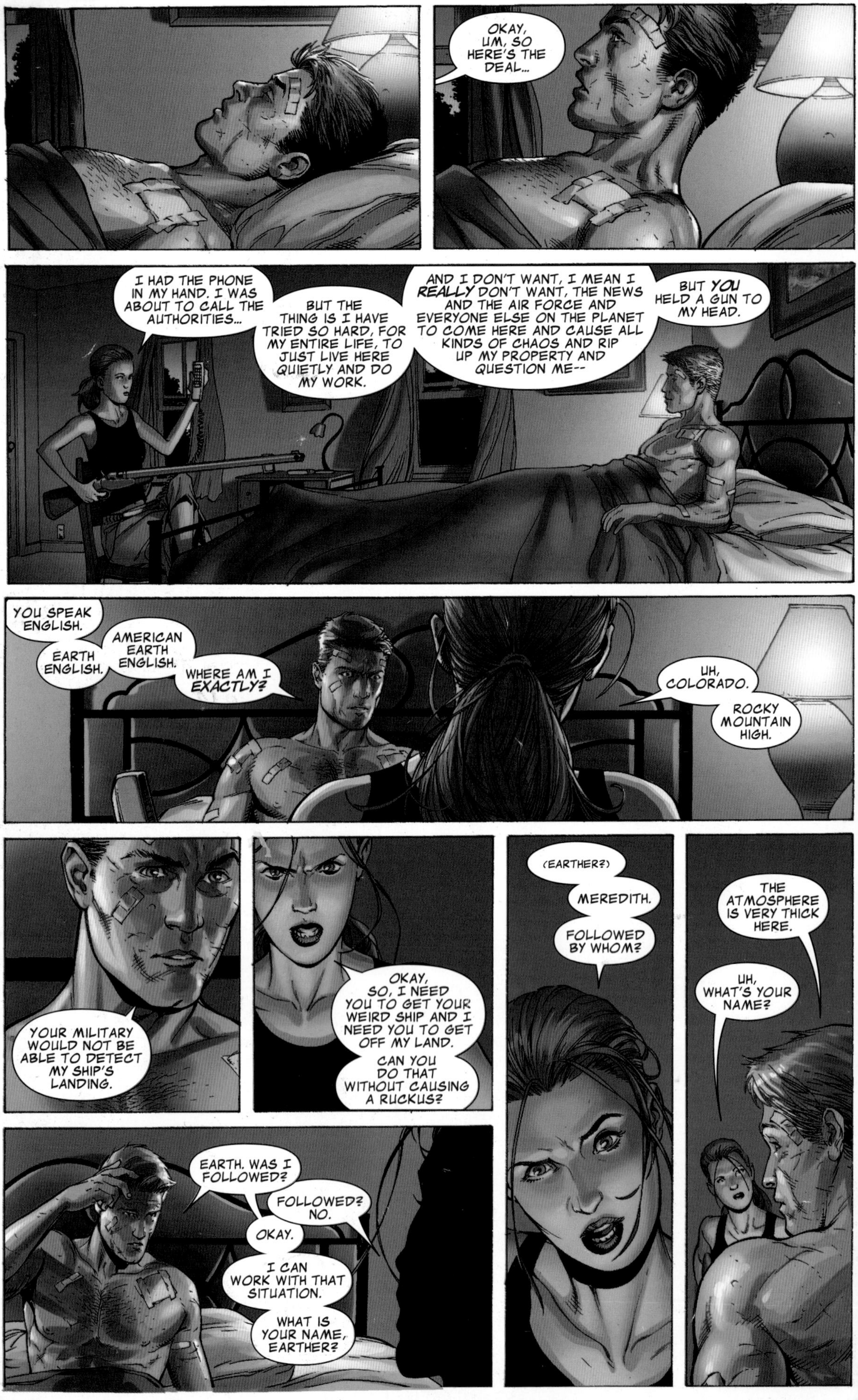
OKAY, UM, SO HERE'S THE DEAL...
I HAD THE PHONE IN MY HAND. I WAS ABOUT TO CALL THE AUTHORITIES...
BUT THE THING IS I HAVE TRIED SO HARD, FOR MY ENTIRE LIFE, TO JUST LIVE HERE QUIETLY AND DO MY WORK.
AND I DON'T WANT, I MEAN I REALLY DON'T WANT, THE NEWS AND THE AIR FORCE AND EVERYONE ELSE ON THE PLANET TO COME HERE AND CAUSE ALL KINDS OF CHAOS AND RIP UP MY PROPERTY AND QUESTION ME--
BUT YOU HELD A GUN TO MY HEAD.
YOU SPEAK ENGLISH.
EARTH ENGLISH.
AMERICAN EARTH ENGLISH.
WHERE AM I EXACTLY?
UH, COLORADO.
ROCKY MOUNTAIN HIGH.
YOUR MILITARY WOULD NOT BE ABLE TO DETECT MY SHIP'S LANDING.
OKAY, SO, I NEED YOU TO GET YOUR WEIRD SHIP AND I NEED YOU TO GET OFF MY LAND.
CAN YOU DO THAT WITHOUT CAUSING A RUCKUS?
EARTH. WAS I FOLLOWED?
FOLLOWED? NO.
OKAY.
I CAN WORK WITH THAT SITUATION.
WHAT IS YOUR NAME, EARTHER?
(EARTHER?)
MEREDITH.
FOLLOWED BY WHOM?
THE ATMOSPHERE IS VERY THICK HERE.
UH, WHAT'S YOUR NAME?

MY NAME IS J'SON OF SPARTAX.

YOUR KINDNESS IS APPRECIATED.

I HOPE I WILL BE ABLE TO RETURN IT.

ARE YOU A PILOT?

I'M FROM SPARTAX. I AM OF THE THRONE.

IS THAT-- WHAT IS THAT?

I WILL NEED TO FIX MY SHIP AND GET BACK TO MY PEOPLE. I WILL TRY TO DO SO AS QUICKLY AS I CAN.

OH MY GOD. ARE YOU KIDDING ME?

ARE YOU FROM--ARE YOU FROM SPACE?

I'M FROM SPARTAX.

I'VE TOLD YOU THIS A FEW TIMES.

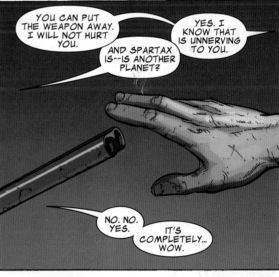

YOU CAN PUT THE WEAPON AWAY. I WILL NOT HURT YOU.

AND SPARTAX IS--IS ANOTHER PLANET?

YES. I KNOW THAT IS UNNERVING TO YOU.

NO. NO. YES.

IT'S COMPLETELY... WOW.

DO YOU-- DO YOU NEED A TOOLBOX OR--?

YOU'RE A FUNNY EARTHER.

NO. I HAVE THE TOOLS. BUT IT MAY TAKE SOME TIME.

EARTHER?

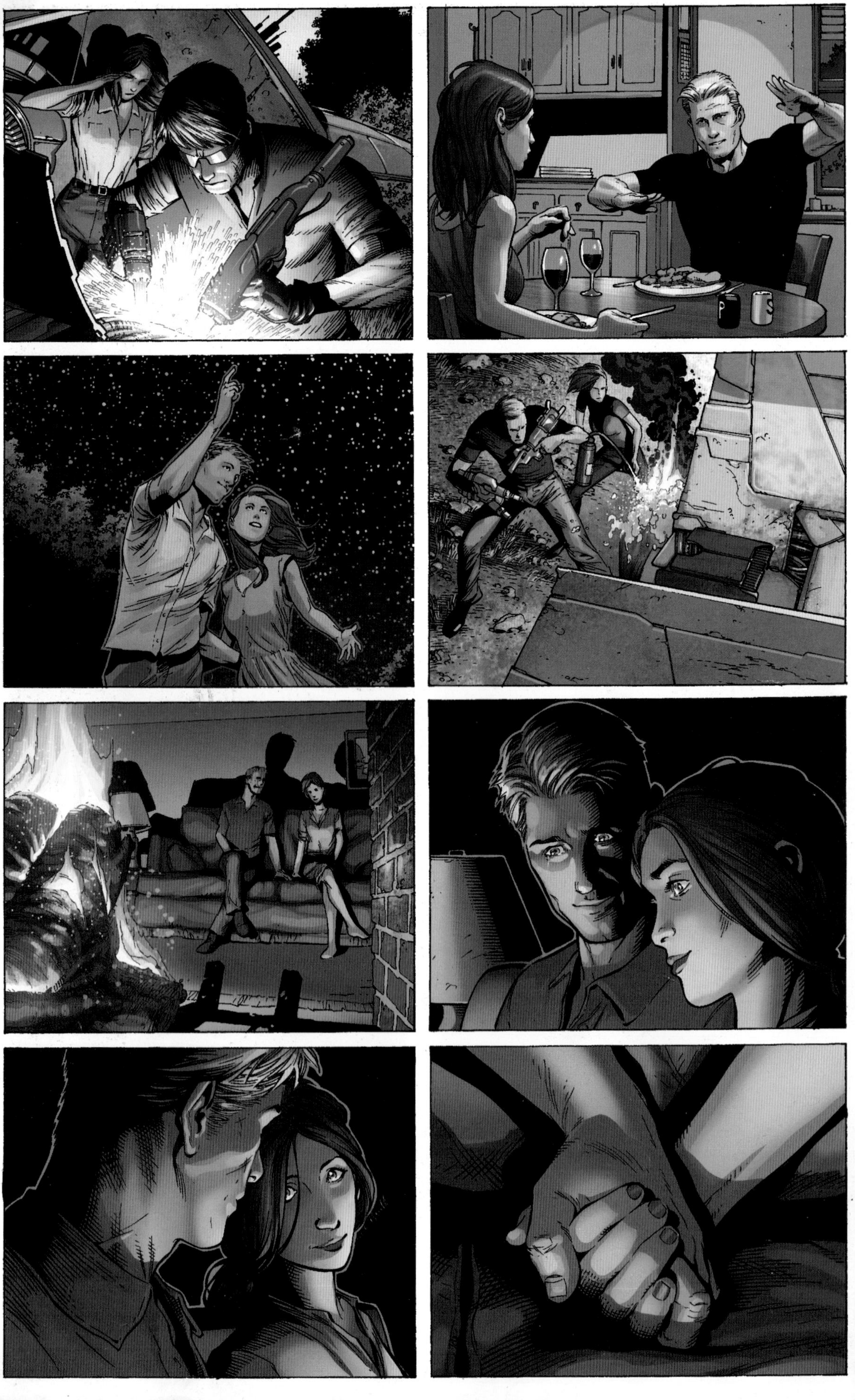
P
S

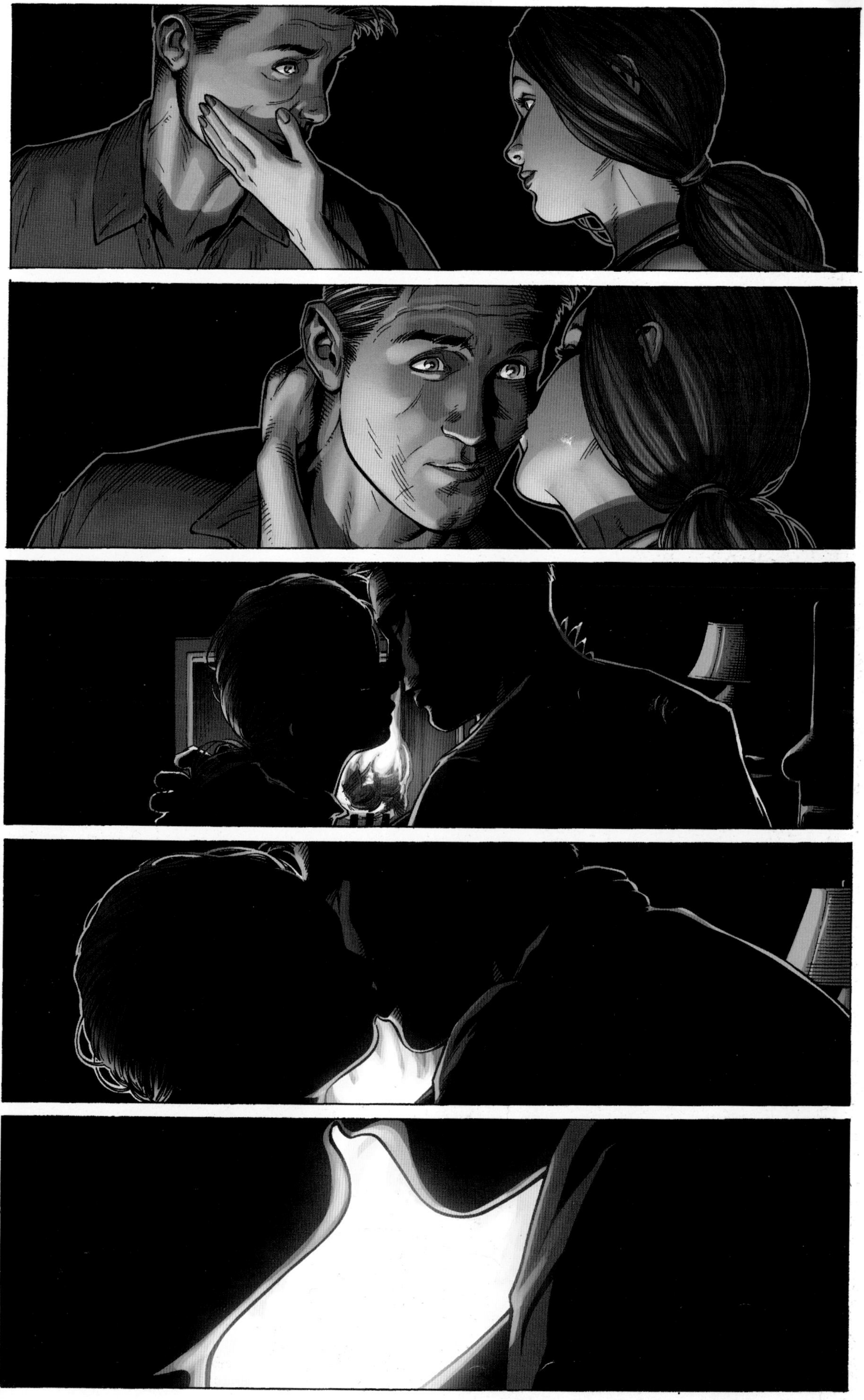

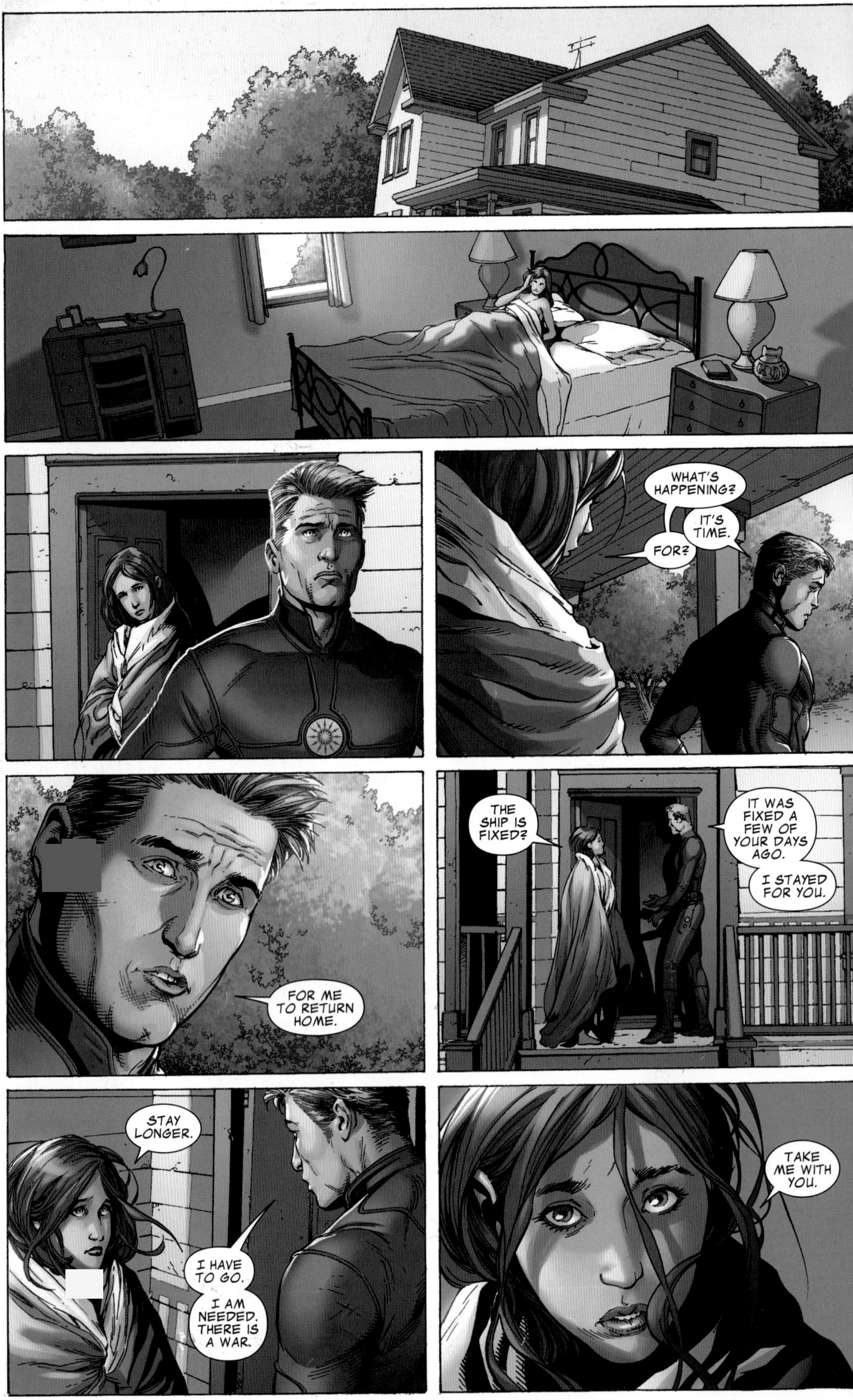
WHAT'S HAPPENING?
IT'S TIME.
FOR?
FOR ME TO RETURN HOME.
THE SHIP IS FIXED?
IT WAS FIXED A FEW OF YOUR DAYS AGO.
I STAYED FOR YOU.
STAY LONGER.
I HAVE TO GO.
I AM NEEDED. THERE IS A WAR.
TAKE ME WITH YOU.

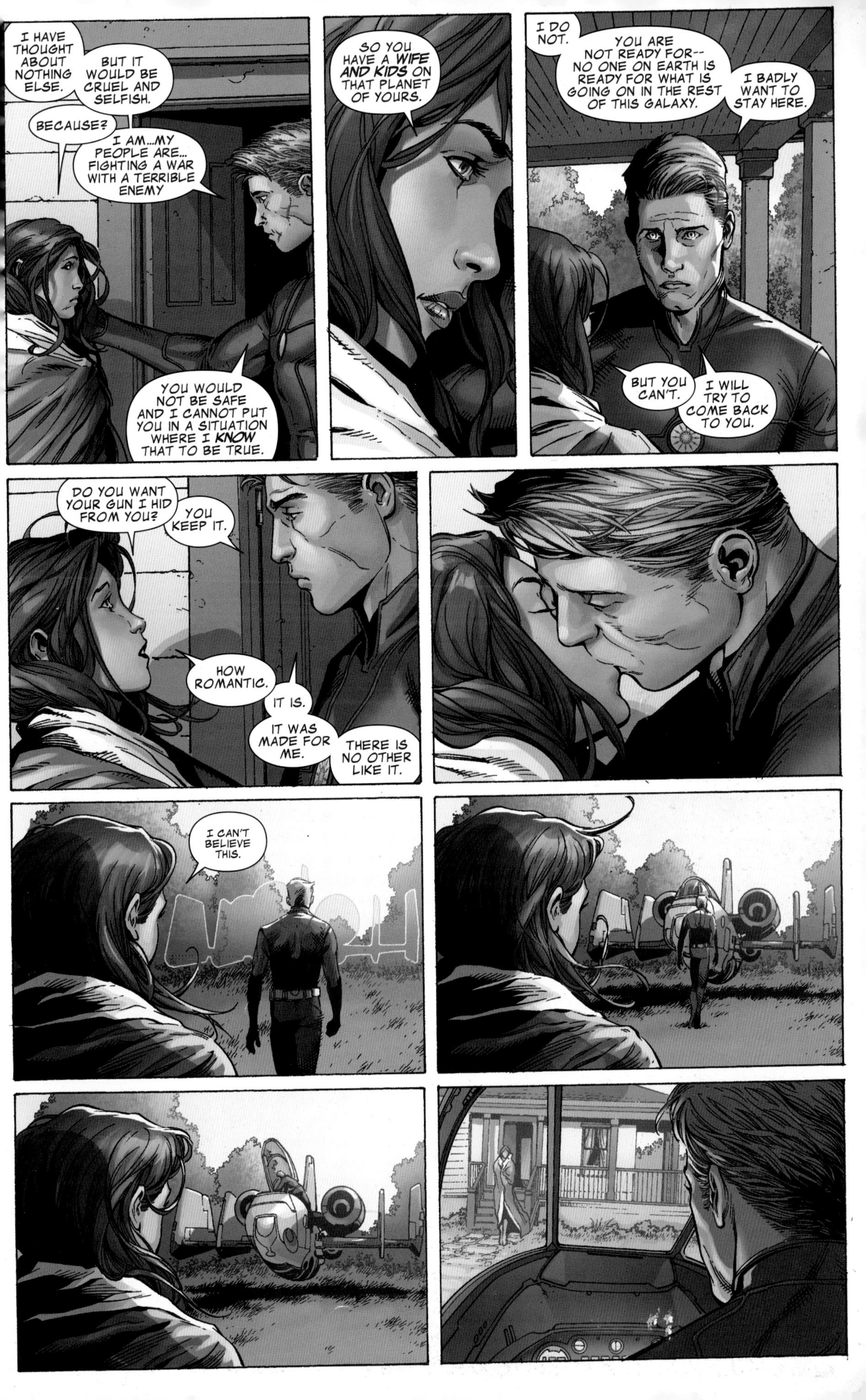
I HAVE THOUGHT ABOUT NOTHING ELSE.
BUT IT WOULD BE CRUEL AND SELFISH.
BECAUSE?
I AM...MY PEOPLE ARE... FIGHTING A WAR WITH A TERRIBLE ENEMY
YOU WOULD NOT BE SAFE AND I CANNOT PUT YOU IN A SITUATION WHERE I KNOW THAT TO BE TRUE.
SO YOU HAVE A WIFE AND KIDS ON THAT PLANET OF YOURS.
I DO NOT.
YOU ARE NOT READY FOR-- NO ONE ON EARTH IS READY FOR WHAT IS GOING ON IN THE REST OF THIS GALAXY.
I BADLY WANT TO STAY HERE.
BUT YOU CAN'T.
I WILL TRY TO COME BACK TO YOU.
DO YOU WANT YOUR GUN I HID FROM YOU?
YOU KEEP IT.
HOW ROMANTIC.
IT IS.
IT WAS MADE FOR ME.
THERE IS NO OTHER LIKE IT.
I CAN'T BELIEVE THIS.

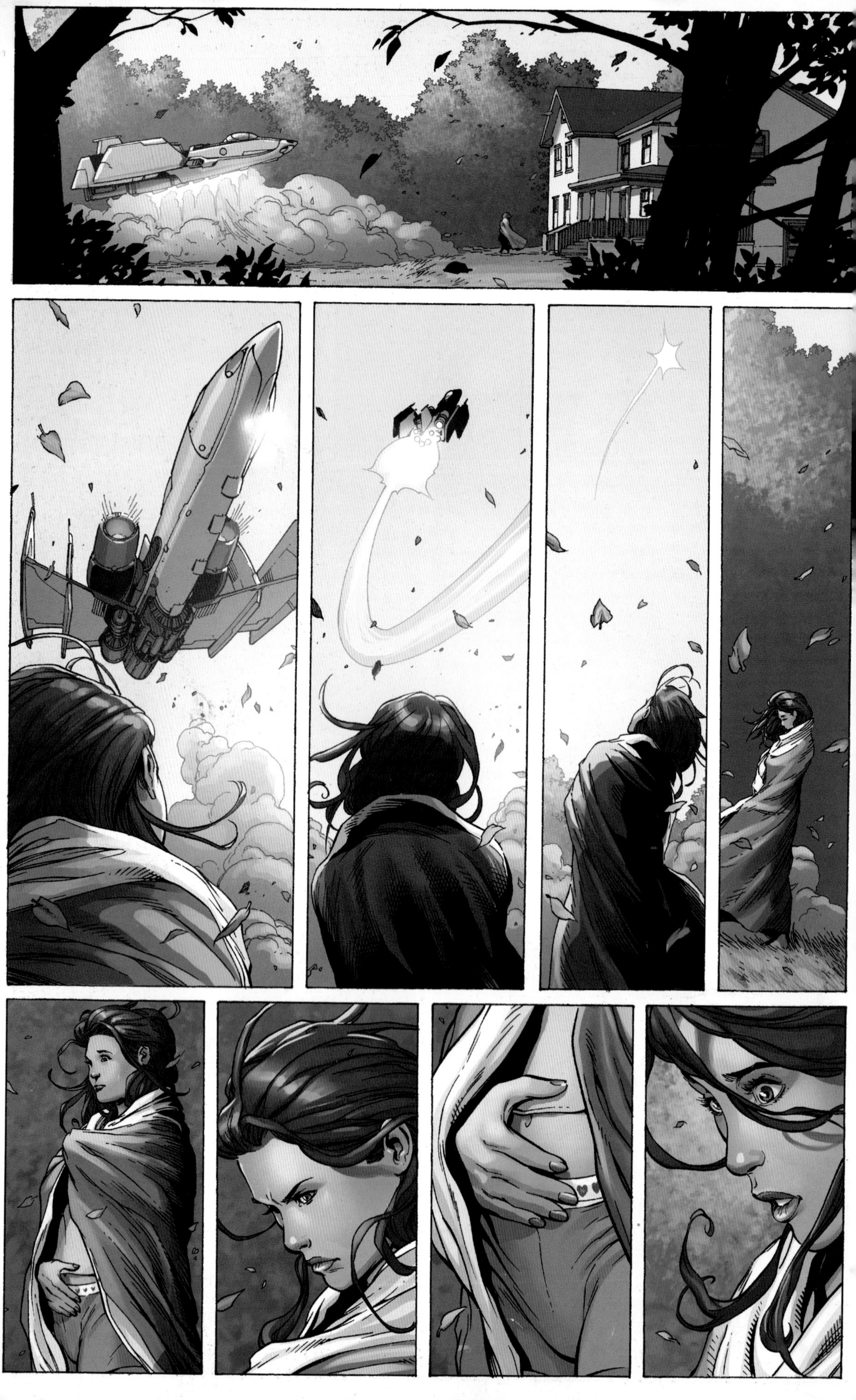

PETER QUILL!!

DID YOU DO YOUR MATH HOMEWORK?

I'M TAKIN' A BREAK.

WHAT DID I SAY ABOUT READING THAT CRAP?

IT'S NOT CRAP, MOM.

I'M READING.

THIS IS READING.

THAT IS NOT READING.

YOU SHOULD READ IT. IT'LL BLOW YOUR MIND OUT THROUGH THE TOP OF YOUR HEAD AND THEN IT'LL--

GO FINISH YOUR HOMEWORK.

UGH!!

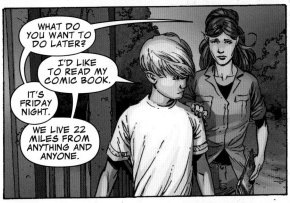

WHAT DO YOU WANT TO DO LATER?

I'D LIKE TO READ MY COMIC BOOK.

IT'S FRIDAY NIGHT.

WE LIVE 22 MILES FROM ANYTHING AND ANYONE.

WOW.

WHAT?

YOU LOOK JUST LIKE YOUR FATHER, ALL OF A SUDDEN.

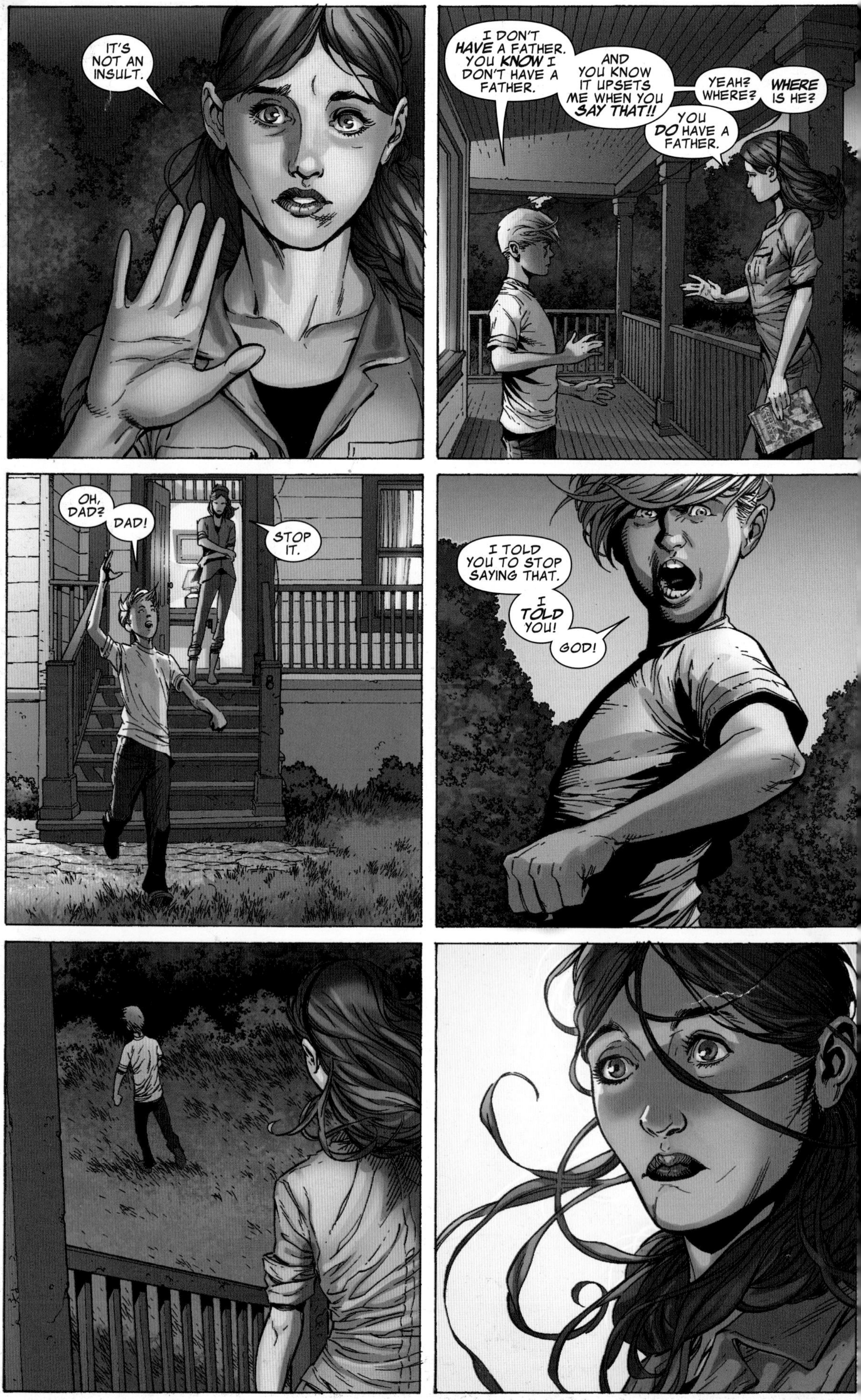
IT'S NOT AN INSULT.
I DON'T HAVE A FATHER. YOU KNOW I DON'T HAVE A FATHER.
AND YOU KNOW IT UPSETS ME WHEN YOU SAY THAT!!
YOU DO HAVE A FATHER.
YEAH? WHERE?
WHERE IS HE?
OH, DAD?
DAD!
STOP IT.
I TOLD YOU TO STOP SAYING THAT.
I TOLD YOU!
GOD!

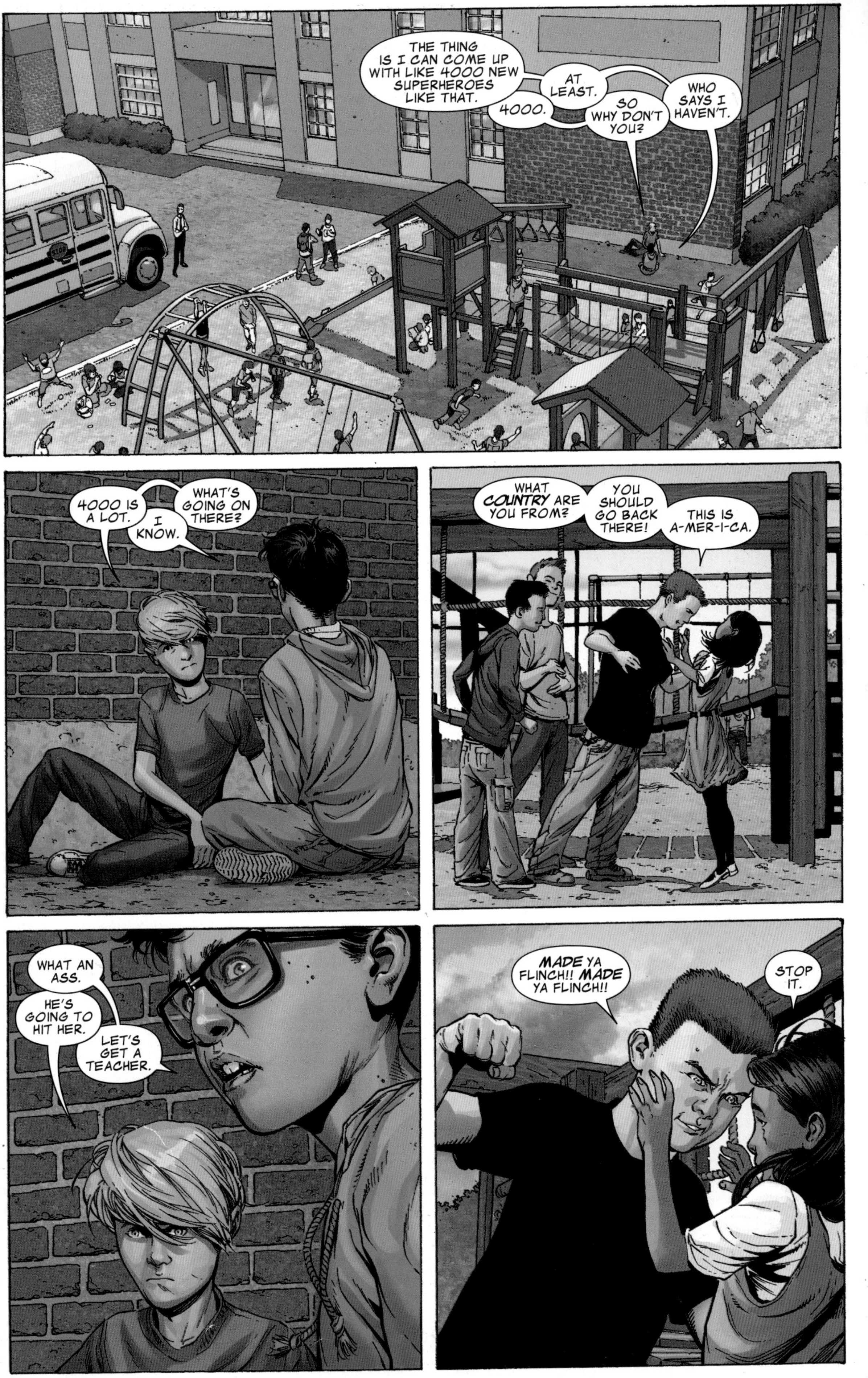
THE THING IS I CAN COME UP WITH LIKE 4000 NEW SUPERHEROES LIKE THAT.
4000.
AT LEAST.
SO WHY DON'T YOU?
WHO SAYS I HAVEN'T.
4000 IS A LOT.
I KNOW.
WHAT'S GOING ON THERE?
WHAT COUNTRY ARE YOU FROM?
YOU SHOULD GO BACK THERE!
THIS IS A-MER-I-CA.
WHAT AN ASS.
HE'S GOING TO HIT HER.
LET'S GET A TEACHER.
MADE YA FLINCH!! MADE YA FLINCH!!
STOP IT.

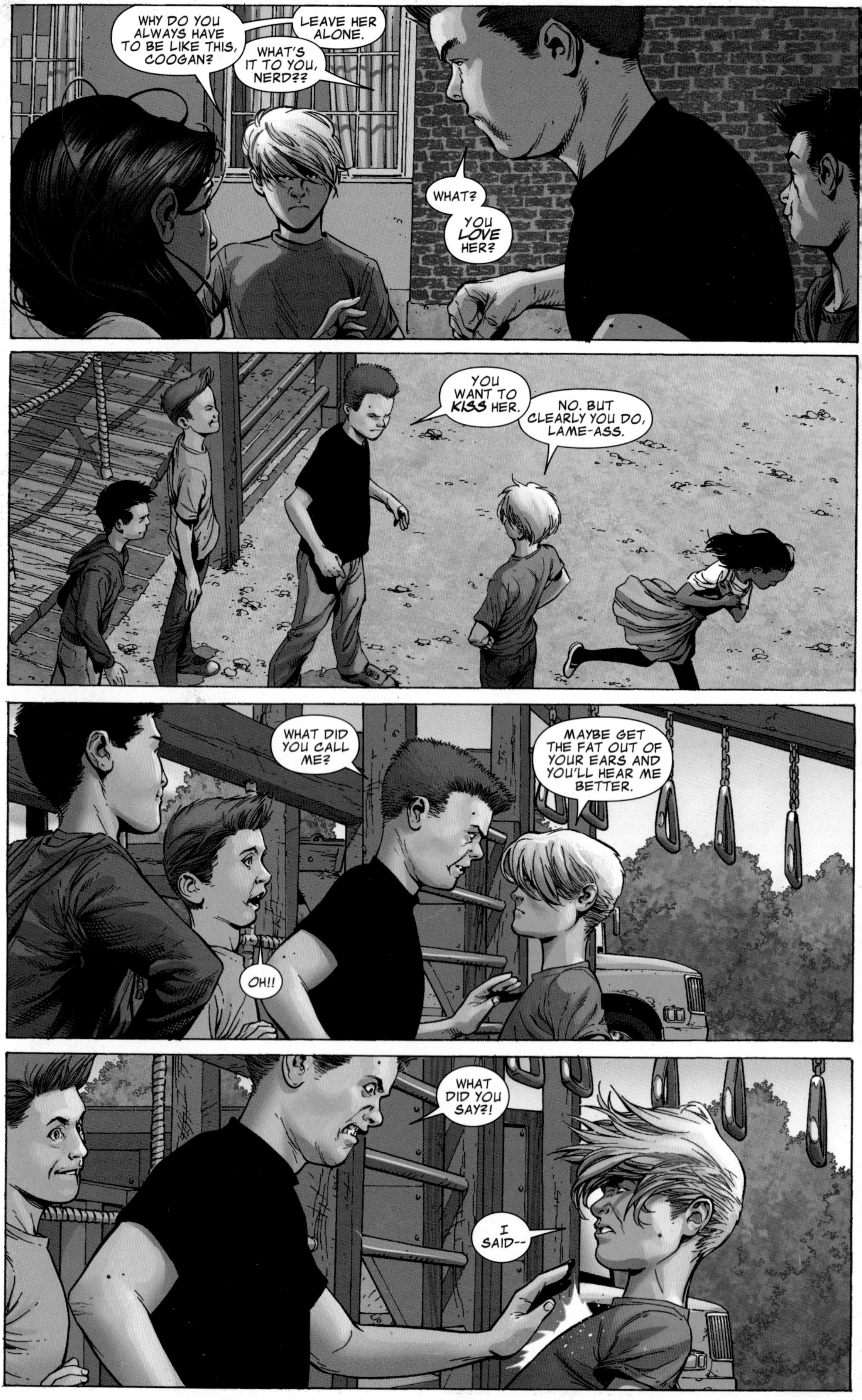
WHY DO YOU ALWAYS HAVE TO BE LIKE THIS, COOGAN?
LEAVE HER ALONE.
WHAT'S IT TO YOU, NERD??
WHAT?
YOU LOVE HER?
YOU WANT TO KISS HER.
NO. BUT CLEARLY YOU DO, LAME-ASS.
WHAT DID YOU CALL ME?
MAYBE GET THE FAT OUT OF YOUR EARS AND YOU'LL HEAR ME BETTER.
OH!!
WHAT DID YOU SAY?!
I SAID--

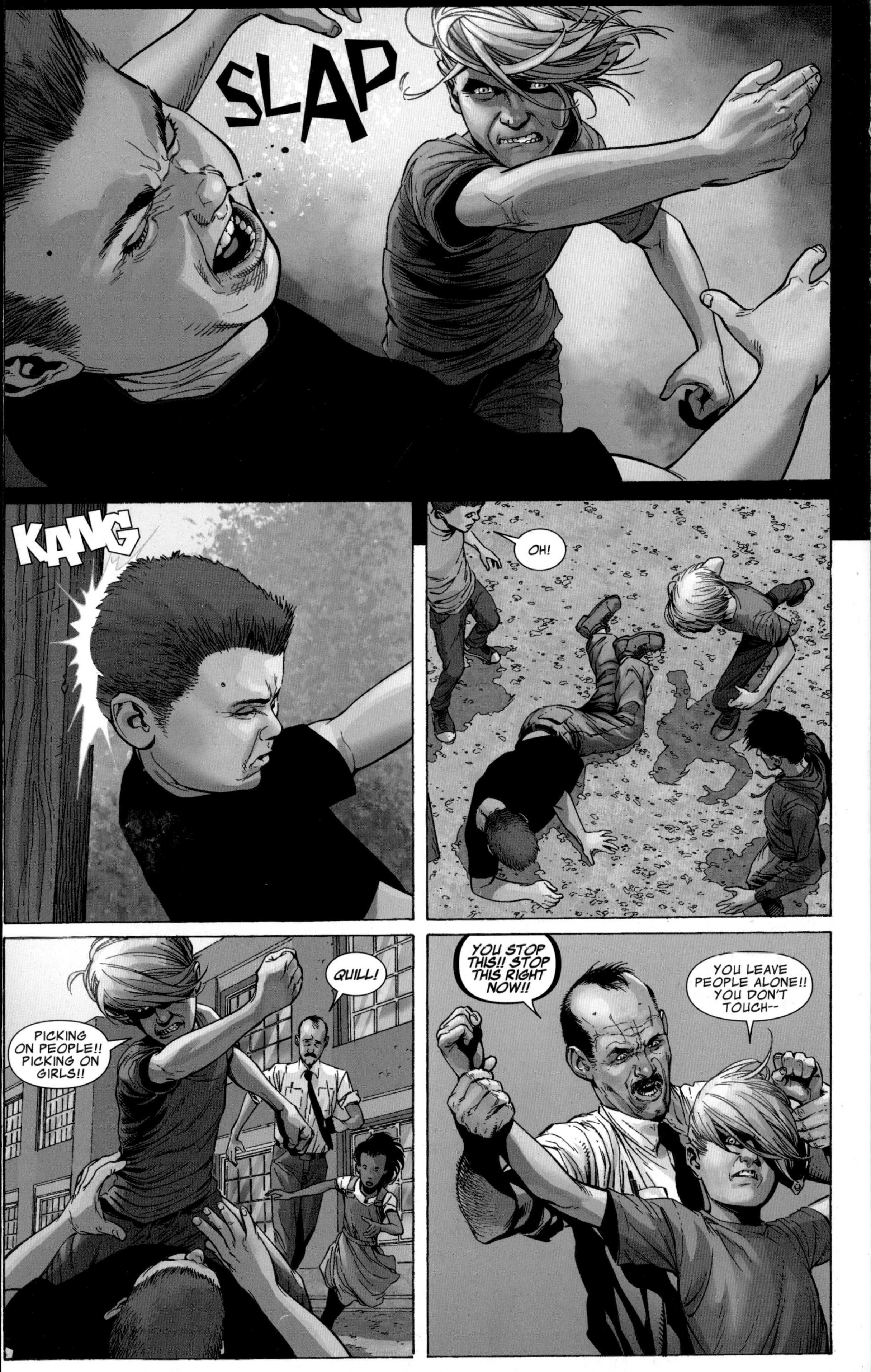
SLAP
KANG
OH!
PICKING ON PEOPLE!! PICKING ON GIRLS!!
QUILL!
YOU STOP THIS!! STOP THIS RIGHT NOW!!
YOU LEAVE PEOPLE ALONE!! YOU DON'T TOUCH--

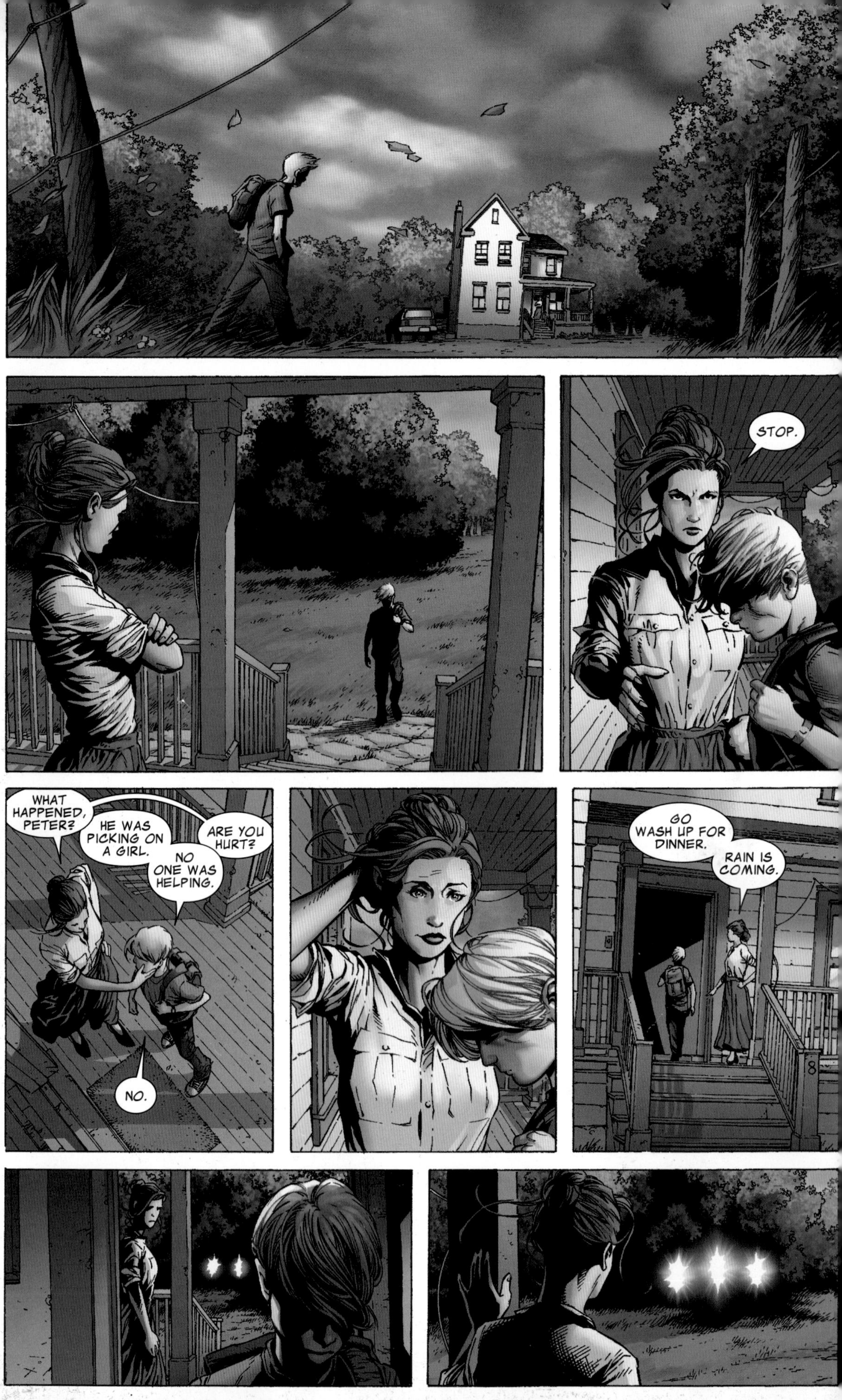
STOP.
WHAT HAPPENED, PETER?
HE WAS PICKING ON A GIRL.
NO ONE WAS HELPING.
ARE YOU HURT?
NO.
GO WASH UP FOR DINNER.
RAIN IS COMING.
8

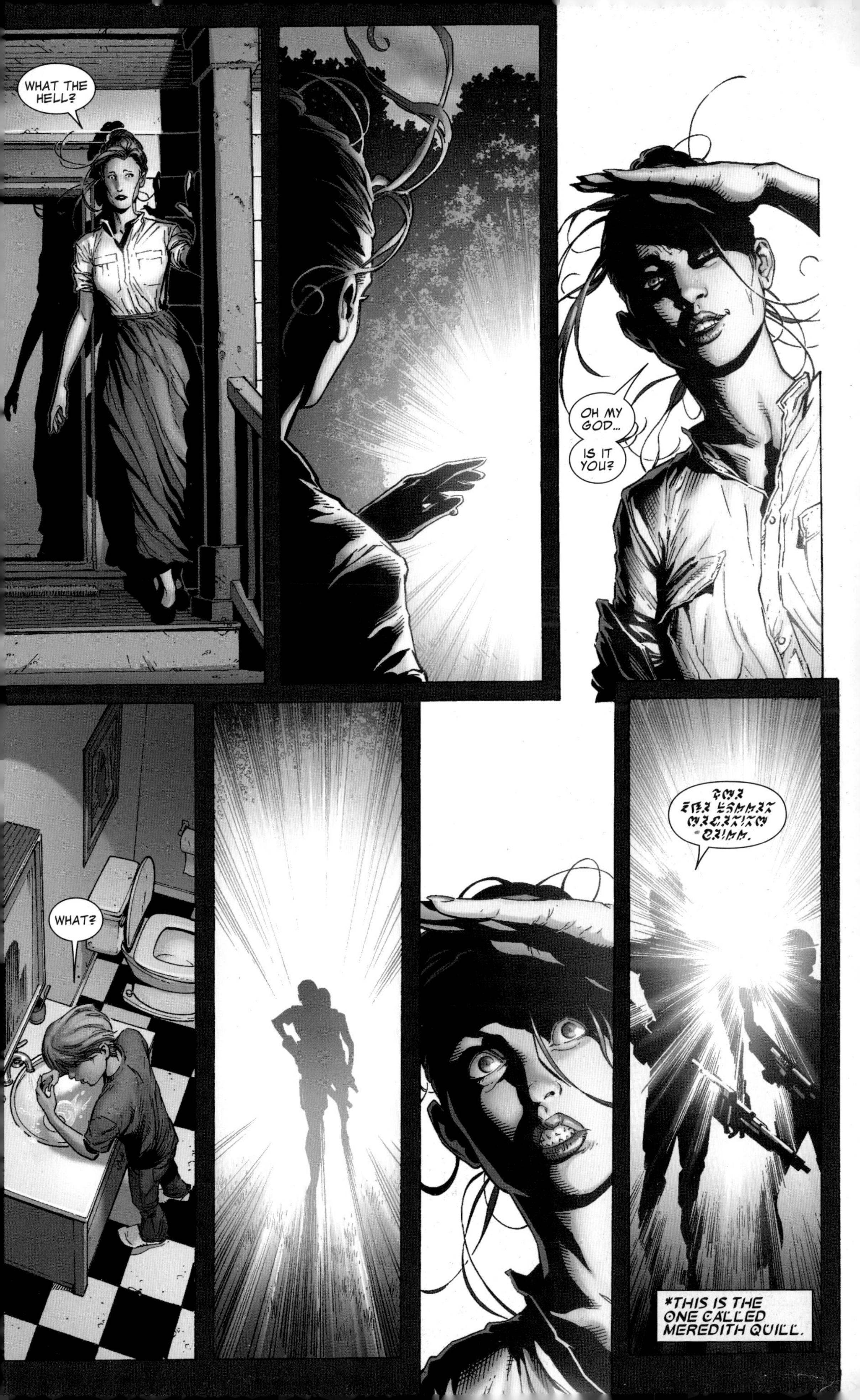
WHAT THE HELL?
OH MY GOD...
IS IT YOU?
WHAT?
*THIS IS THE ONE CALLED MEREDITH QUILL.

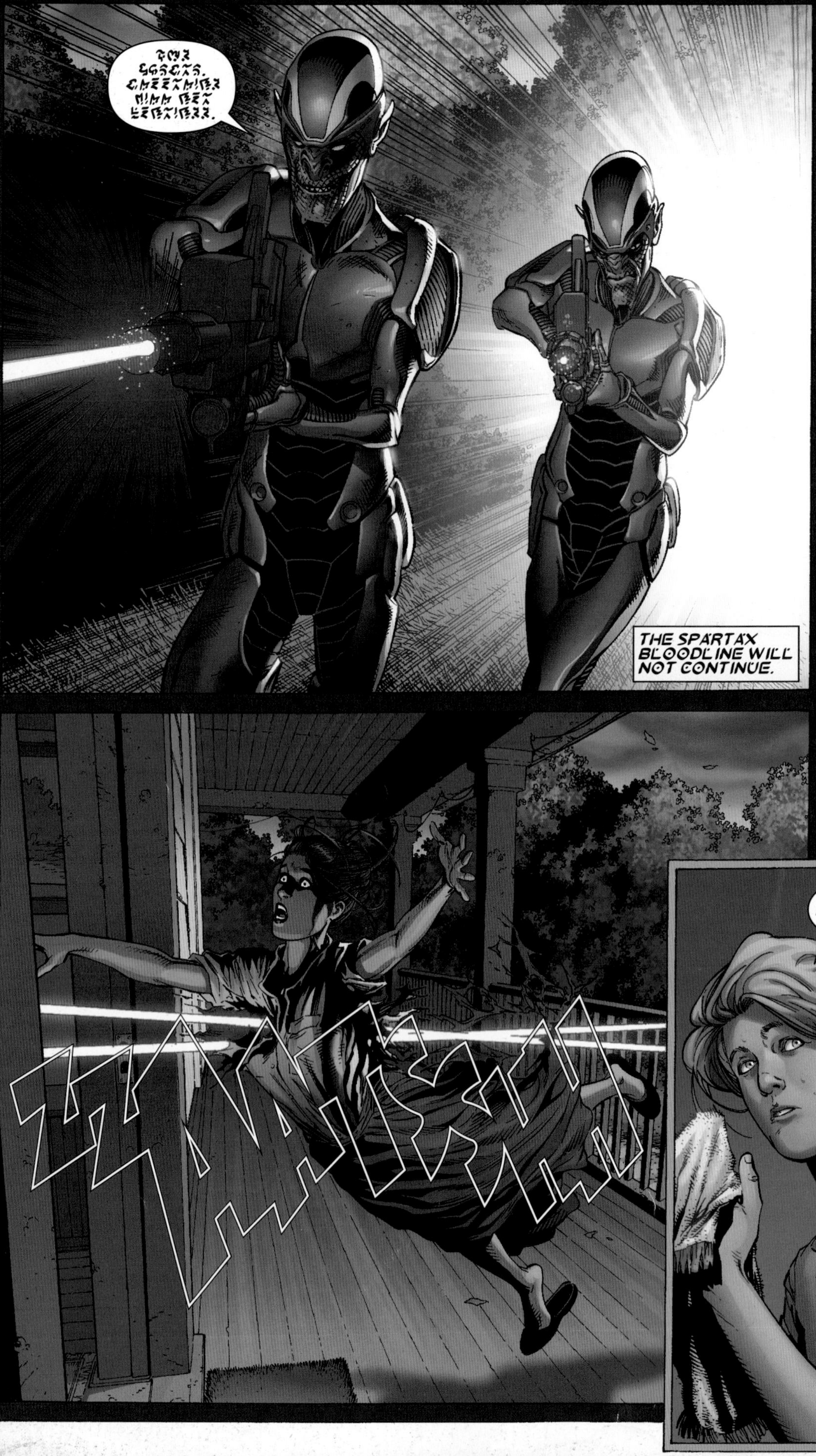
THE SPARTAX BLOODLINE WILL NOT CONTINUE.
MOM?

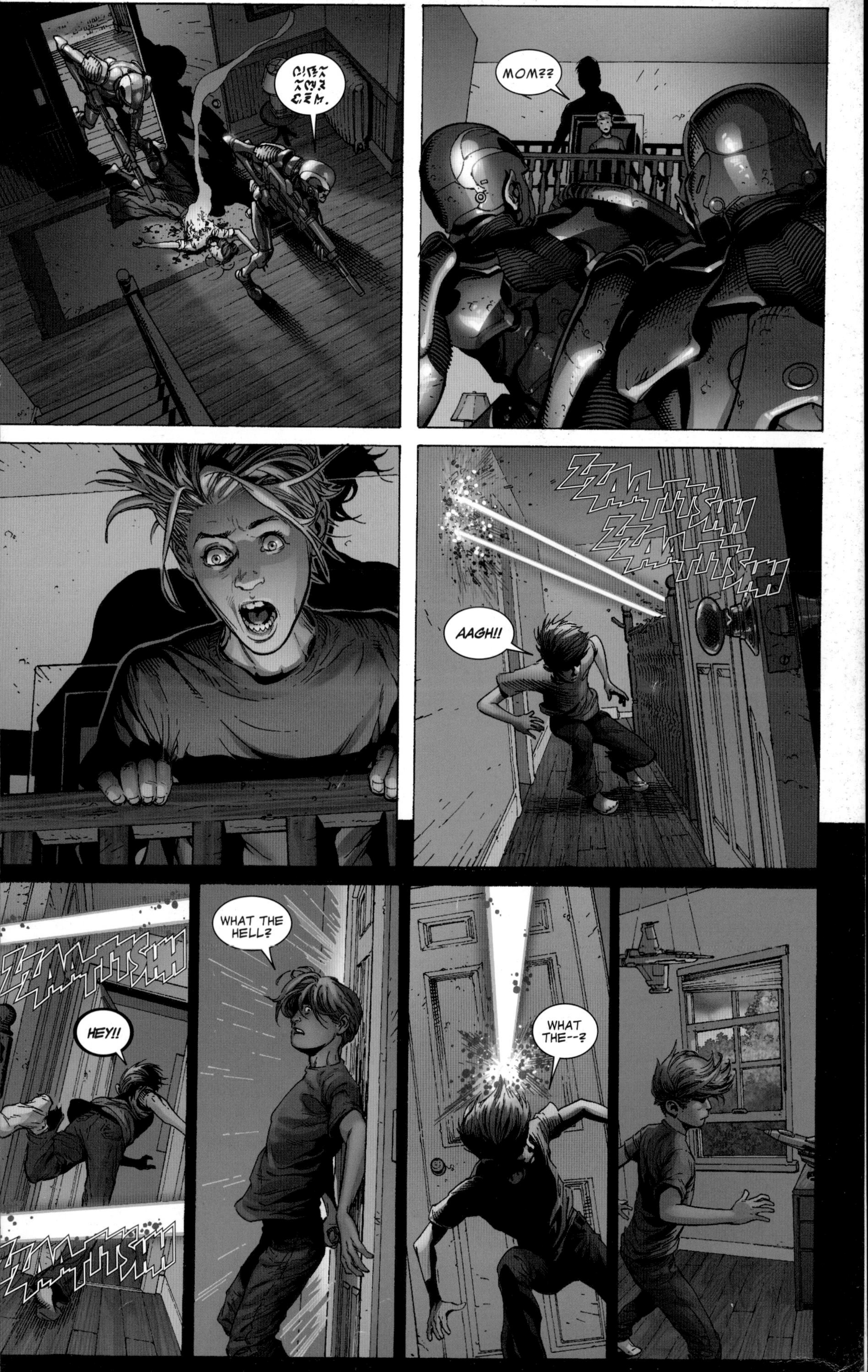
MOM??
AAGH!!
HEY!!
WHAT THE HELL?
WHAT THE--?

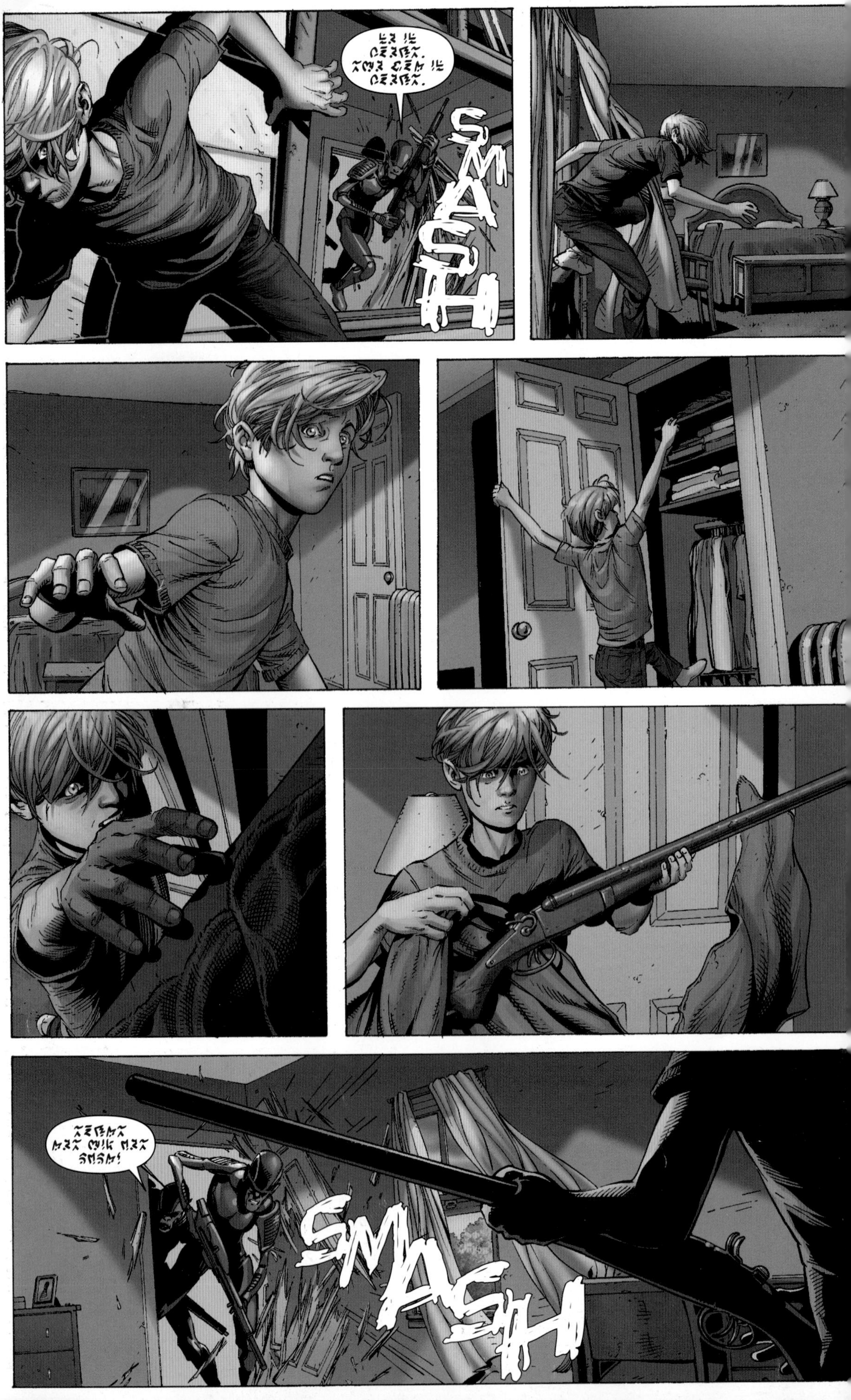
SMASH
SMASH

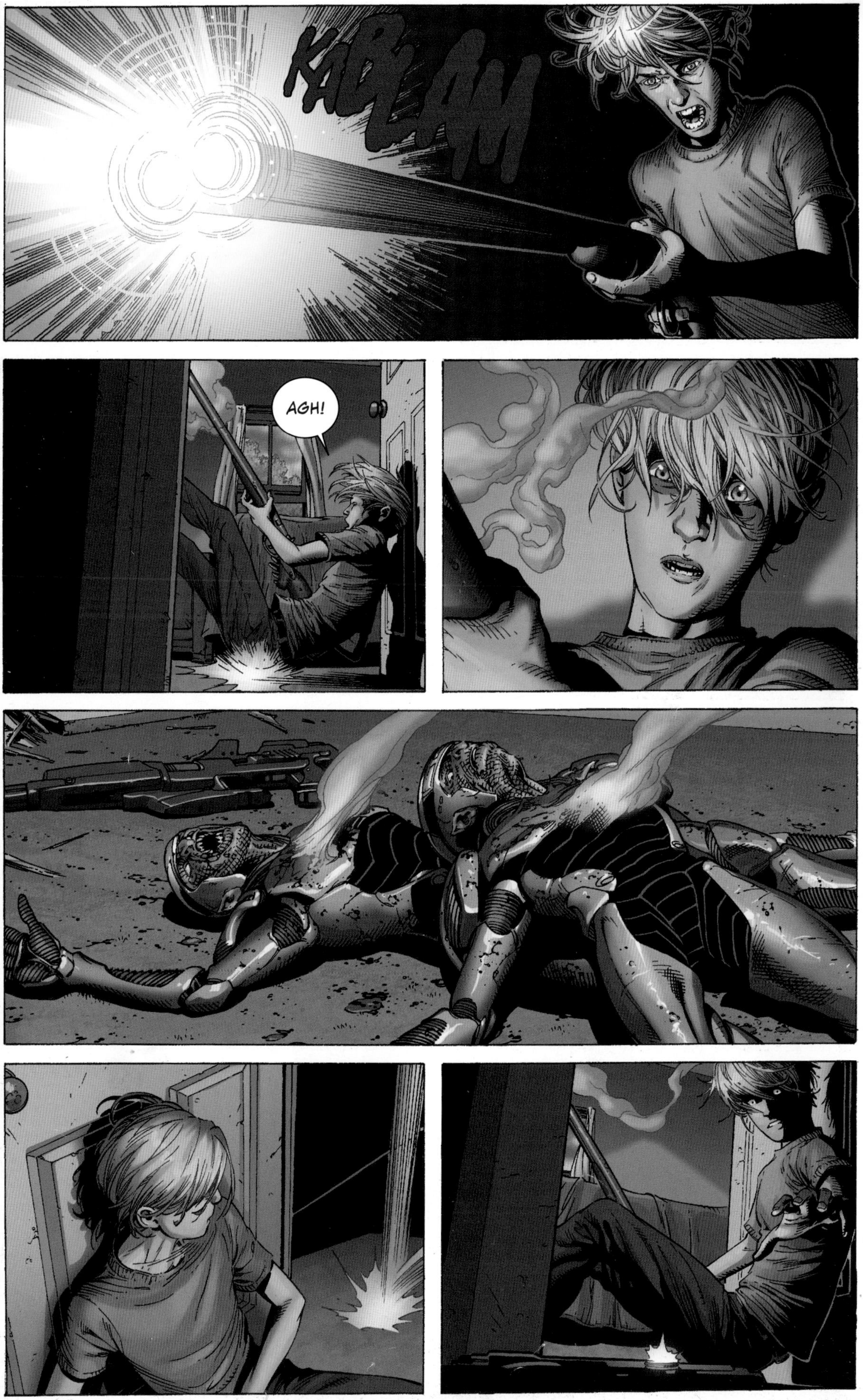
KABLAM
AGH!

MOM HAD A--?

WHAT IS THIS?

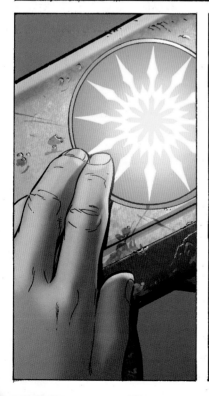

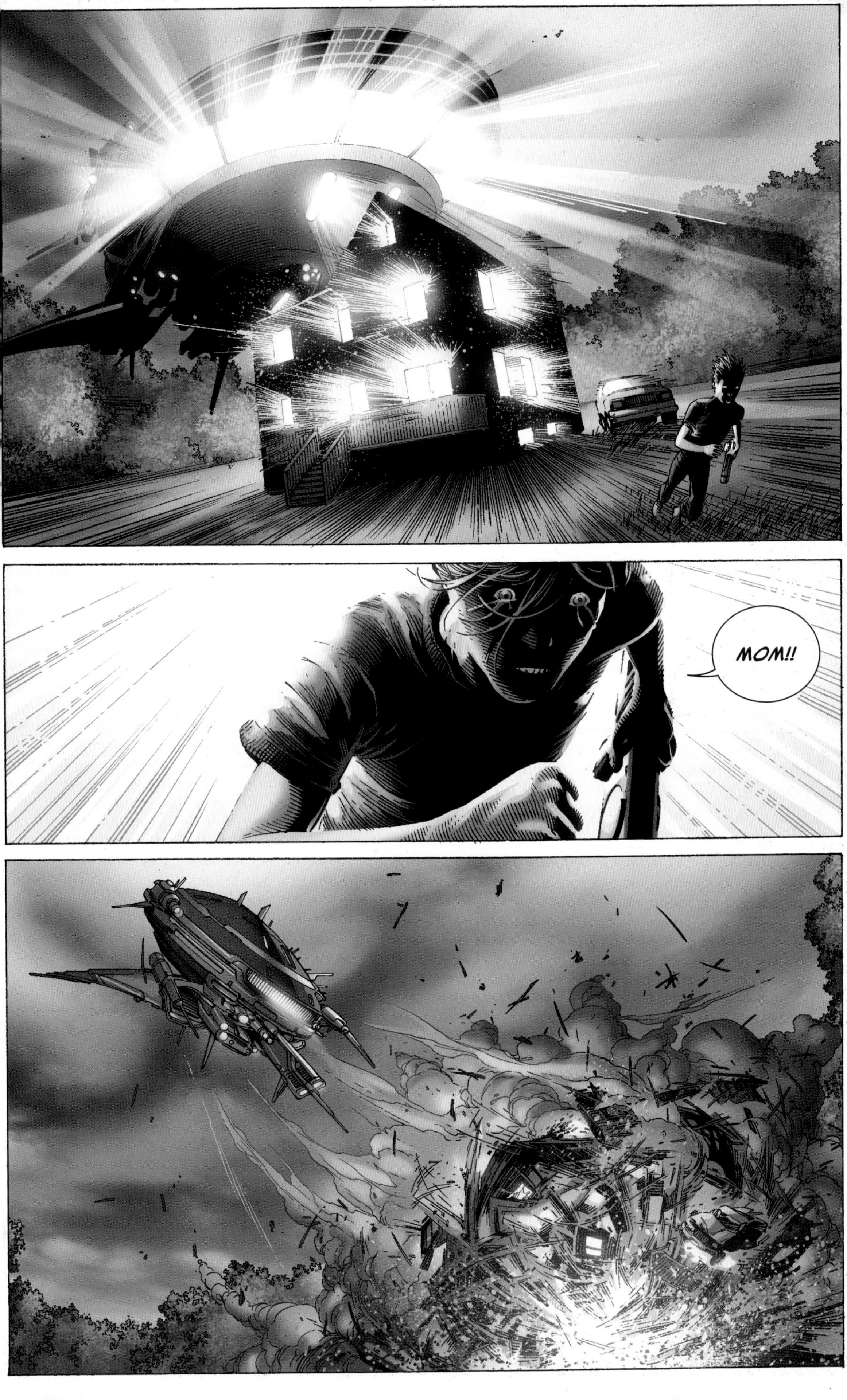
MOM!!

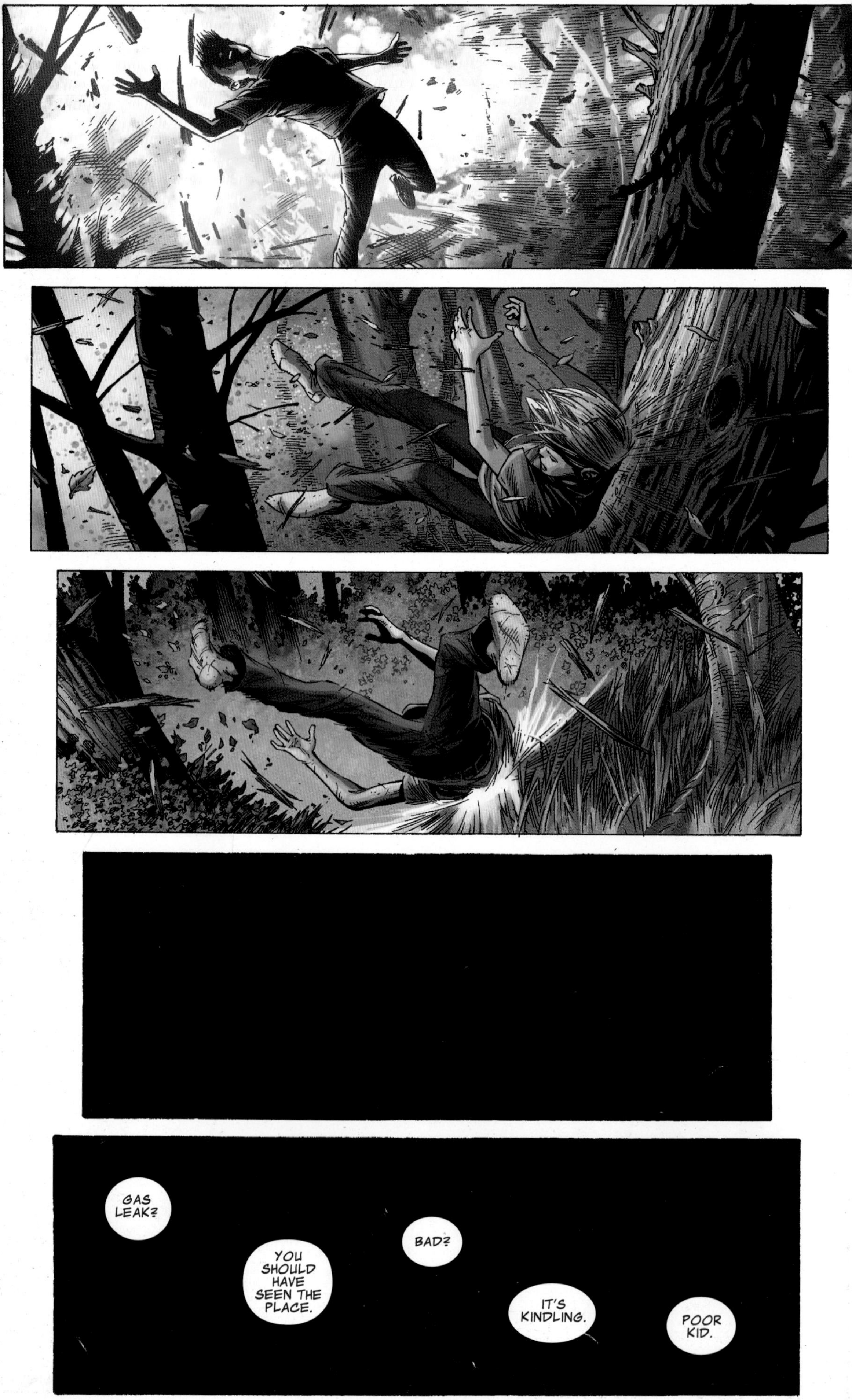
GAS LEAK?
YOU SHOULD HAVE SEEN THE PLACE.
BAD?
IT'S KINDLING.
POOR KID.

4000...
UH, I THINK HE'S AWAKE.
PETER?
PETER, DON'T TRY TO TALK.
NURSE HOLLOWAY, CAN YOU TELL THE FRONT DESK THE PATIENT IS AWAKE?
WE'LL NEED SOMEONE FROM CHILD PSYCHIATRIC DOWN HERE ASAP.
PETER, DO YOU REMEMBER MEETING ME YESTERDAY?
NO.
THAT'S OKAY.
YOU WERE PRETTY OUT OF IT.
DO YOU REMEMBER WHAT HAPPENED TO YOU?

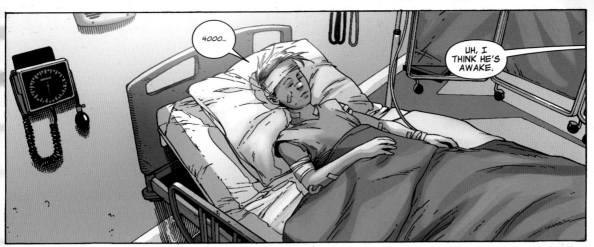

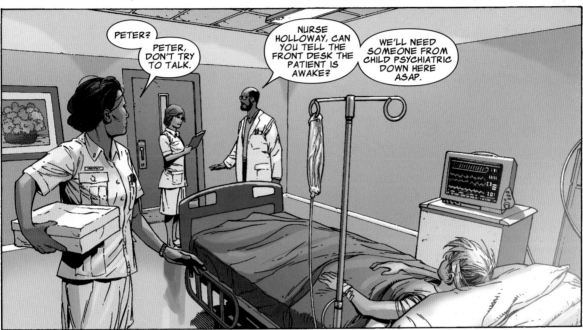

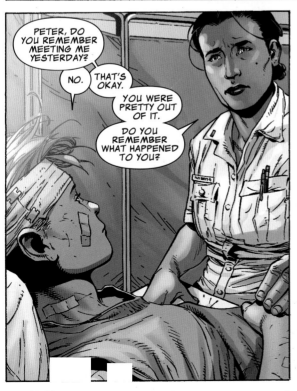

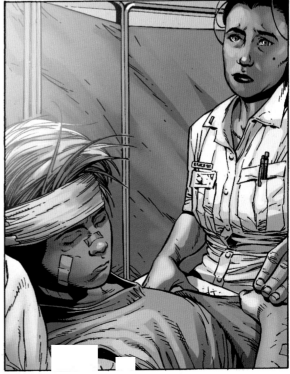

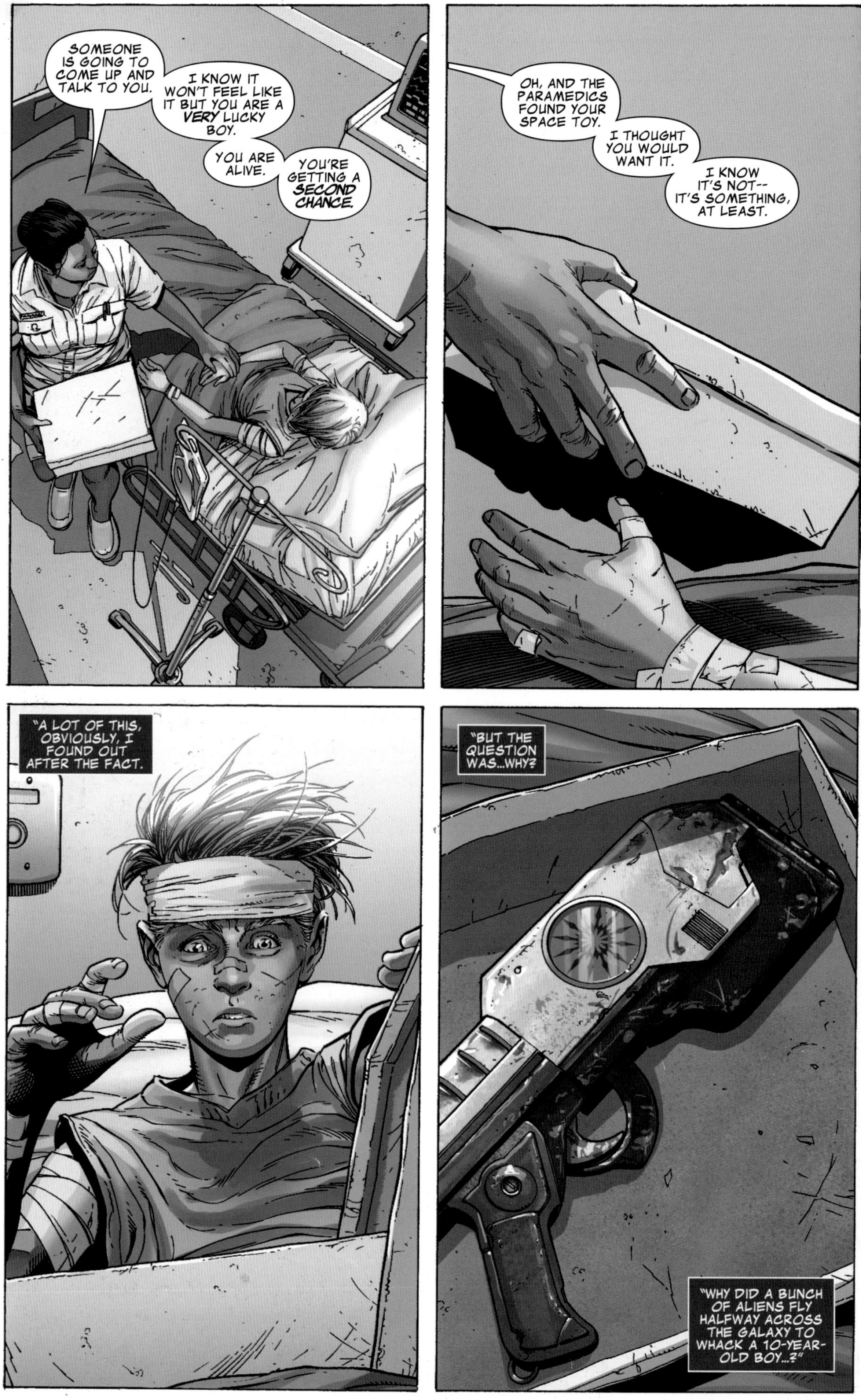
SOMEONE IS GOING TO COME UP AND TALK TO YOU.
I KNOW IT WON'T FEEL LIKE IT BUT YOU ARE A VERY LUCKY BOY.
YOU ARE ALIVE.
YOU'RE GETTING A SECOND CHANCE.
OH, AND THE PARAMEDICS FOUND YOUR SPACE TOY.
I THOUGHT YOU WOULD WANT IT.
I KNOW IT'S NOT-- IT'S SOMETHING, AT LEAST.
"A LOT OF THIS, OBVIOUSLY, I FOUND OUT AFTER THE FACT.
"BUT THE QUESTION WAS...WHY?
"WHY DID A BUNCH OF ALIENS FLY HALFWAY ACROSS THE GALAXY TO WHACK A 10-YEAR-OLD BOY...?"

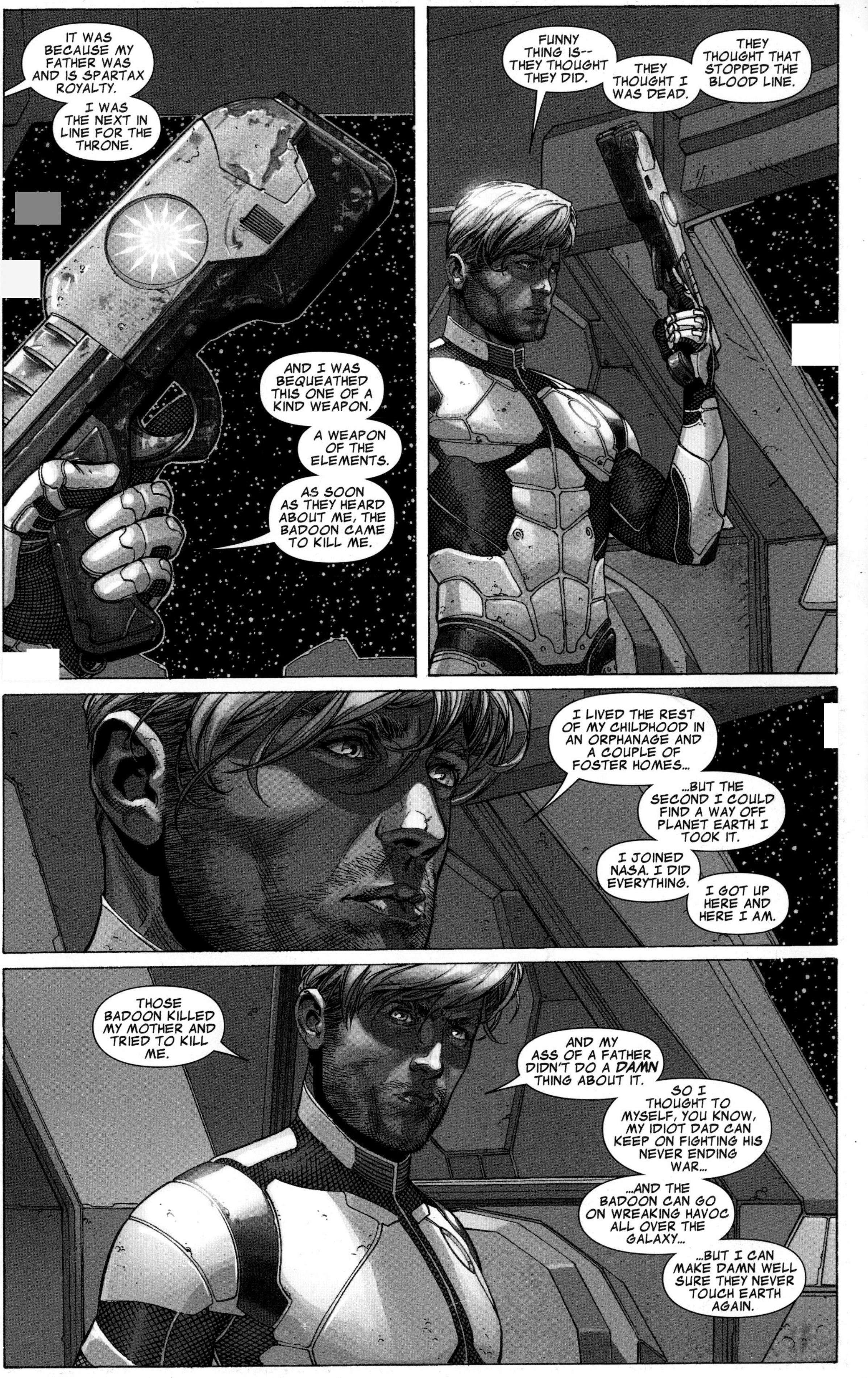
IT WAS BECAUSE MY FATHER WAS AND IS SPARTAX ROYALTY.
I WAS THE NEXT IN LINE FOR THE THRONE.
AND I WAS BEQUEATHED THIS ONE OF A KIND WEAPON.
A WEAPON OF THE ELEMENTS.
AS SOON AS THEY HEARD ABOUT ME, THE BADOON CAME TO KILL ME.
FUNNY THING IS-- THEY THOUGHT THEY DID.
THEY THOUGHT I WAS DEAD.
THEY THOUGHT THAT STOPPED THE BLOOD LINE.
I LIVED THE REST OF MY CHILDHOOD IN AN ORPHANAGE AND A COUPLE OF FOSTER HOMES...
...BUT THE SECOND I COULD FIND A WAY OFF PLANET EARTH I TOOK IT.
I JOINED NASA. I DID EVERYTHING.
I GOT UP HERE AND HERE I AM.
THOSE BADOON KILLED MY MOTHER AND TRIED TO KILL ME.
AND MY ASS OF A FATHER DIDN'T DO A *DAMN* THING ABOUT IT.
SO I THOUGHT TO MYSELF, YOU KNOW, MY IDIOT DAD CAN KEEP ON FIGHTING HIS NEVER ENDING WAR...
...AND THE BADOON CAN GO ON WREAKING HAVOC ALL OVER THE GALAXY...
...BUT I CAN MAKE DAMN WELL SURE THEY NEVER TOUCH EARTH AGAIN.

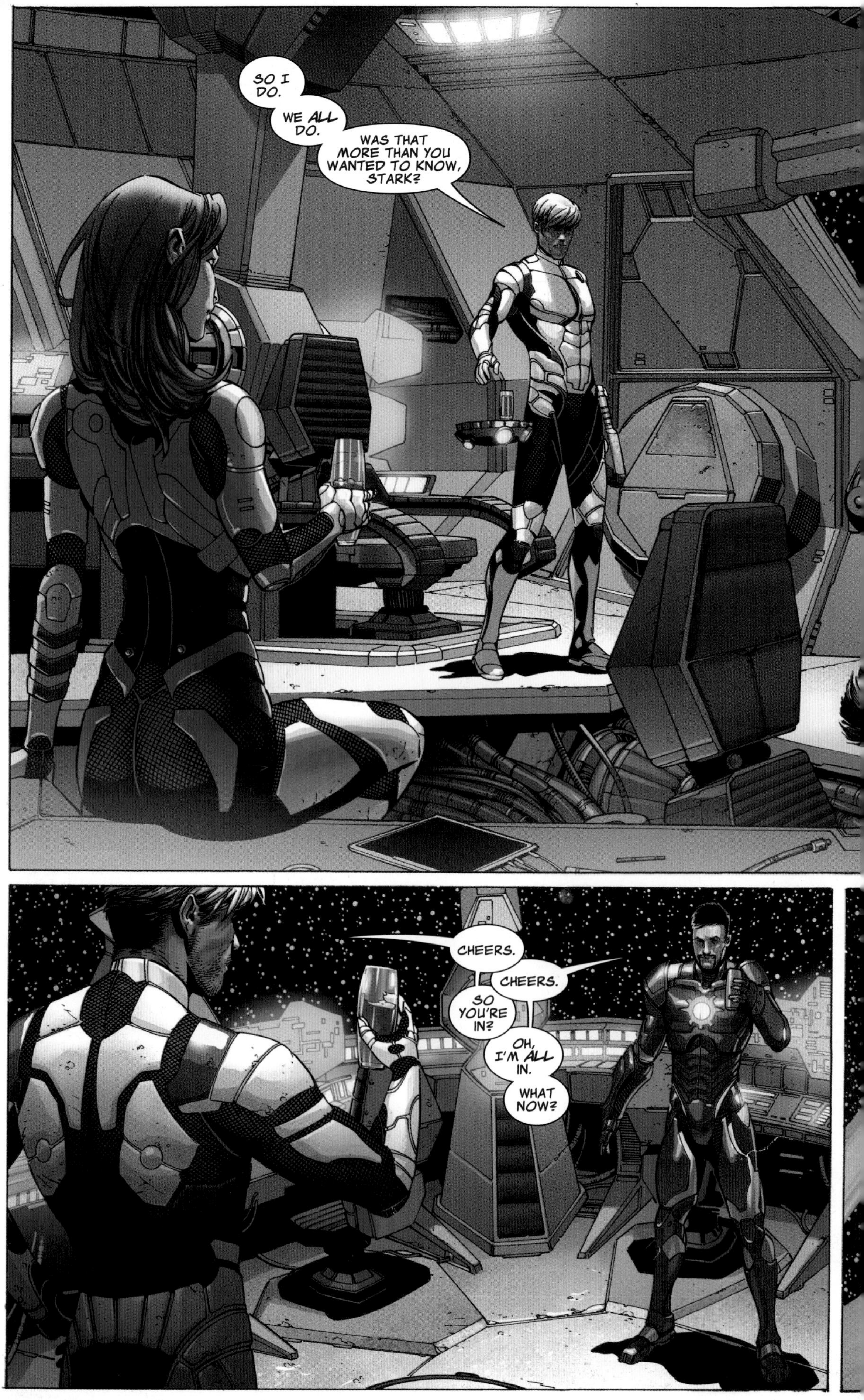
SO I DO.
WE ALL DO.
WAS THAT MORE THAN YOU WANTED TO KNOW, STARK?
CHEERS.
CHEERS.
SO YOU'RE IN?
OH, I'M ALL IN.
WHAT NOW?

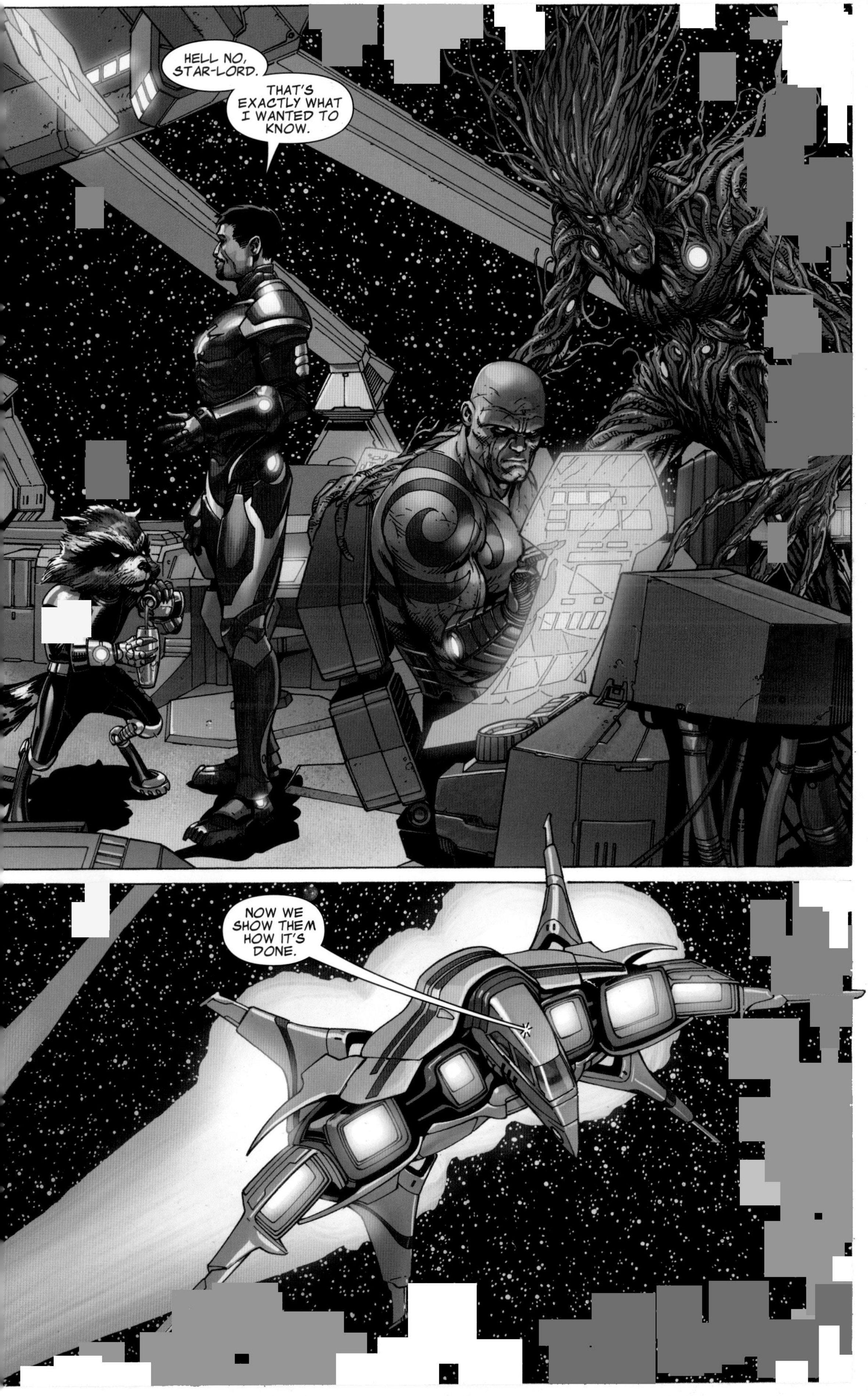
HELL NO, STAR-LORD.
THAT'S EXACTLY WHAT I WANTED TO KNOW.
NOW WE SHOW THEM HOW IT'S DONE.

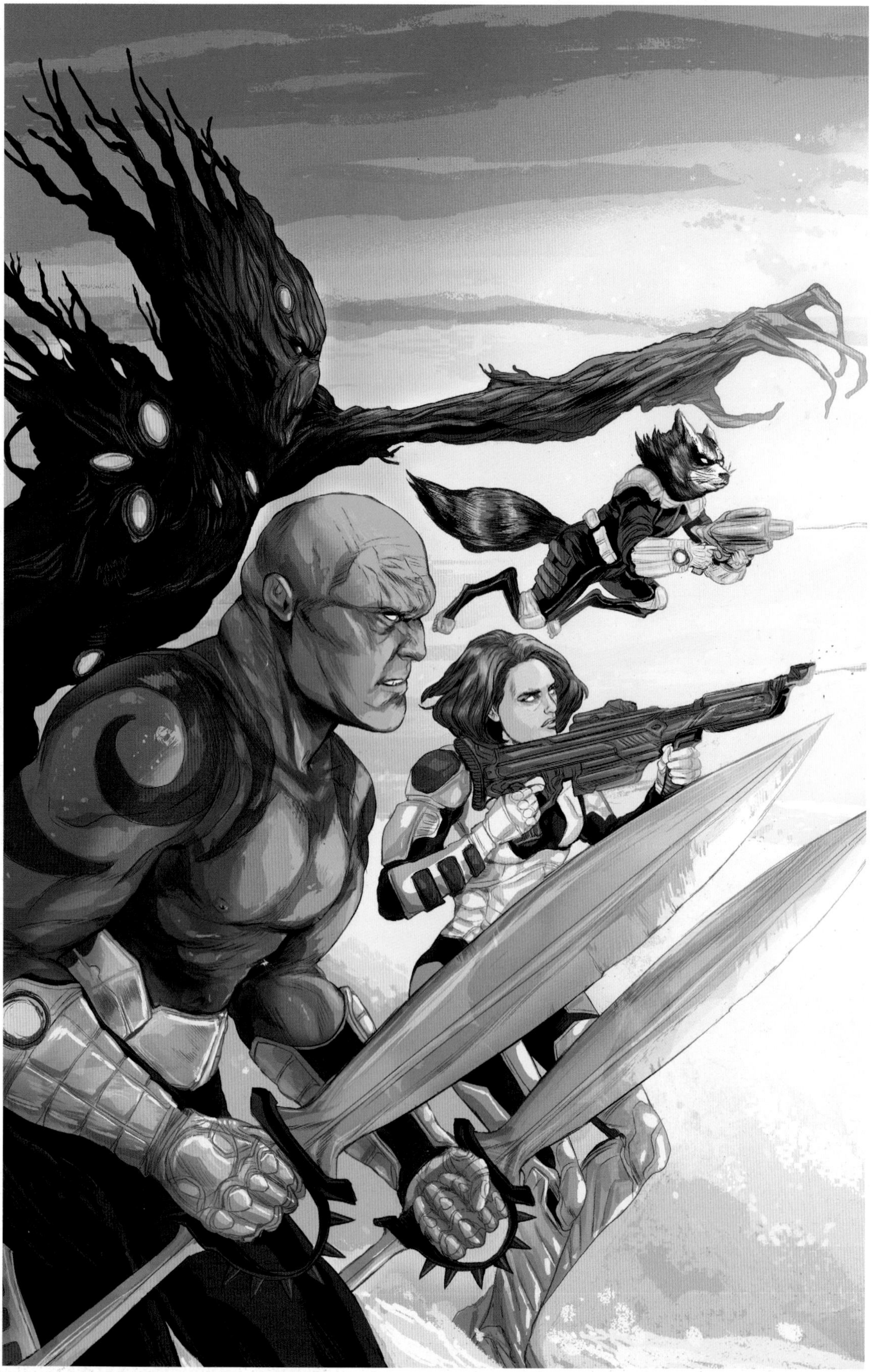

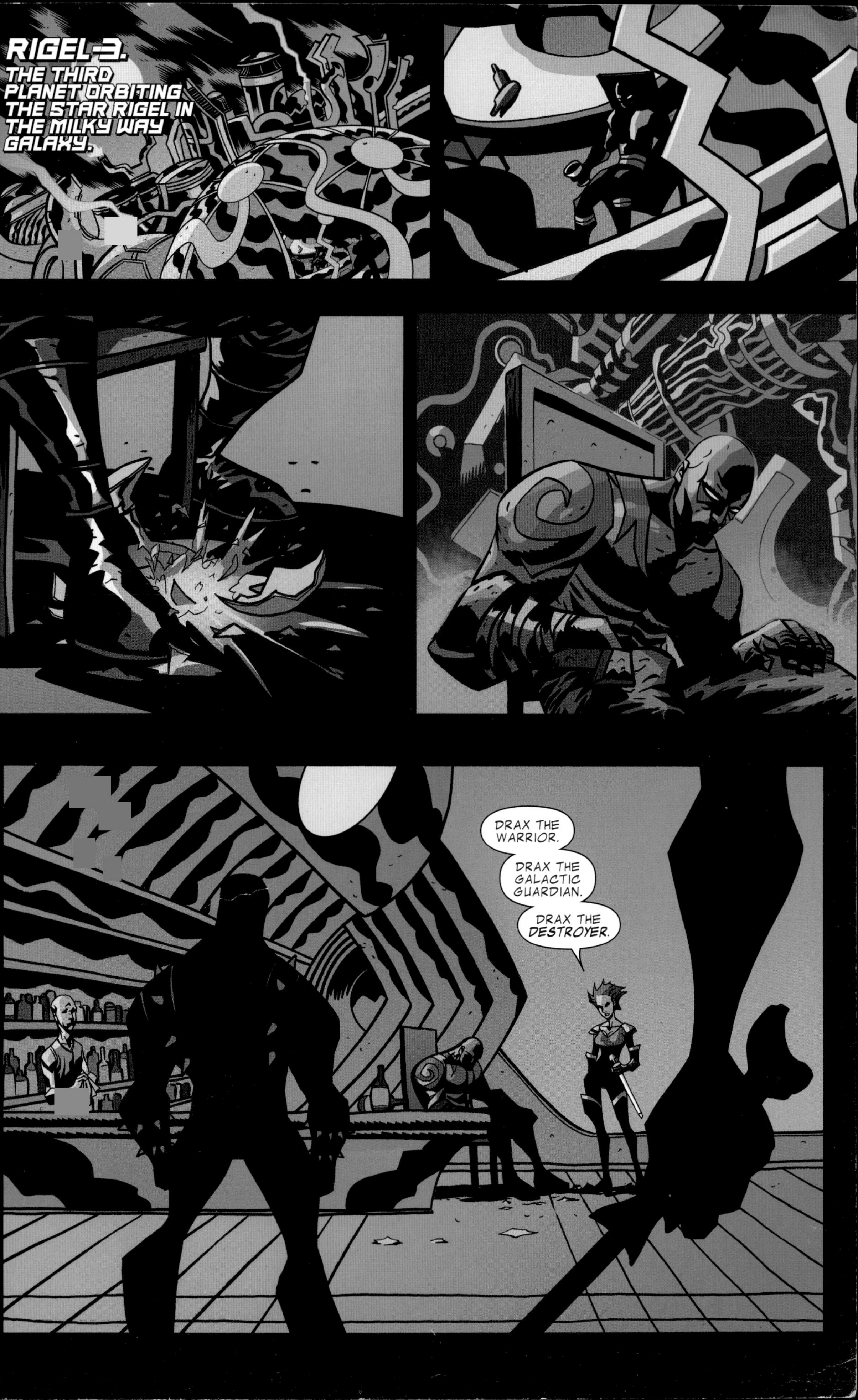
RIGEL-3.
THE THIRD PLANET ORBITING THE STAR RIGEL IN THE MILKY WAY GALAXY.
DRAX THE WARRIOR.
DRAX THE GALACTIC GUARDIAN.
DRAX THE *DESTROYER*.

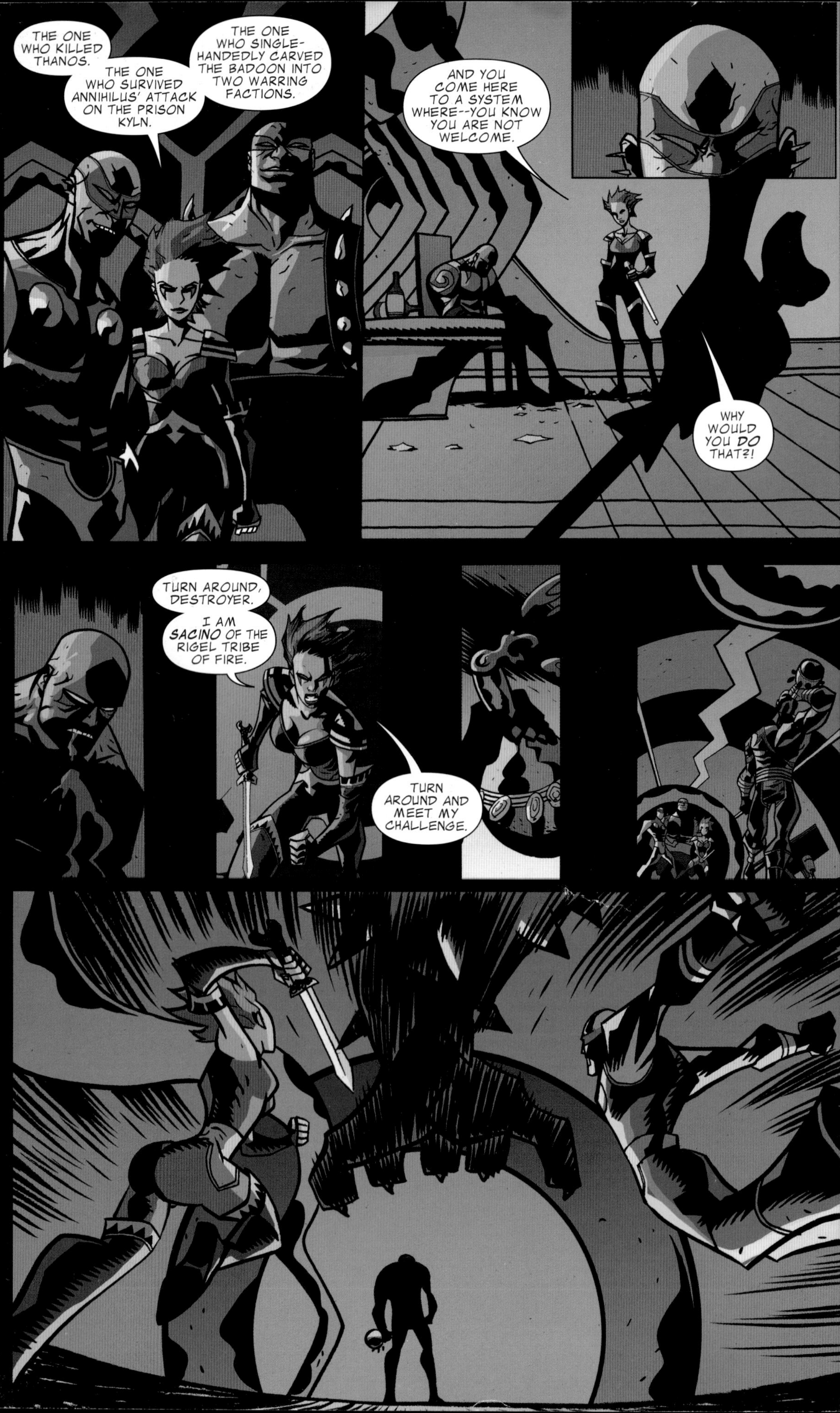
THE ONE WHO KILLED THANOS.
THE ONE WHO SURVIVED ANNIHILUS' ATTACK ON THE PRISON KYLN.
THE ONE WHO SINGLE-HANDEDLY CARVED THE BADOON INTO TWO WARRING FACTIONS.
AND YOU COME HERE TO A SYSTEM WHERE--YOU KNOW YOU ARE NOT WELCOME.
WHY WOULD YOU DO THAT?!
TURN AROUND, DESTROYER.
I AM SACINO OF THE RIGEL TRIBE OF FIRE.
TURN AROUND AND MEET MY CHALLENGE.

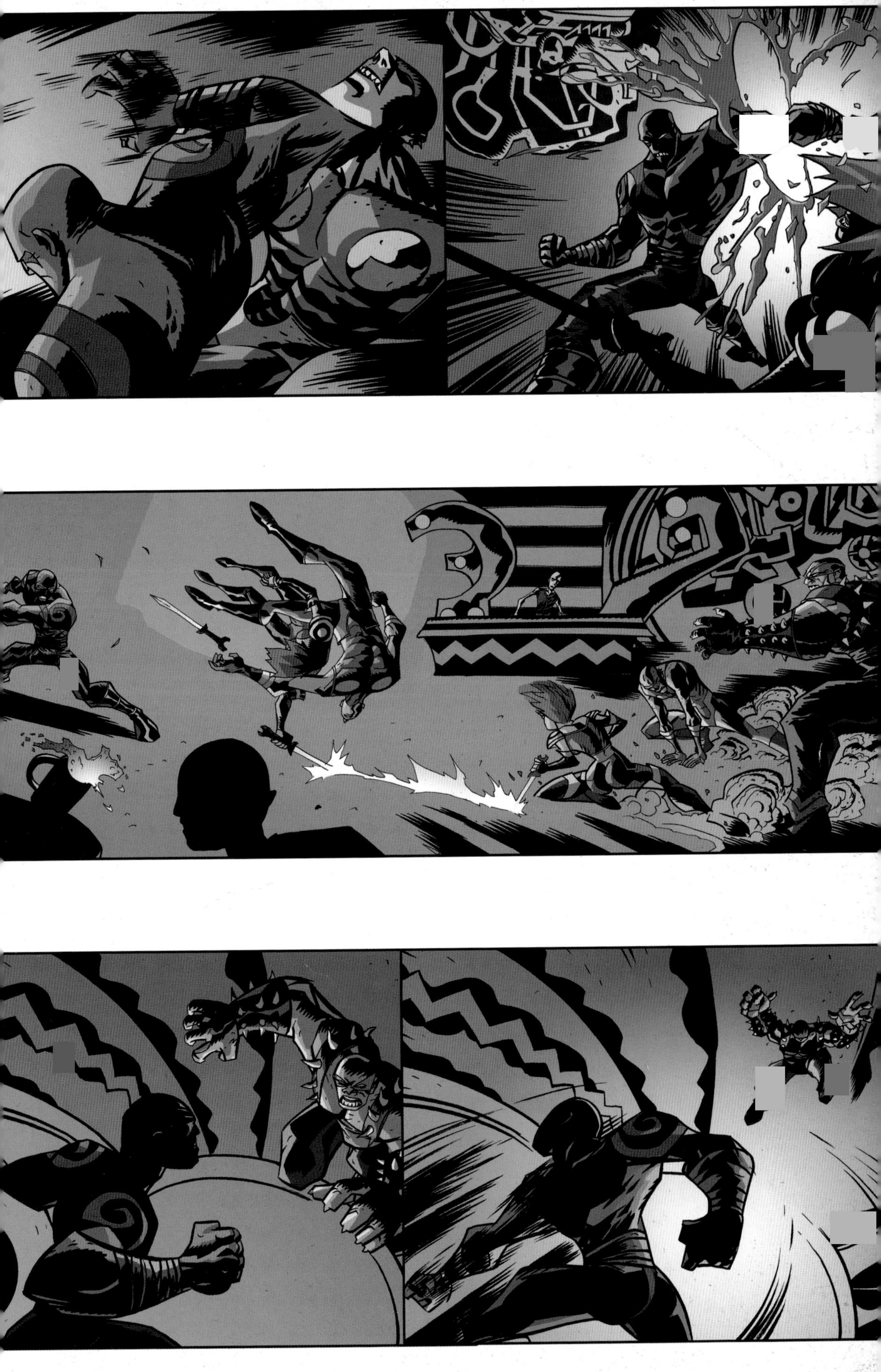

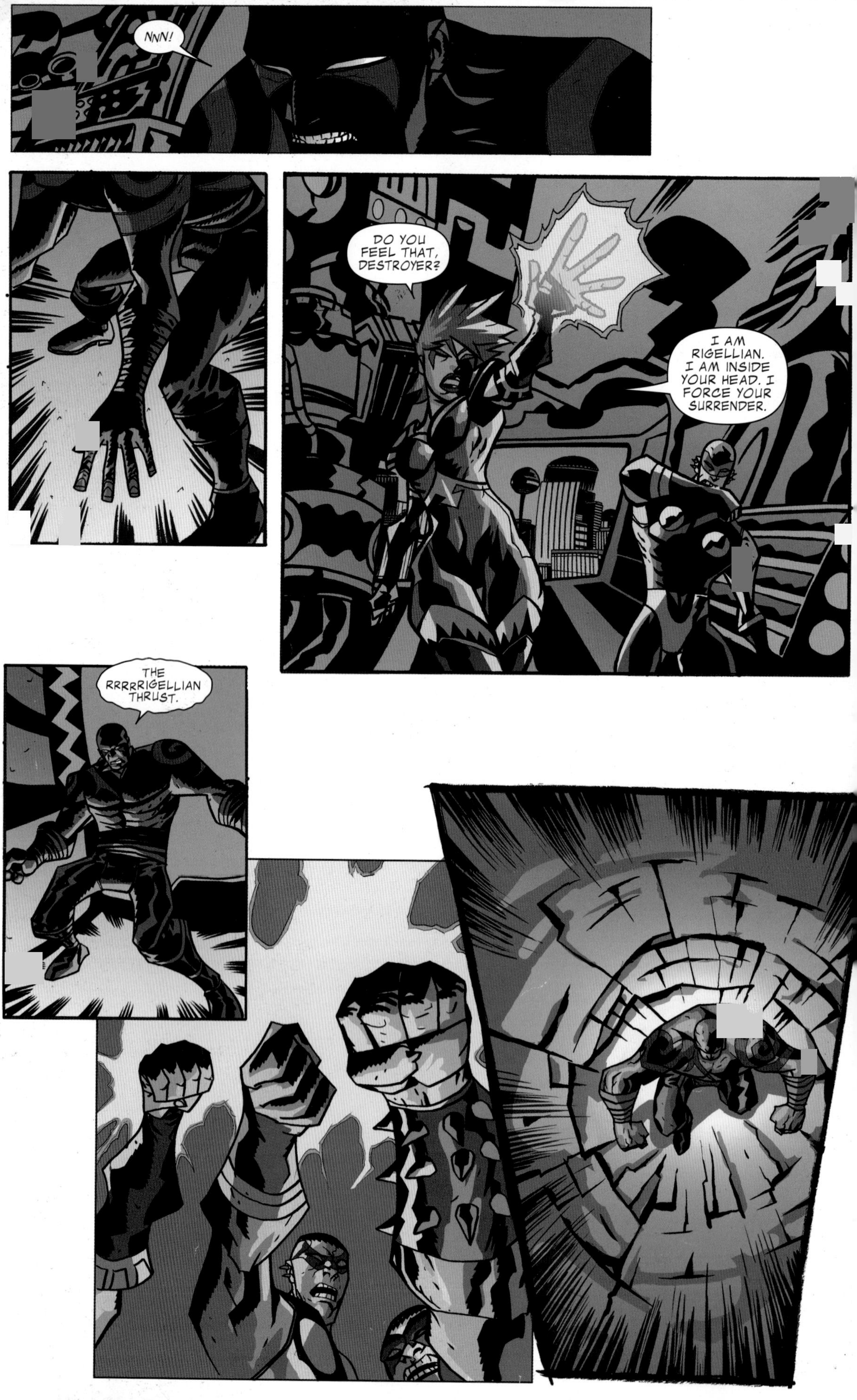
NNN!
DO YOU FEEL THAT, DESTROYER?
I AM RIGELLIAN. I AM INSIDE YOUR HEAD. I FORCE YOUR SURRENDER.
THE RRRRRIGELLIAN THRUST.

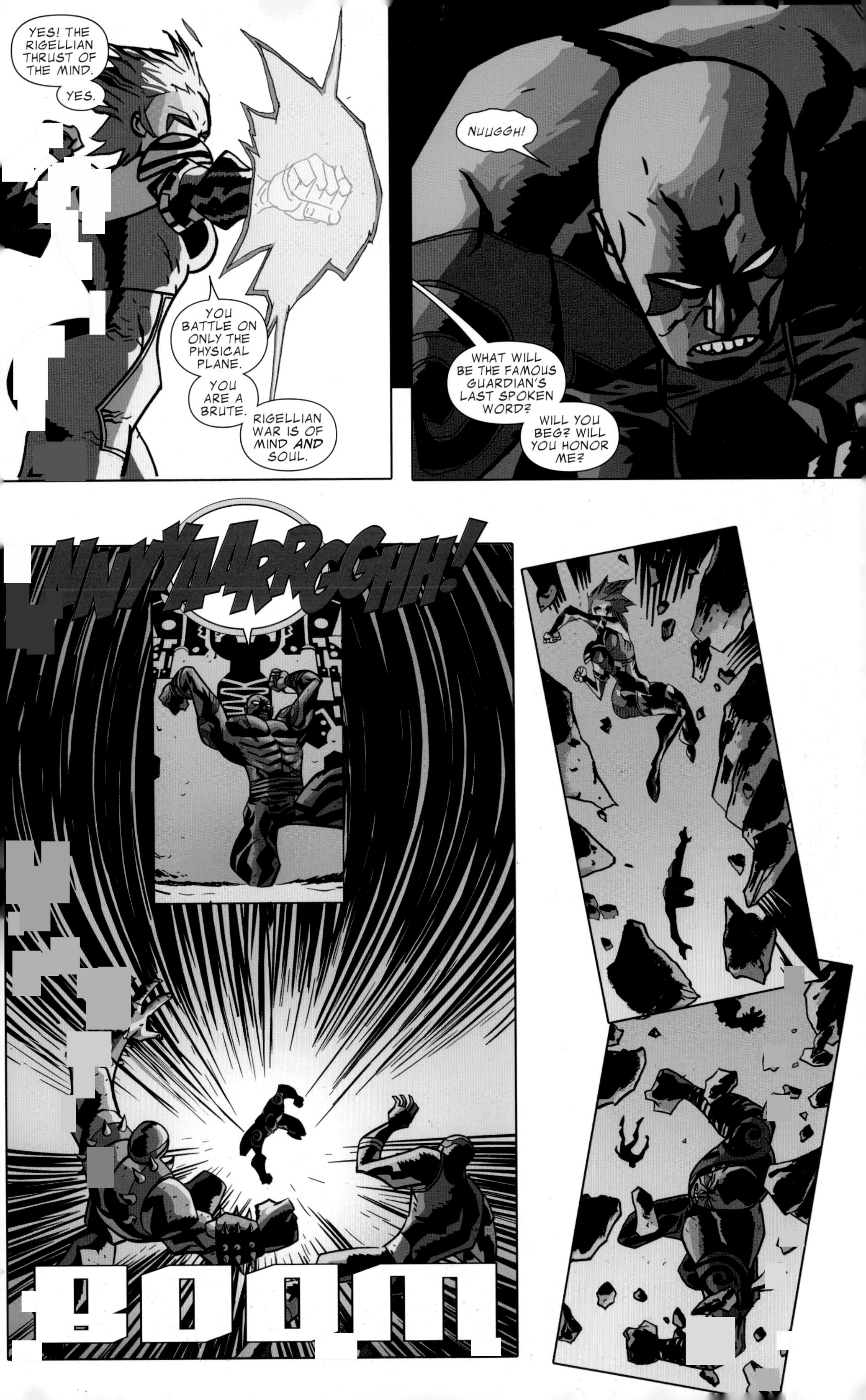
YES! THE RIGELLIAN THRUST OF THE MIND.
YES.
NUUGGH!
YOU BATTLE ON ONLY THE PHYSICAL PLANE.
YOU ARE A BRUTE.
RIGELLIAN WAR IS OF MIND AND SOUL.
WHAT WILL BE THE FAMOUS GUARDIAN'S LAST SPOKEN WORD?
WILL YOU BEG? WILL YOU HONOR ME?
NNYYAARRGGHH!
BOOM

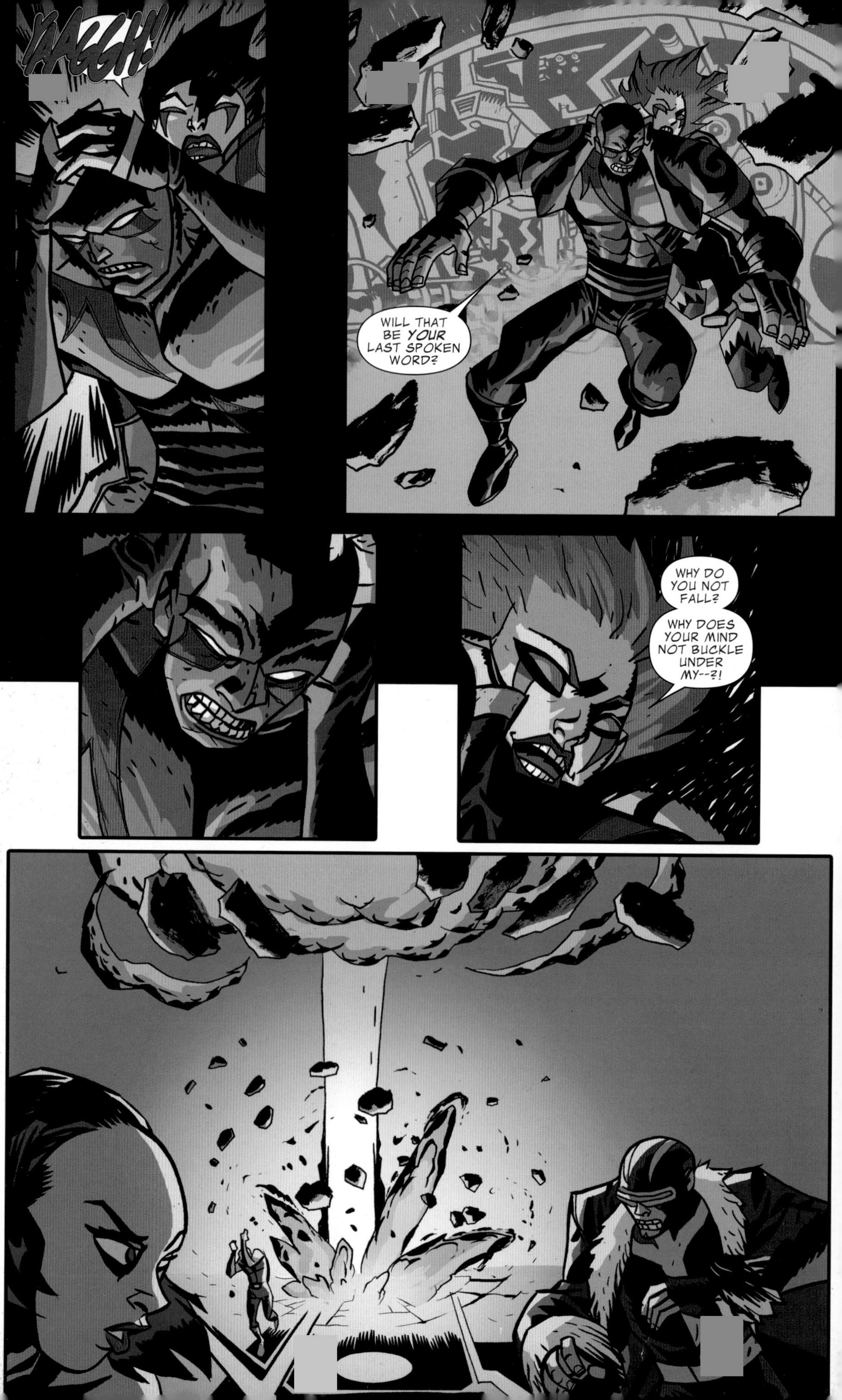
YAAGGH!!
WILL THAT BE YOUR LAST SPOKEN WORD?
WHY DO YOU NOT FALL?
WHY DOES YOUR MIND NOT BUCKLE UNDER MY--?!

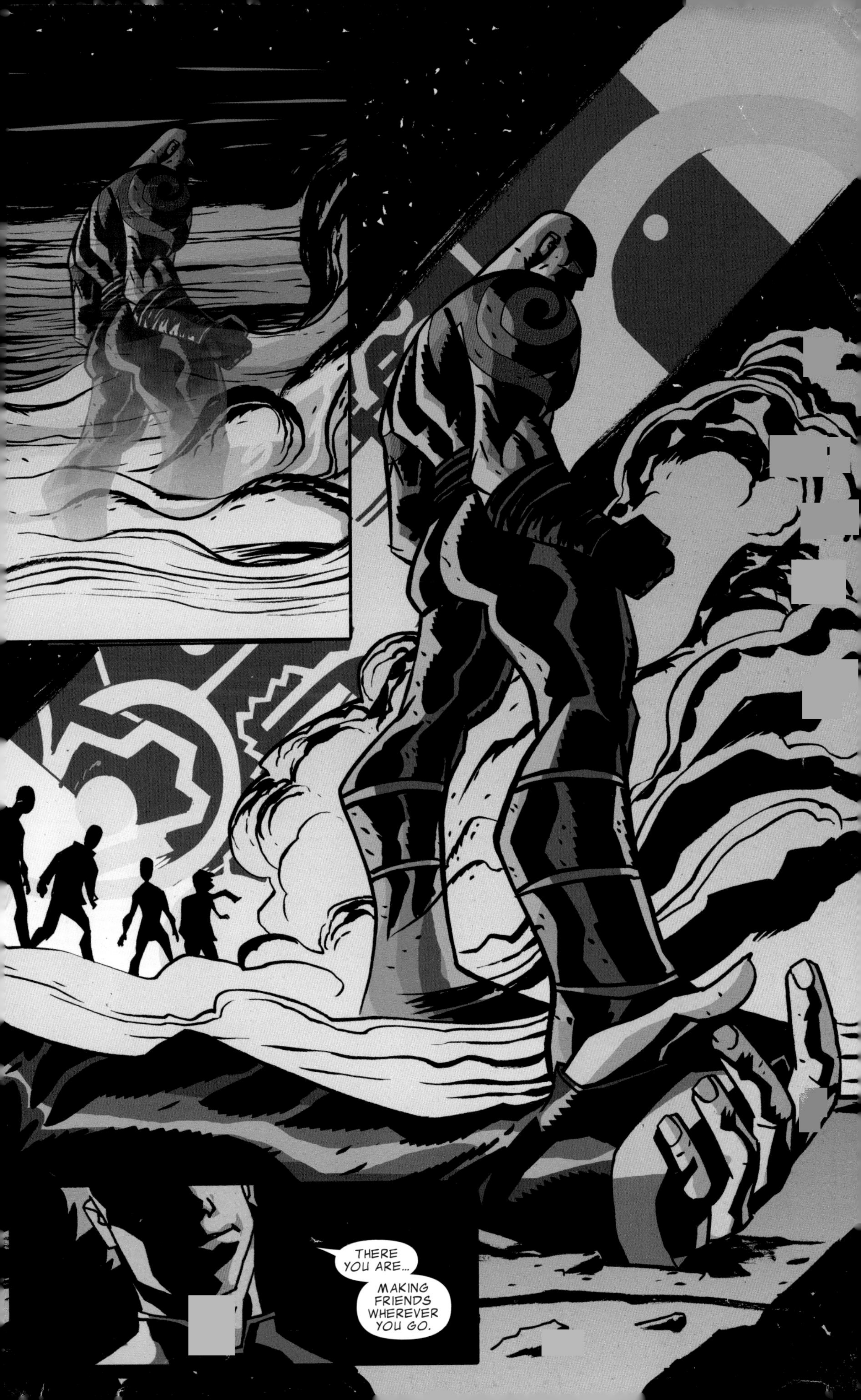
THERE YOU ARE...
MAKING FRIENDS WHEREVER YOU GO.

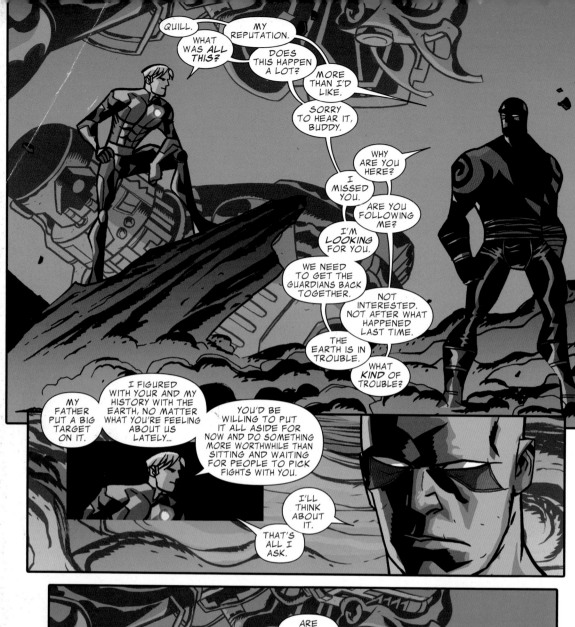

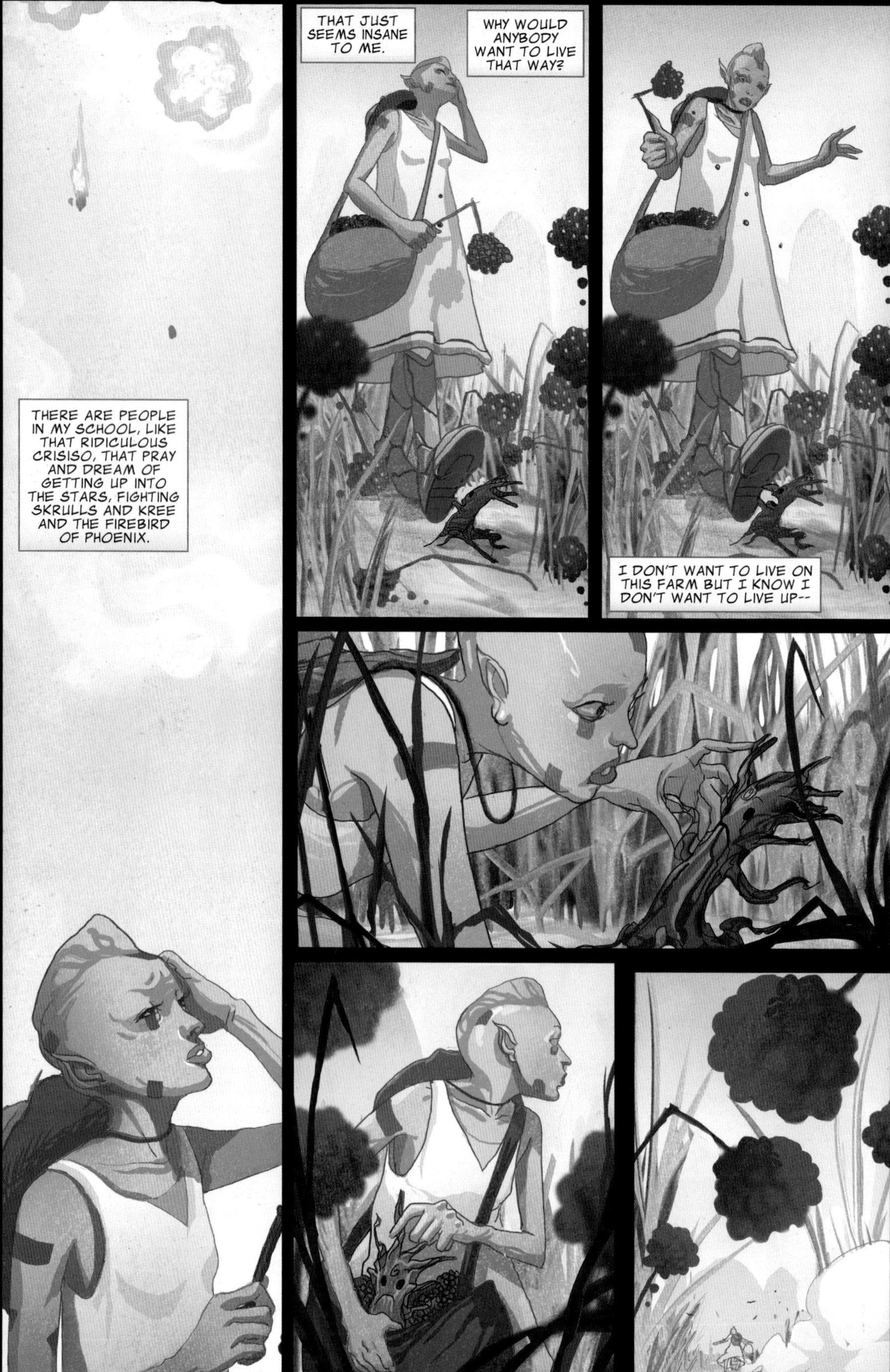
THERE ARE PEOPLE IN MY SCHOOL, LIKE THAT RIDICULOUS CRISISO, THAT PRAY AND DREAM OF GETTING UP INTO THE STARS, FIGHTING SKRULLS AND KREE AND THE FIREBIRD OF PHOENIX.
THAT JUST SEEMS INSANE TO ME.
WHY WOULD ANYBODY WANT TO LIVE THAT WAY?
I DON'T WANT TO LIVE ON THIS FARM BUT I KNOW I DON'T WANT TO LIVE UP--

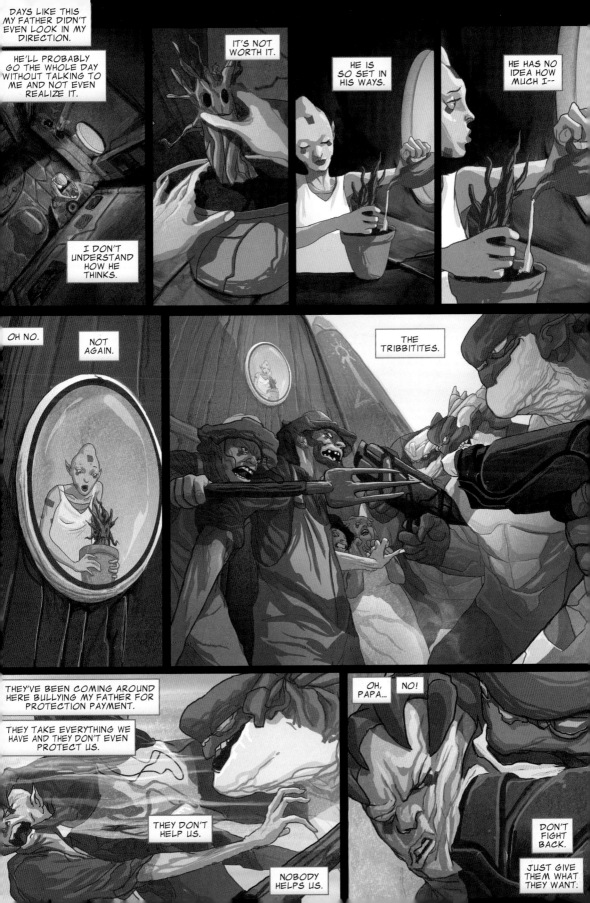

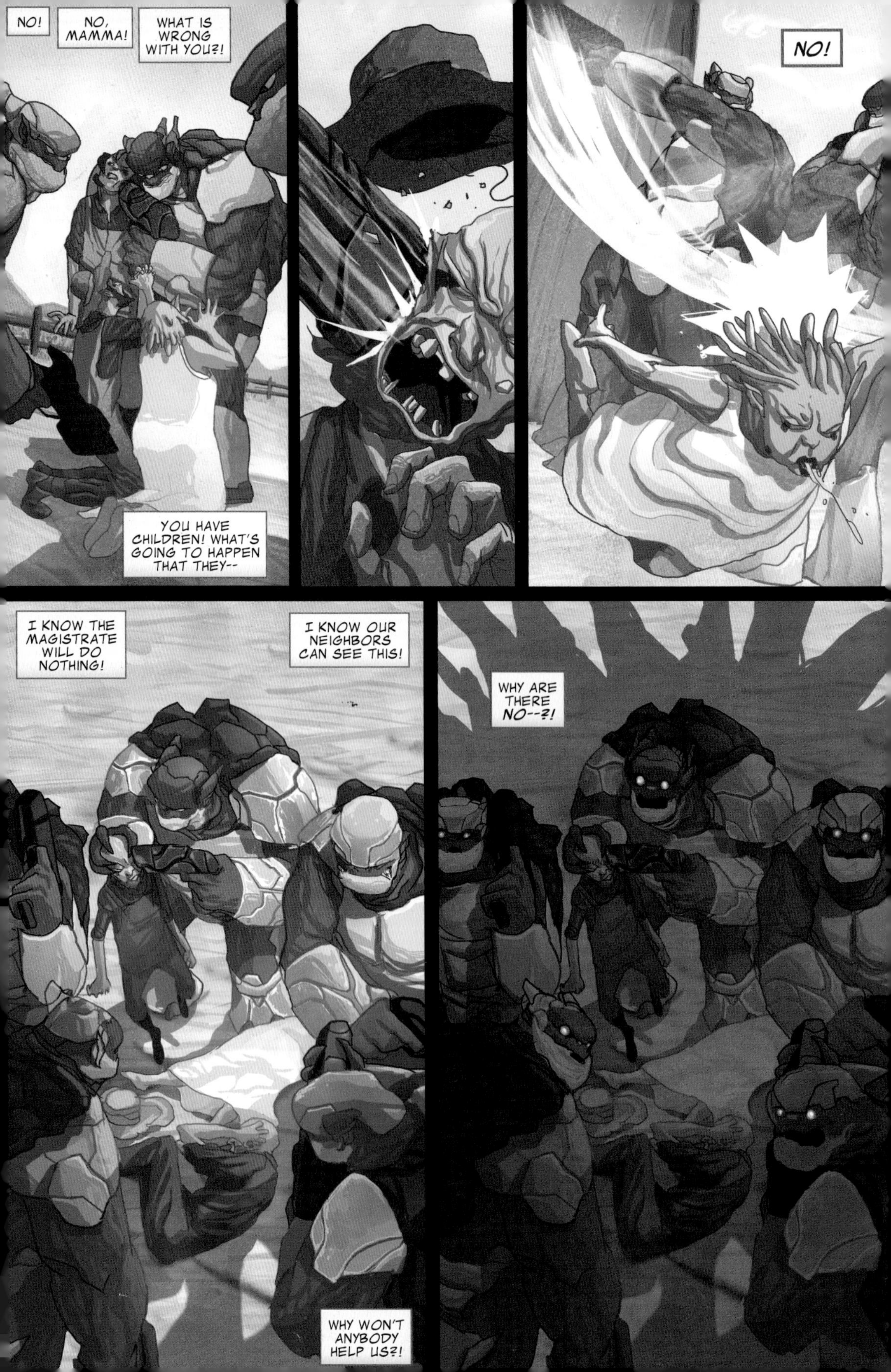
NO!
NO, MAMMA!
WHAT IS WRONG WITH YOU?!
YOU HAVE CHILDREN! WHAT'S GOING TO HAPPEN THAT THEY--
NO!
I KNOW THE MAGISTRATE WILL DO NOTHING!
I KNOW OUR NEIGHBORS CAN SEE THIS!
WHY WON'T ANYBODY HELP US?!
WHY ARE THERE NO--?!

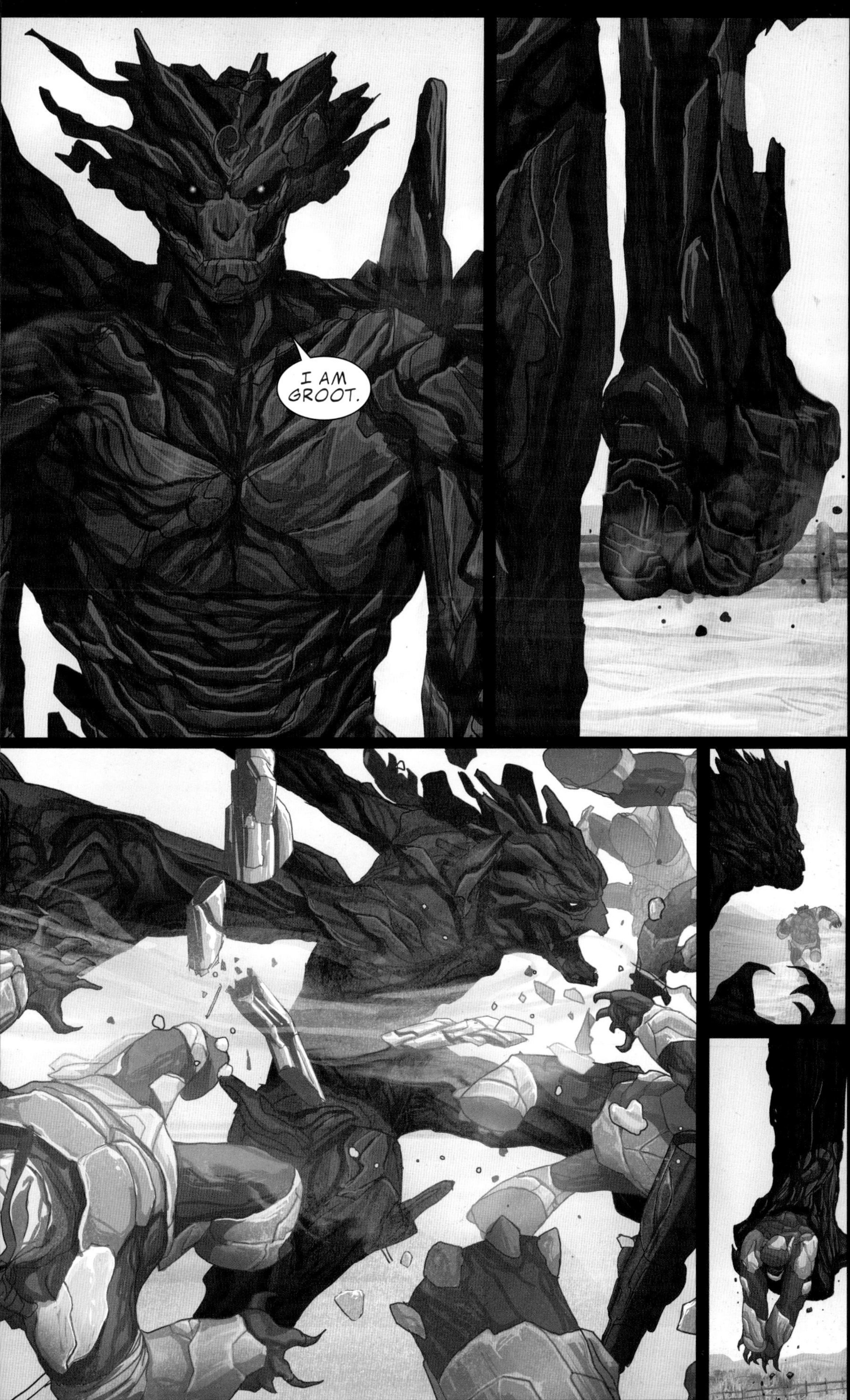
I AM GROOT.

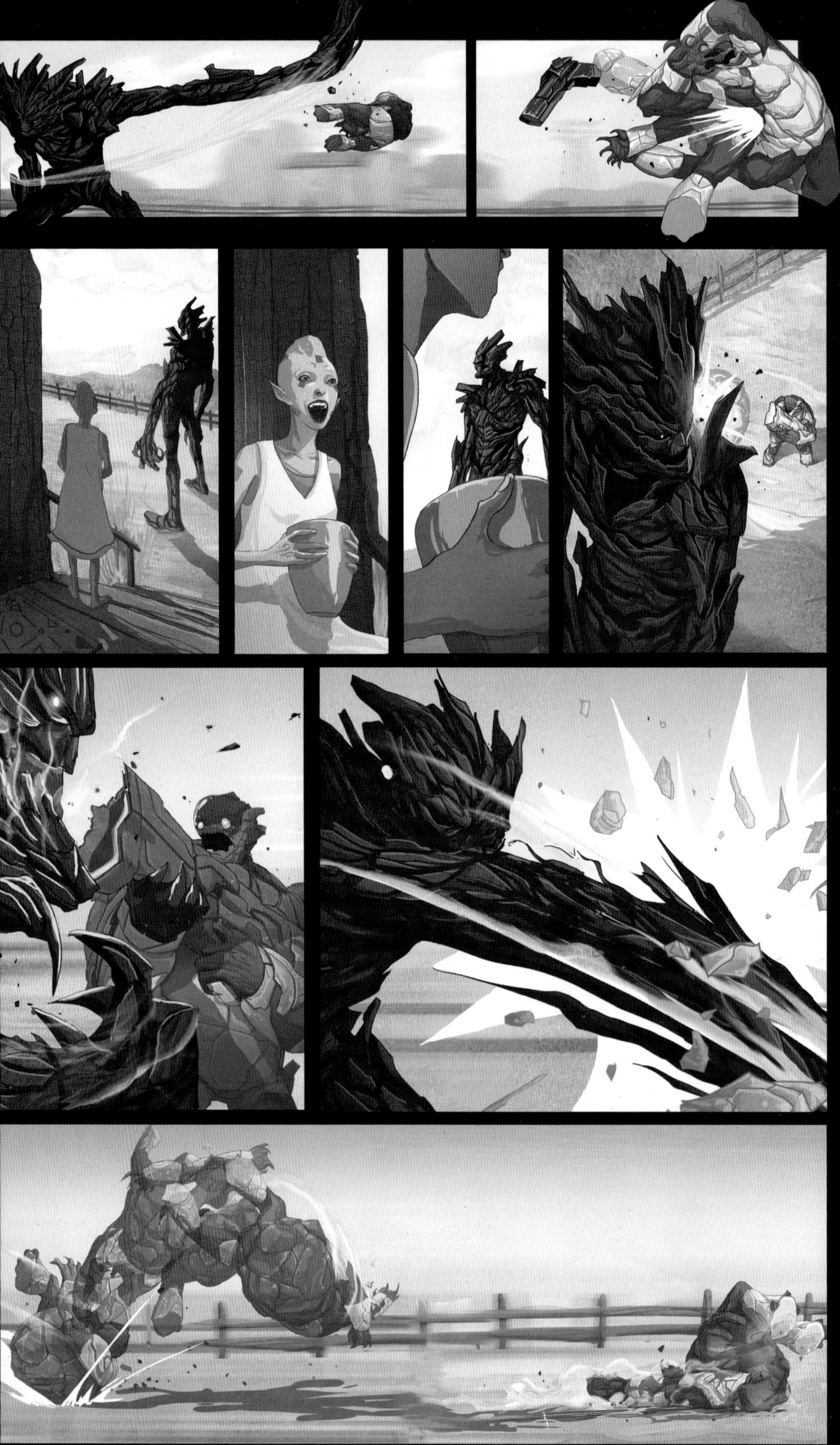

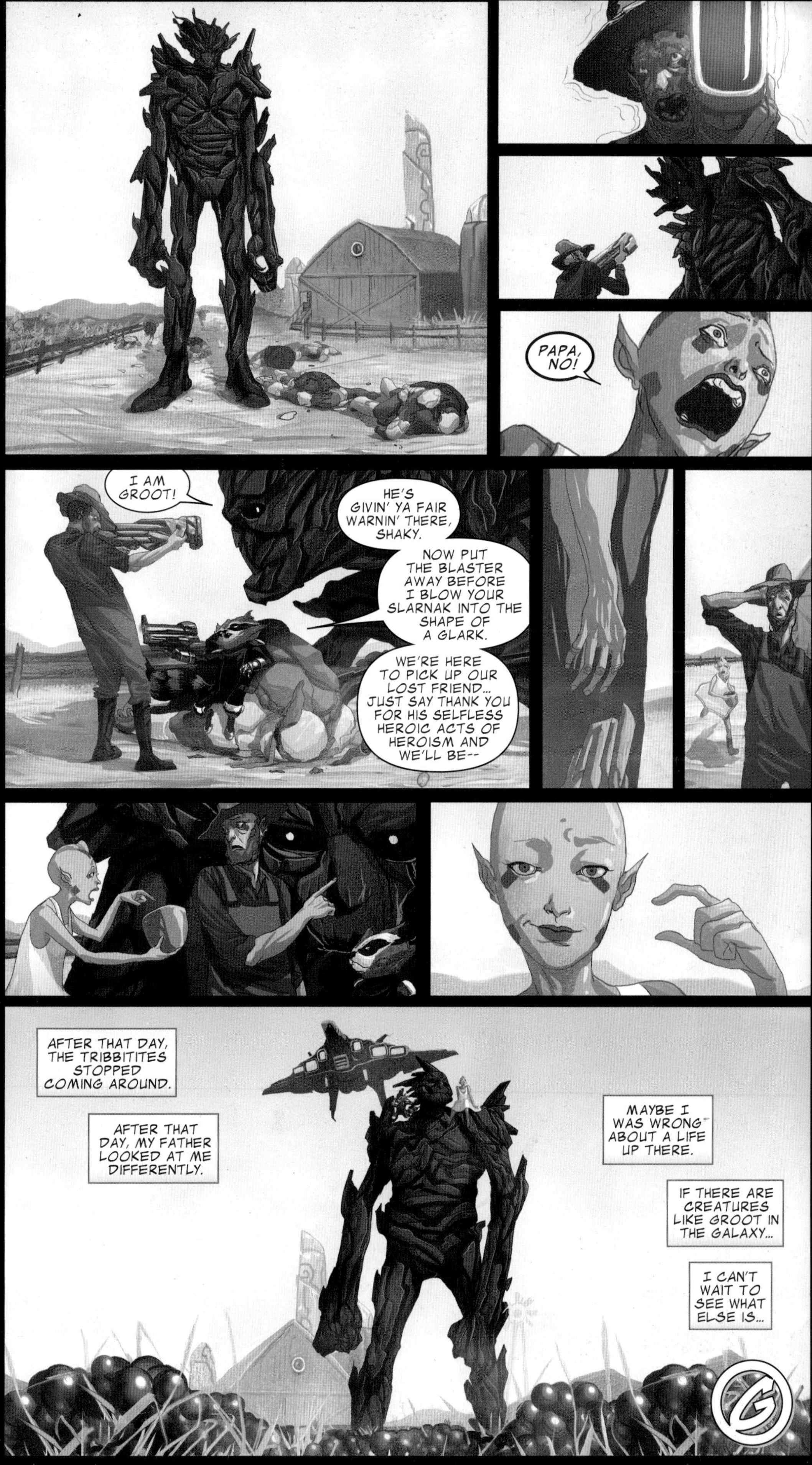
PAPA, NO!
I AM GROOT!
HE'S GIVIN' YA FAIR WARNIN' THERE, SHAKY.
NOW PUT THE BLASTER AWAY BEFORE I BLOW YOUR SLARNAK INTO THE SHAPE OF A GLARK.
WE'RE HERE TO PICK UP OUR LOST FRIEND... JUST SAY THANK YOU FOR HIS SELFLESS HEROIC ACTS OF HEROISM AND WE'LL BE--
AFTER THAT DAY, THE TRIBBITITES STOPPED COMING AROUND.
AFTER THAT DAY, MY FATHER LOOKED AT ME DIFFERENTLY.
MAYBE I WAS WRONG ABOUT A LIFE UP THERE.
IF THERE ARE CREATURES LIKE GROOT IN THE GALAXY...
I CAN'T WAIT TO SEE WHAT ELSE IS...

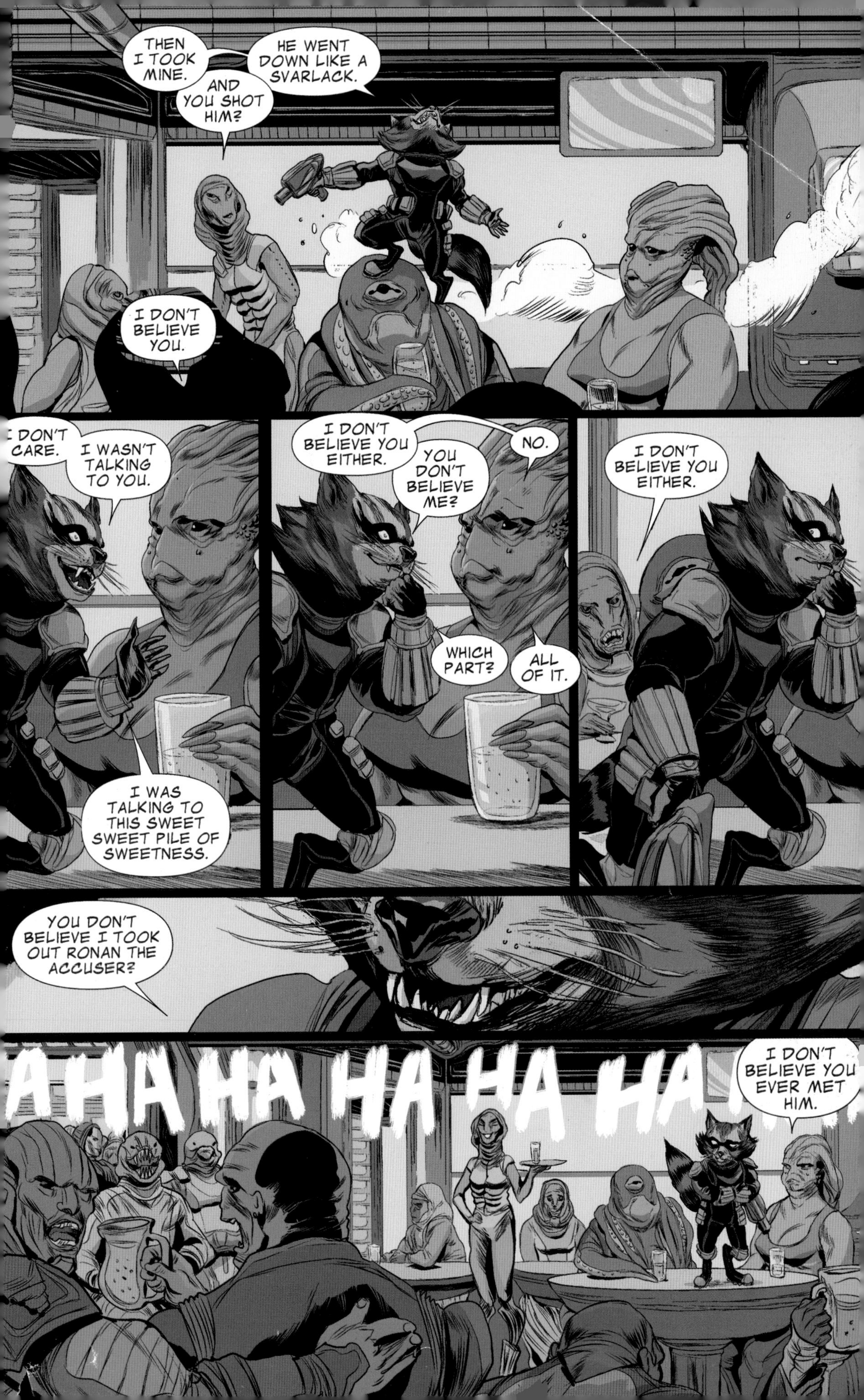
THEN I TOOK MINE.
HE WENT DOWN LIKE A SVARLACK.
AND YOU SHOT HIM?
I DON'T BELIEVE YOU.
I DON'T CARE.
I WASN'T TALKING TO YOU.
I WAS TALKING TO THIS SWEET SWEET PILE OF SWEETNESS.
I DON'T BELIEVE YOU EITHER.
NO.
YOU DON'T BELIEVE ME?
WHICH PART?
ALL OF IT.
I DON'T BELIEVE YOU EITHER.
YOU DON'T BELIEVE I TOOK OUT RONAN THE ACCUSER?
AHAHA HA HA HA HA
I DON'T BELIEVE YOU EVER MET HIM.

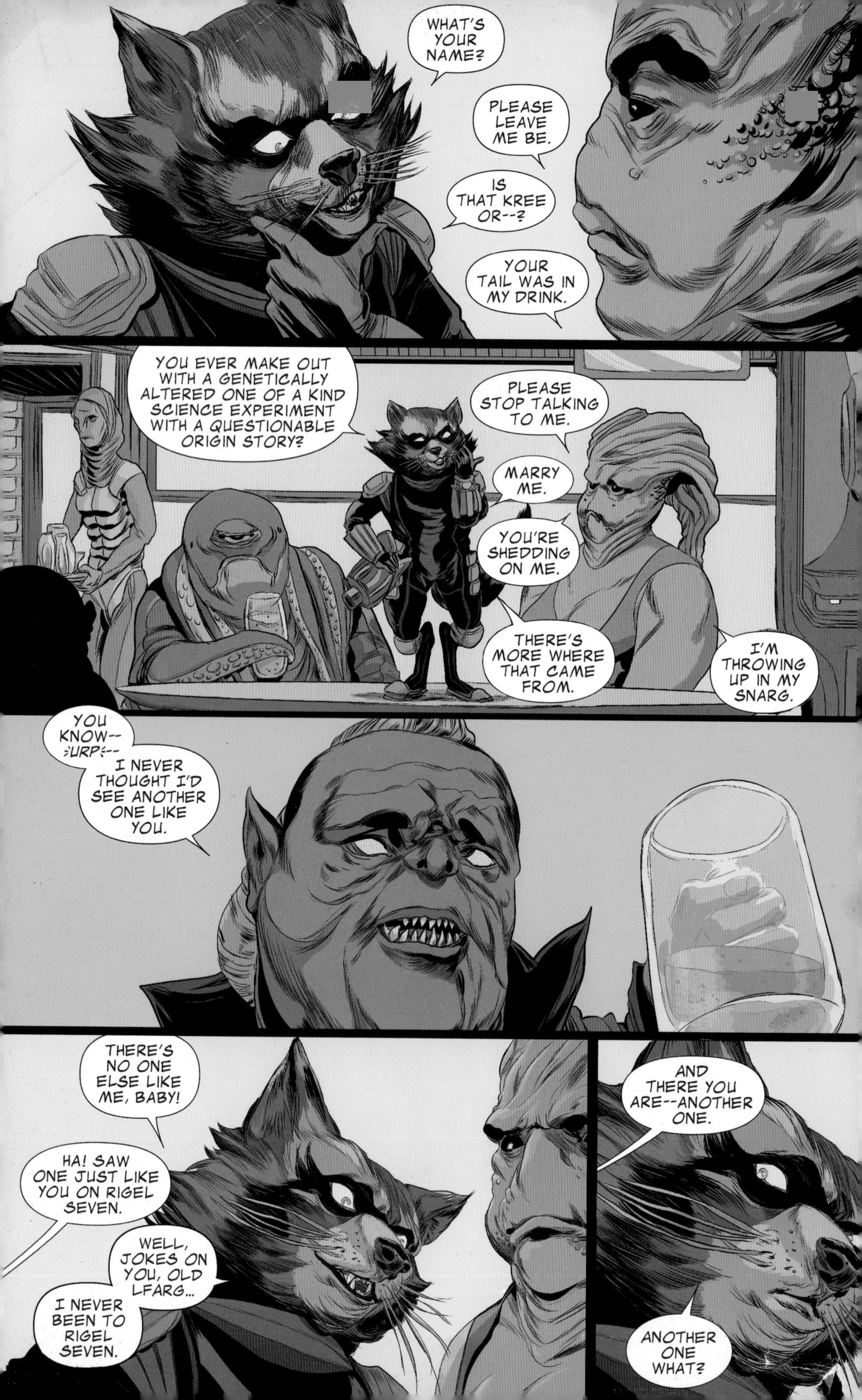
WHAT'S YOUR NAME?
PLEASE LEAVE ME BE.
IS THAT KREE OR--?
YOUR TAIL WAS IN MY DRINK.
YOU EVER MAKE OUT WITH A GENETICALLY ALTERED ONE OF A KIND SCIENCE EXPERIMENT WITH A QUESTIONABLE ORIGIN STORY?
PLEASE STOP TALKING TO ME.
MARRY ME.
YOU'RE SHEDDING ON ME.
THERE'S MORE WHERE THAT CAME FROM.
I'M THROWING UP IN MY SNARG.
YOU KNOW-- ›URP‹-- I NEVER THOUGHT I'D SEE ANOTHER ONE LIKE YOU.
THERE'S NO ONE ELSE LIKE ME, BABY!
HA! SAW ONE JUST LIKE YOU ON RIGEL SEVEN.
WELL, JOKES ON YOU, OLD LFARG...
I NEVER BEEN TO RIGEL SEVEN.
AND THERE YOU ARE--ANOTHER ONE.
ANOTHER ONE WHAT?

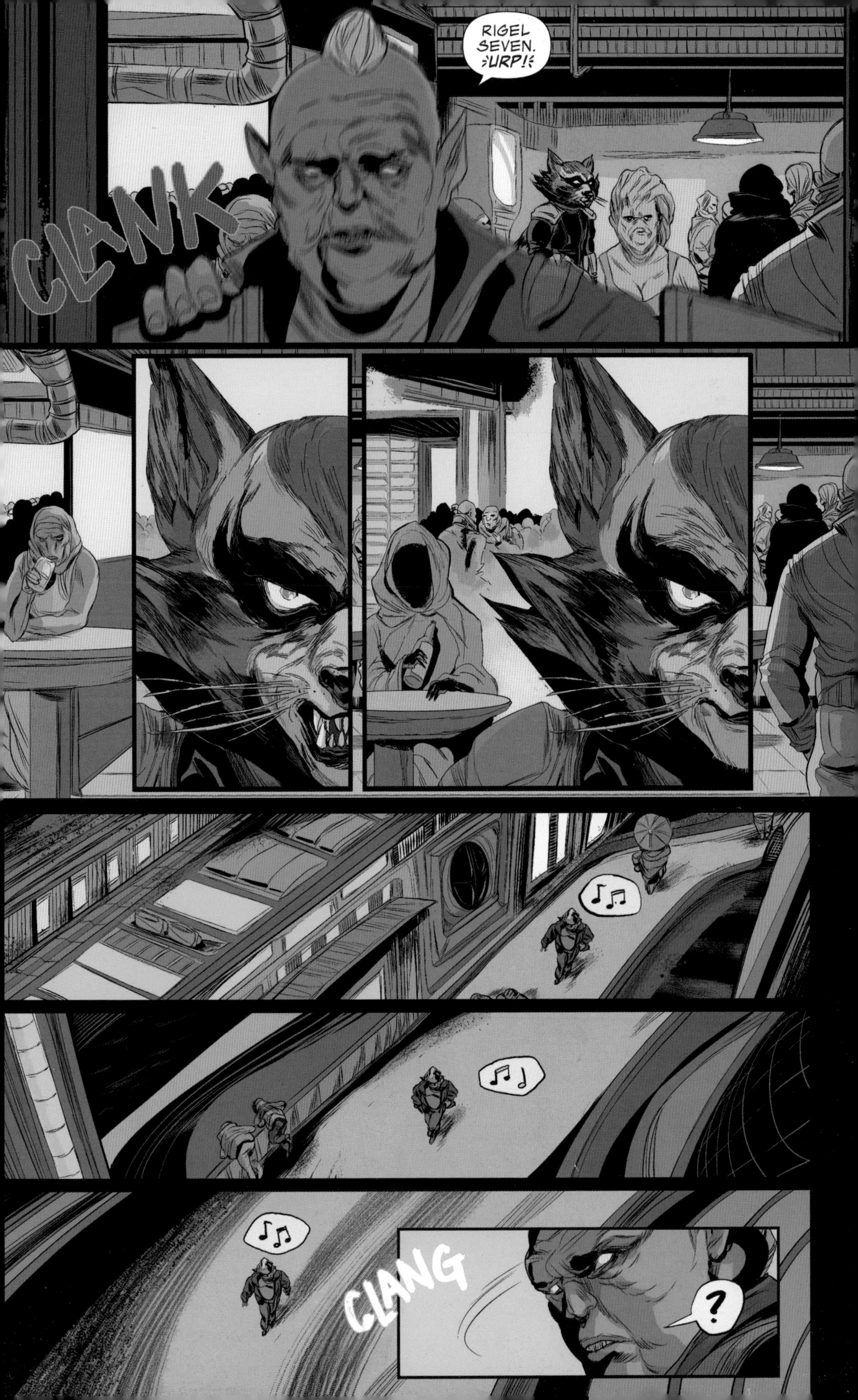
RIGEL SEVEN. *URP!*
CLANK
♫♫
♫♩
♫♫
CLANG
?

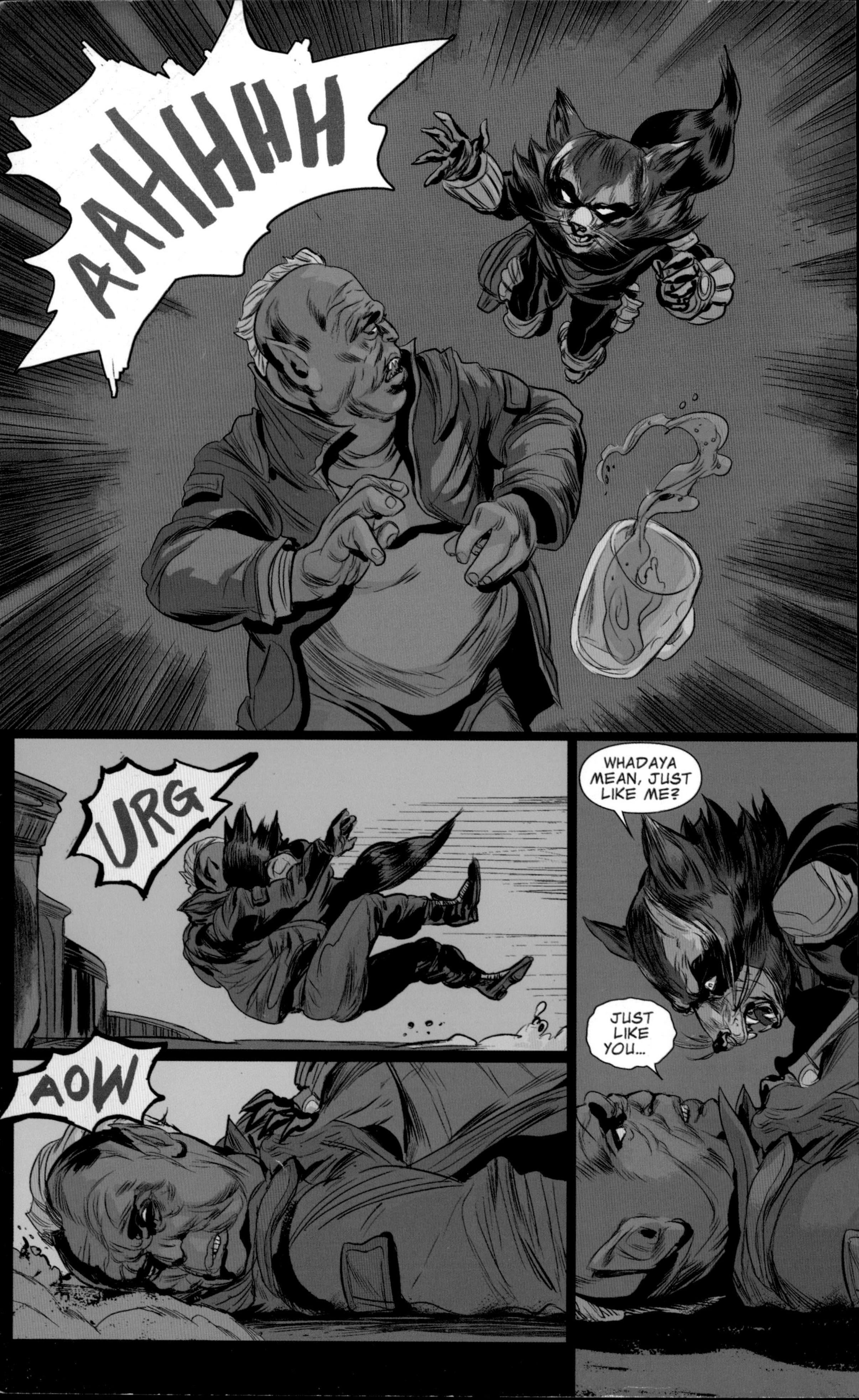
AAHHHH
URG
AOW
WHADAYA MEAN, JUST LIKE ME?
JUST LIKE YOU...

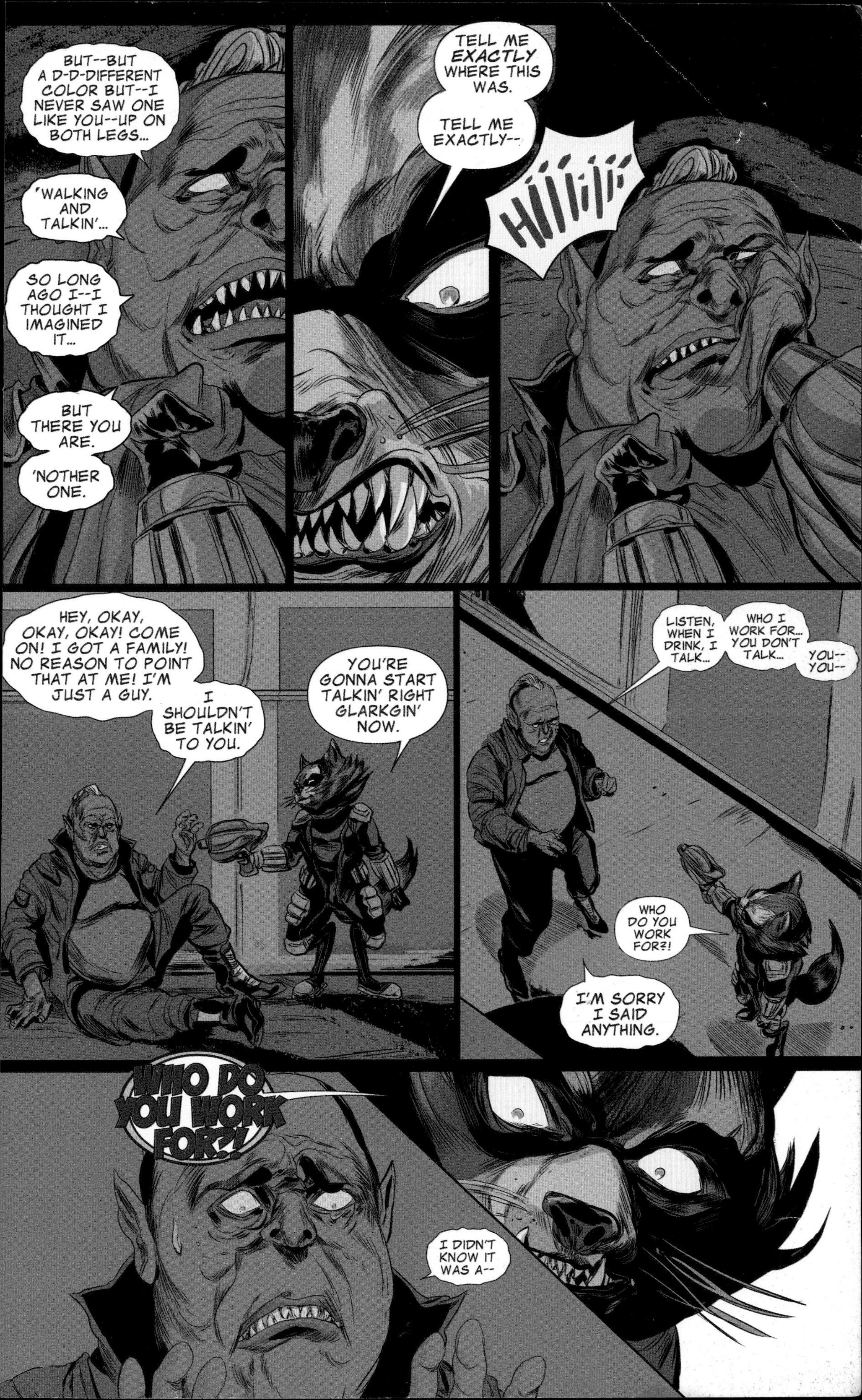

BUT--BUT A D-D-DIFFERENT COLOR BUT--I NEVER SAW ONE LIKE YOU--UP ON BOTH LEGS...
'WALKING AND TALKIN'...
SO LONG AGO I--I THOUGHT I IMAGINED IT...
BUT THERE YOU ARE.
'NOTHER ONE.
TELL ME EXACTLY WHERE THIS WAS.
TELL ME EXACTLY--
HEY, OKAY, OKAY, OKAY! COME ON! I GOT A FAMILY! NO REASON TO POINT THAT AT ME! I'M JUST A GUY.
I SHOULDN'T BE TALKIN' TO YOU.
YOU'RE GONNA START TALKIN' RIGHT GLARKGIN' NOW.
LISTEN, WHEN I DRINK, I TALK...
WHO I WORK FOR... YOU DON'T TALK...
YOU-- YOU--
WHO DO YOU WORK FOR?!
I'M SORRY I SAID ANYTHING.
WHO DO YOU WORK FOR?!
I DIDN'T KNOW IT WAS A--

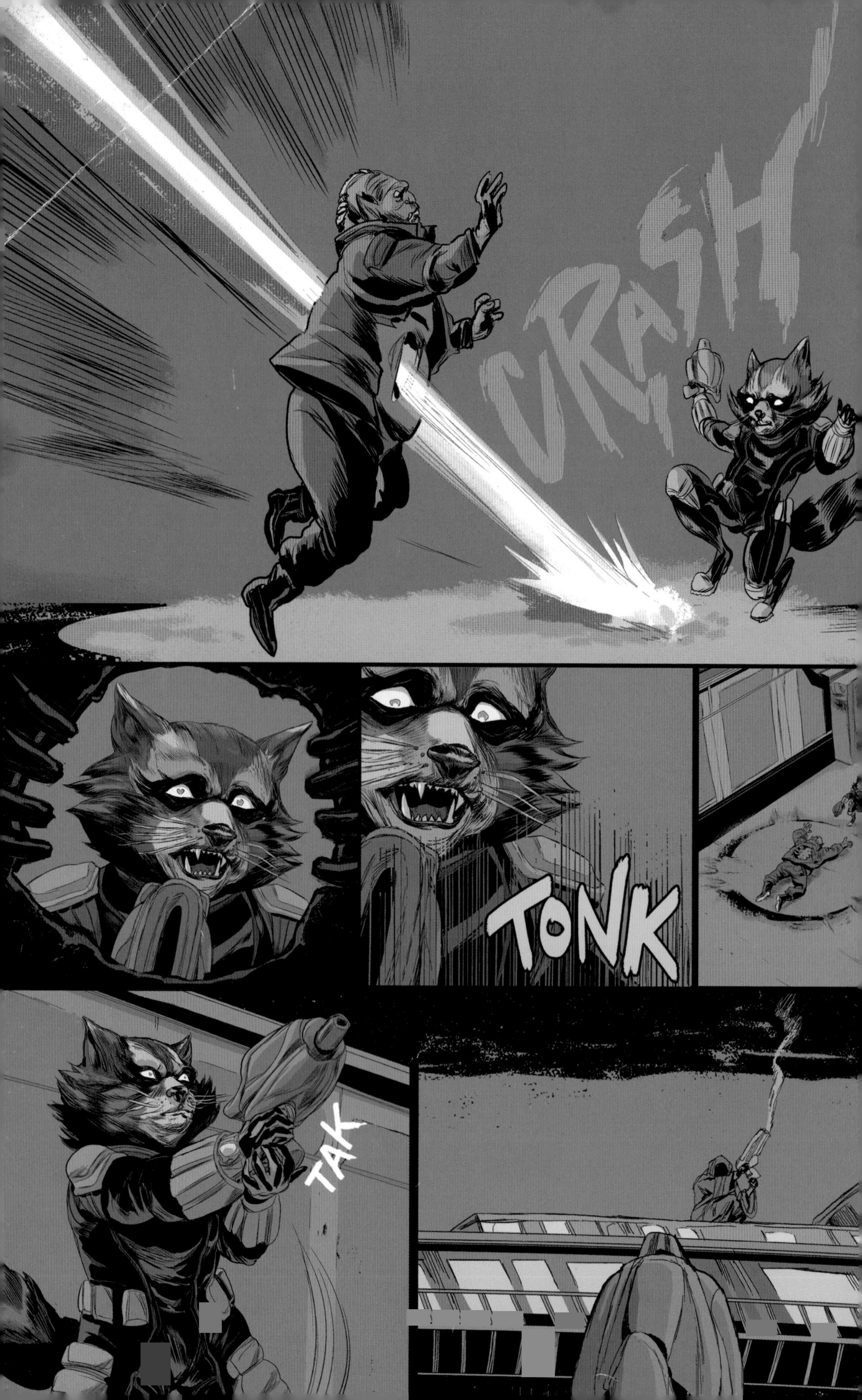
CRASH
TONK
TAK

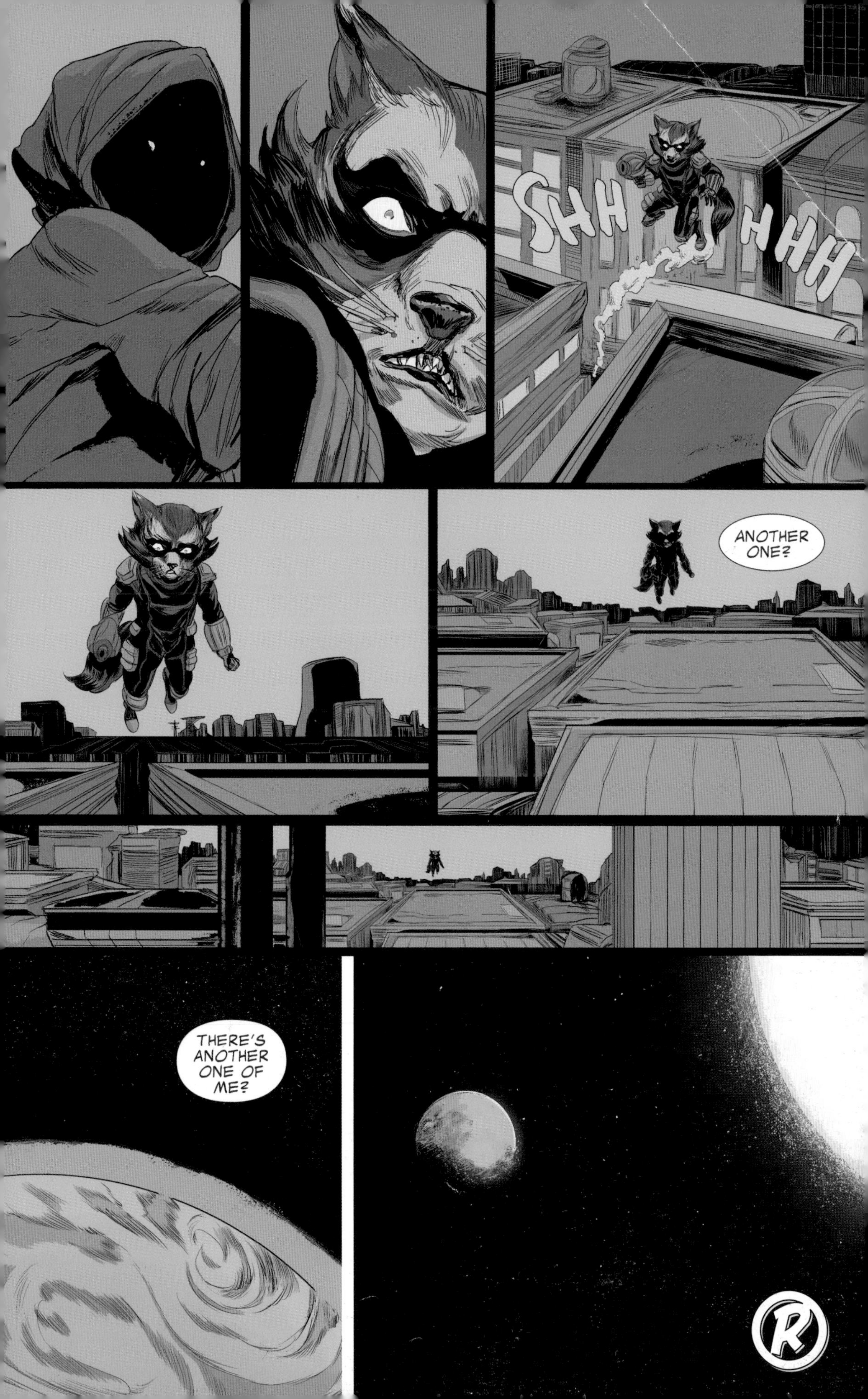
SHHHHH
ANOTHER ONE?
THERE'S ANOTHER ONE OF ME?

TERRAN.

THE SIXTH MOON OF THE
GAS-GIANT PLANET MARMAN.

SEVENTH FROM THE SUN IN A
SOLAR SYSTEM 80,000 LIGHT
YEARS FROM EARTH.

ITS HOST PLANET WAS A VICTIM OF
THE ALL-CONSUMING PHOENIX FORCE.

ALL LIFE WAS WIPED
FROM THE PLANET.

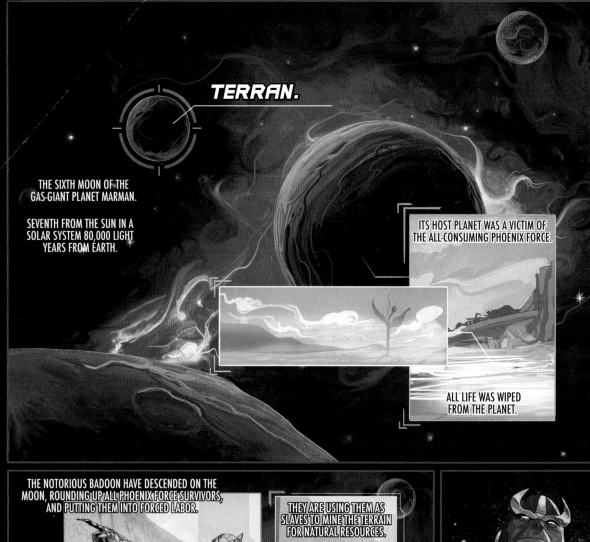

THE NOTORIOUS BADOON HAVE DESCENDED ON THE
MOON, ROUNDING UP ALL PHOENIX FORCE SURVIVORS,
AND PUTTING THEM INTO FORCED LABOR.

THEY ARE USING THEM AS
SLAVES TO MINE THE TERRAIN
FOR NATURAL RESOURCES.

ALL FOR THE GLORY
OF THE MAD TITAN
THANOS.

BUT THANOS HAS A DAUGHTER.

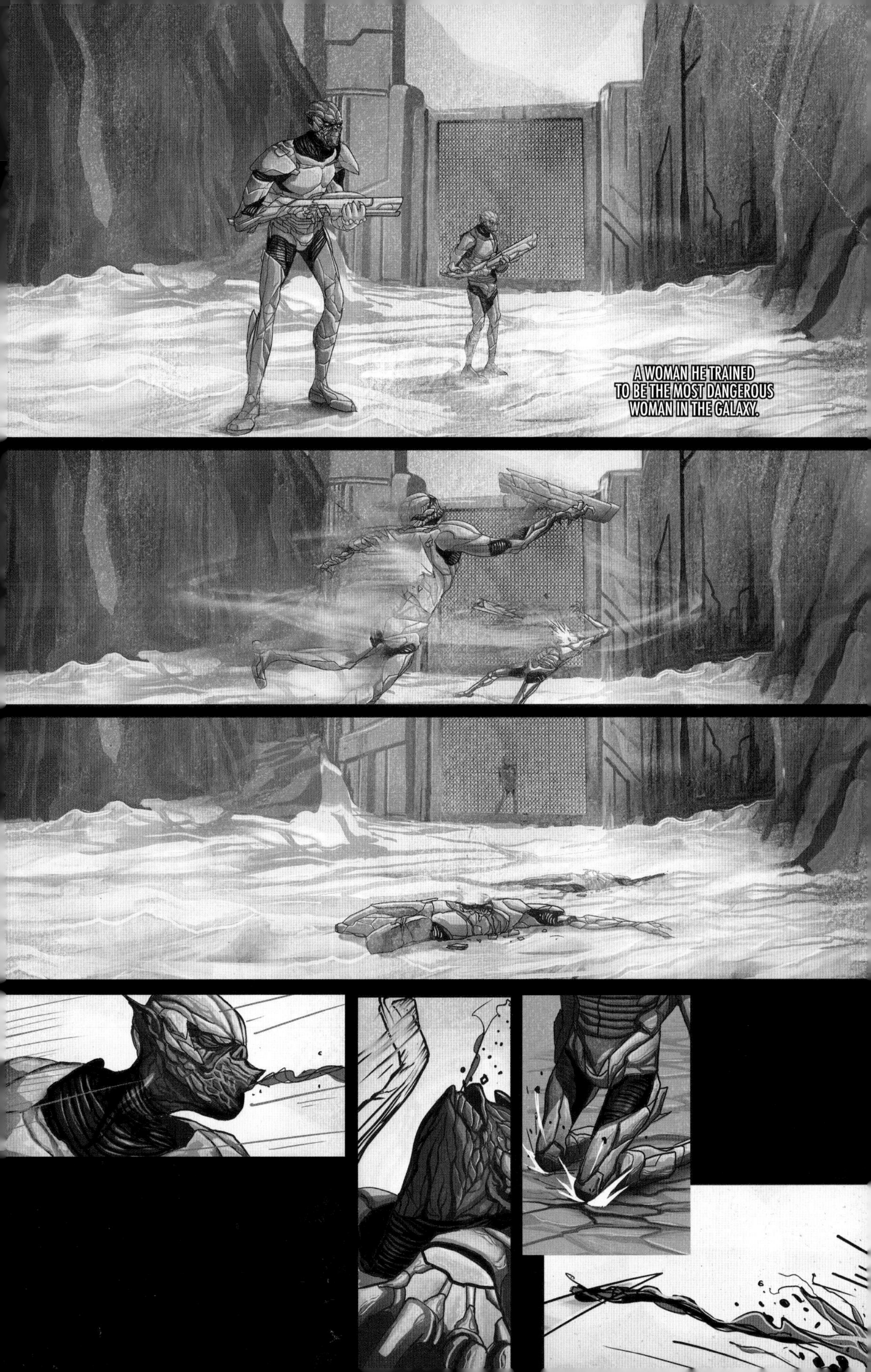
A WOMAN HE TRAINED TO BE THE MOST DANGEROUS WOMAN IN THE GALAXY.

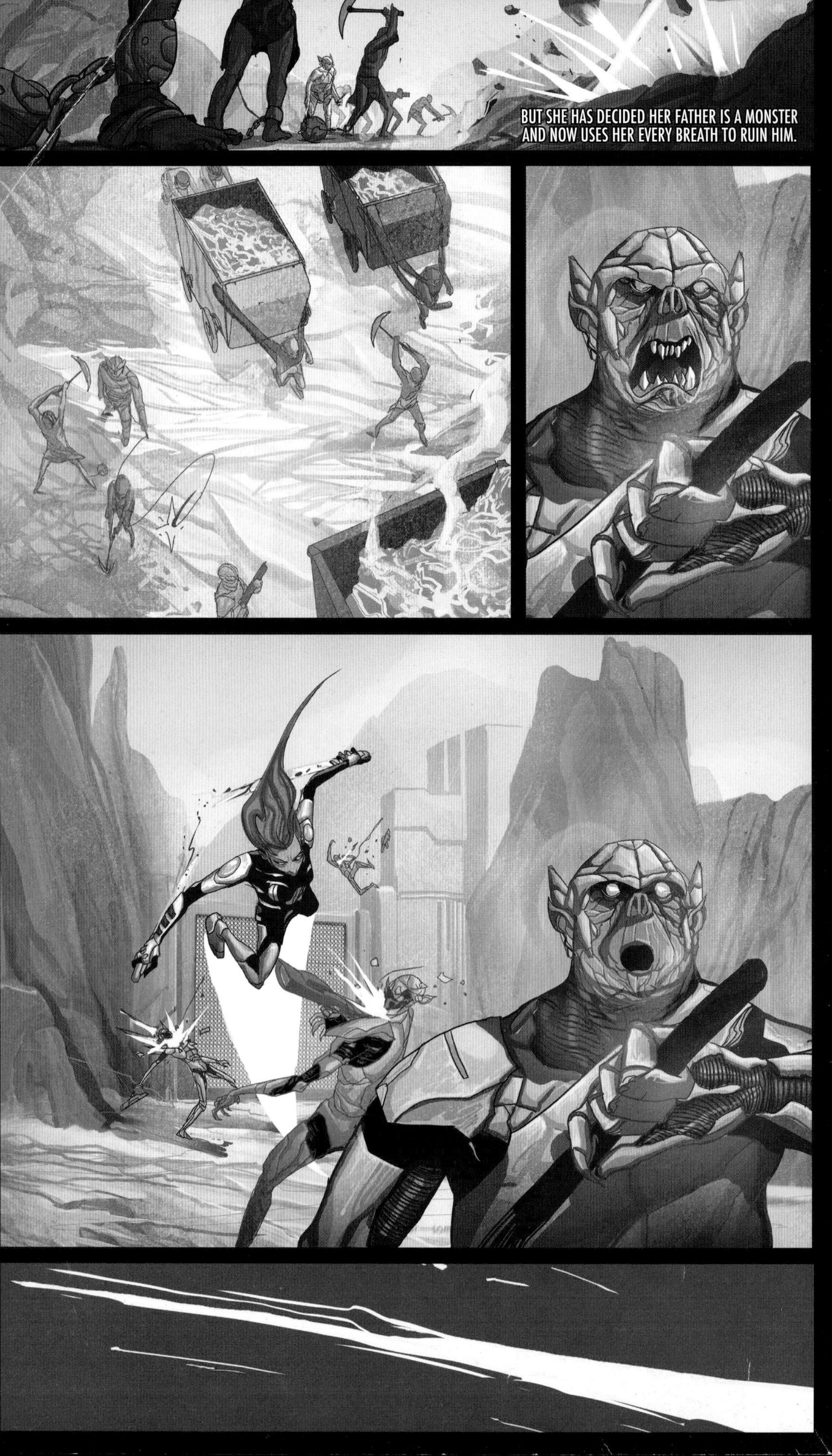
BUT SHE HAS DECIDED HER FATHER IS A MONSTER AND NOW USES HER EVERY BREATH TO RUIN HIM.

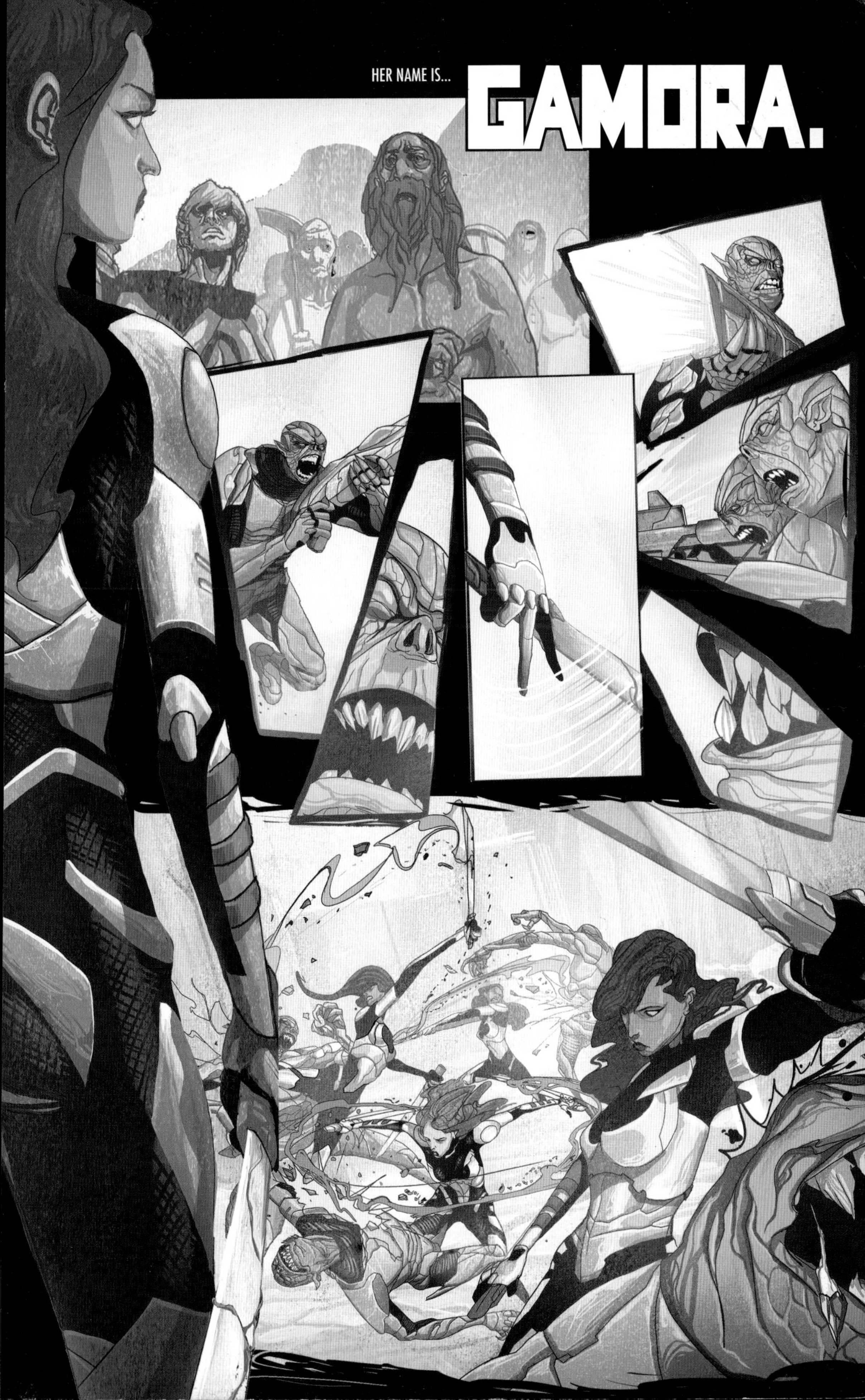
HER NAME IS...
GAMORA.

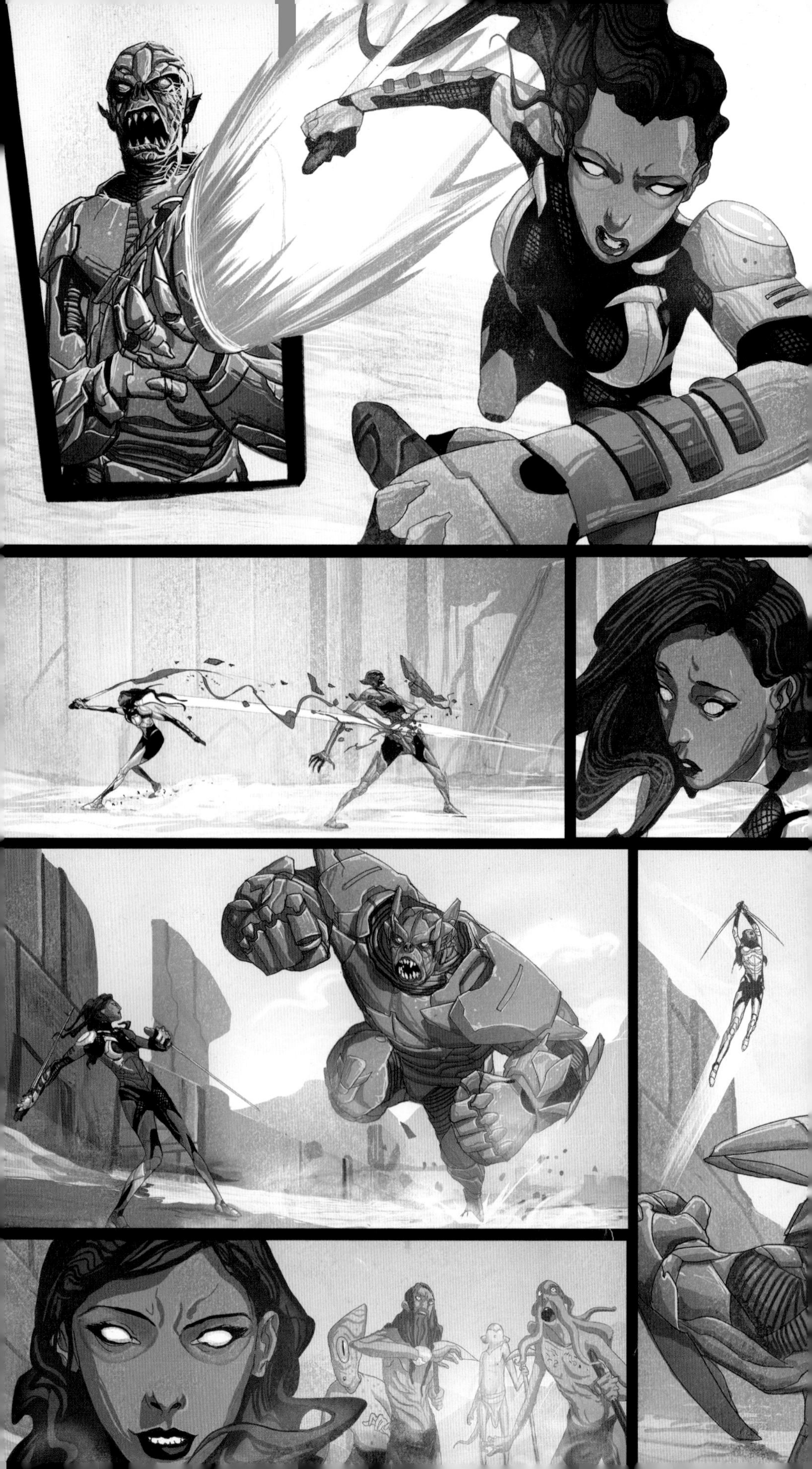

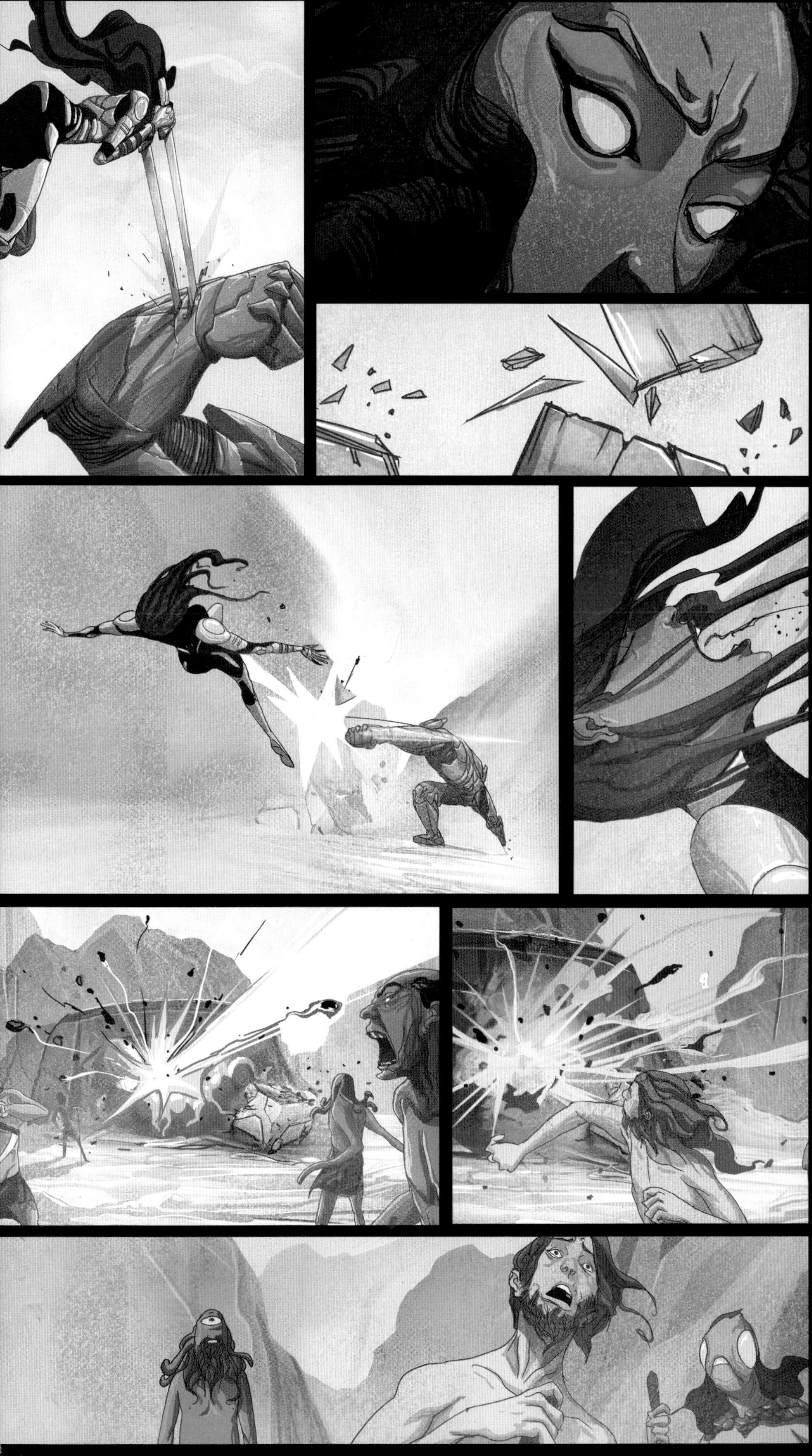

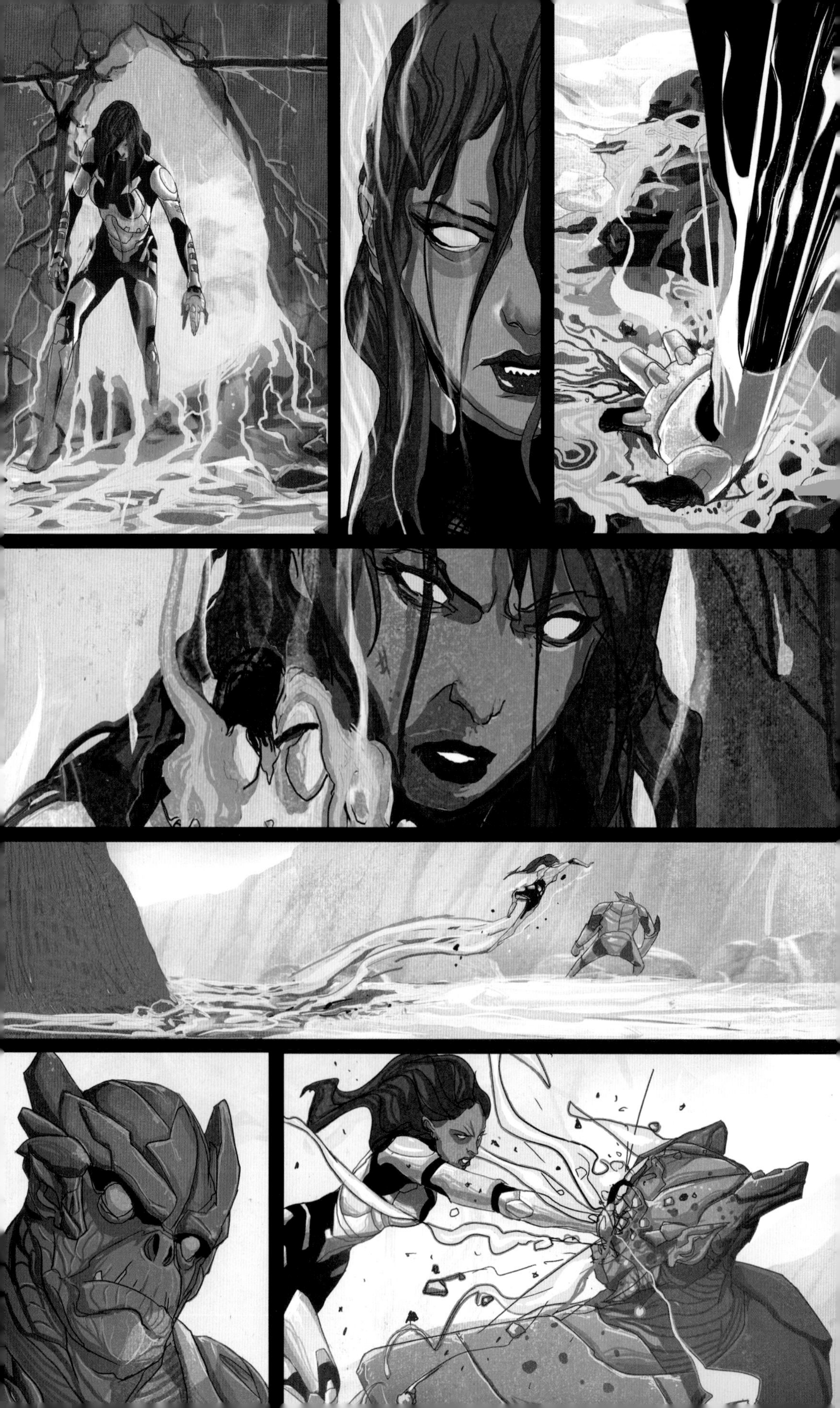

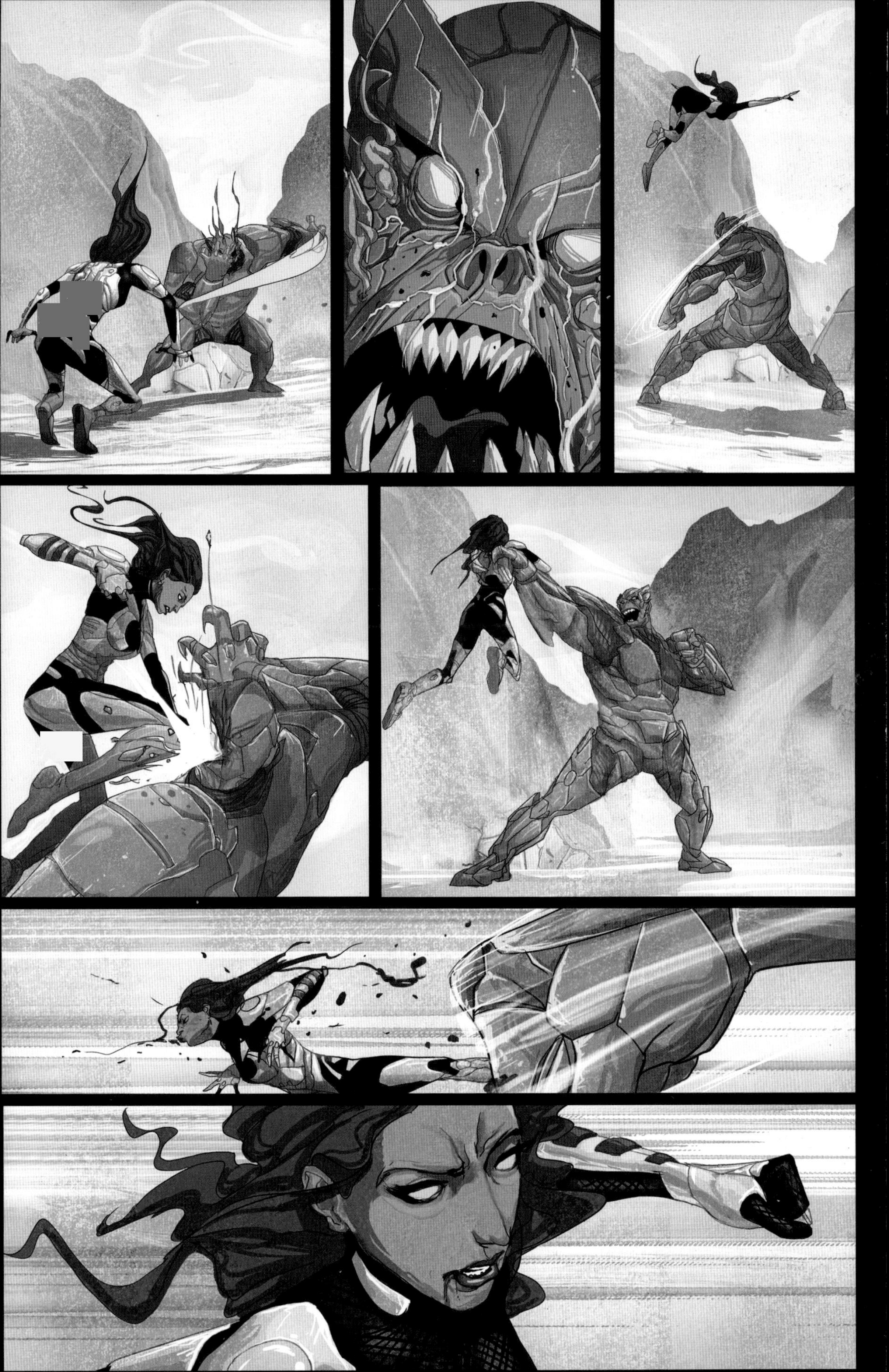

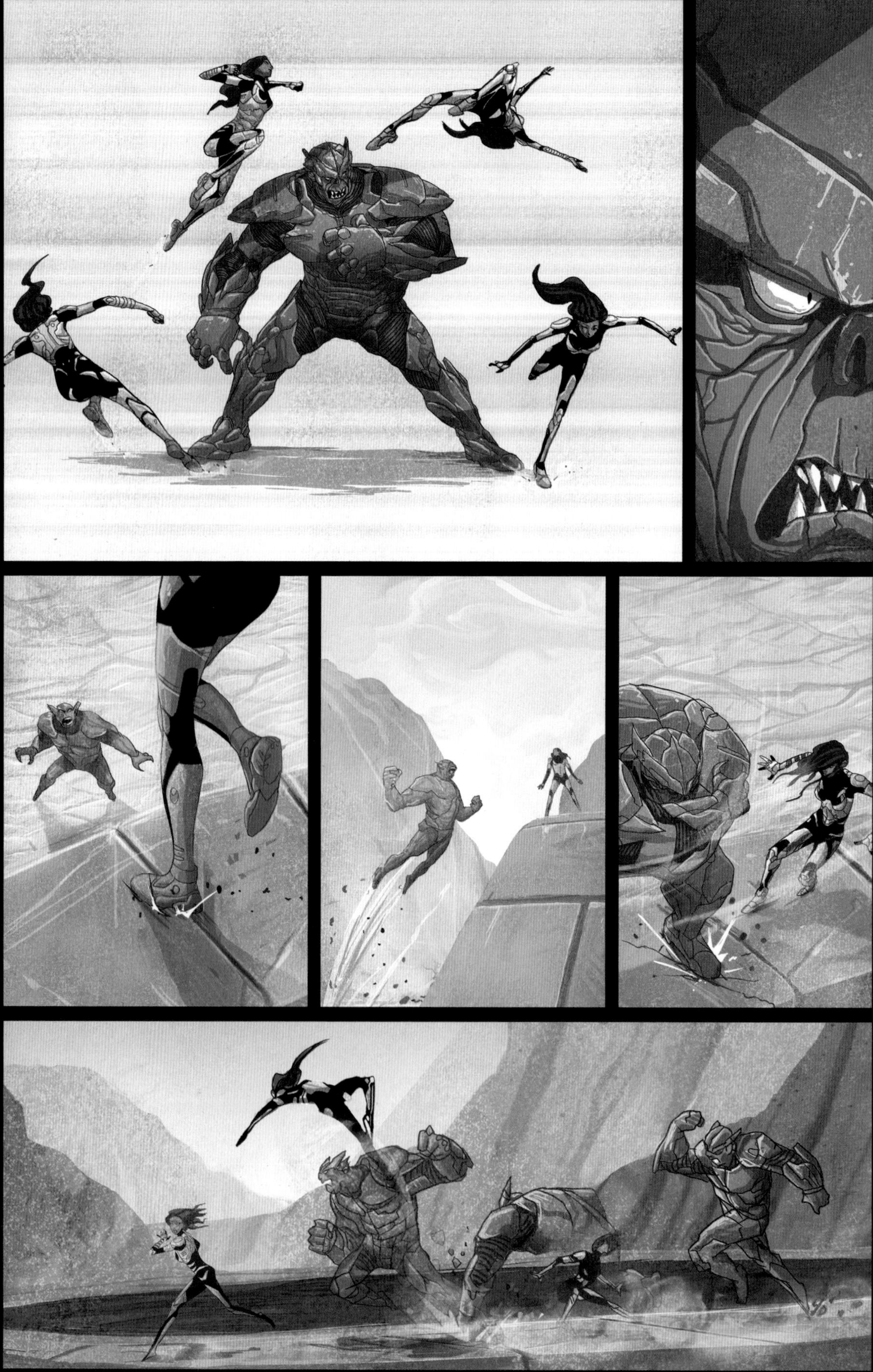

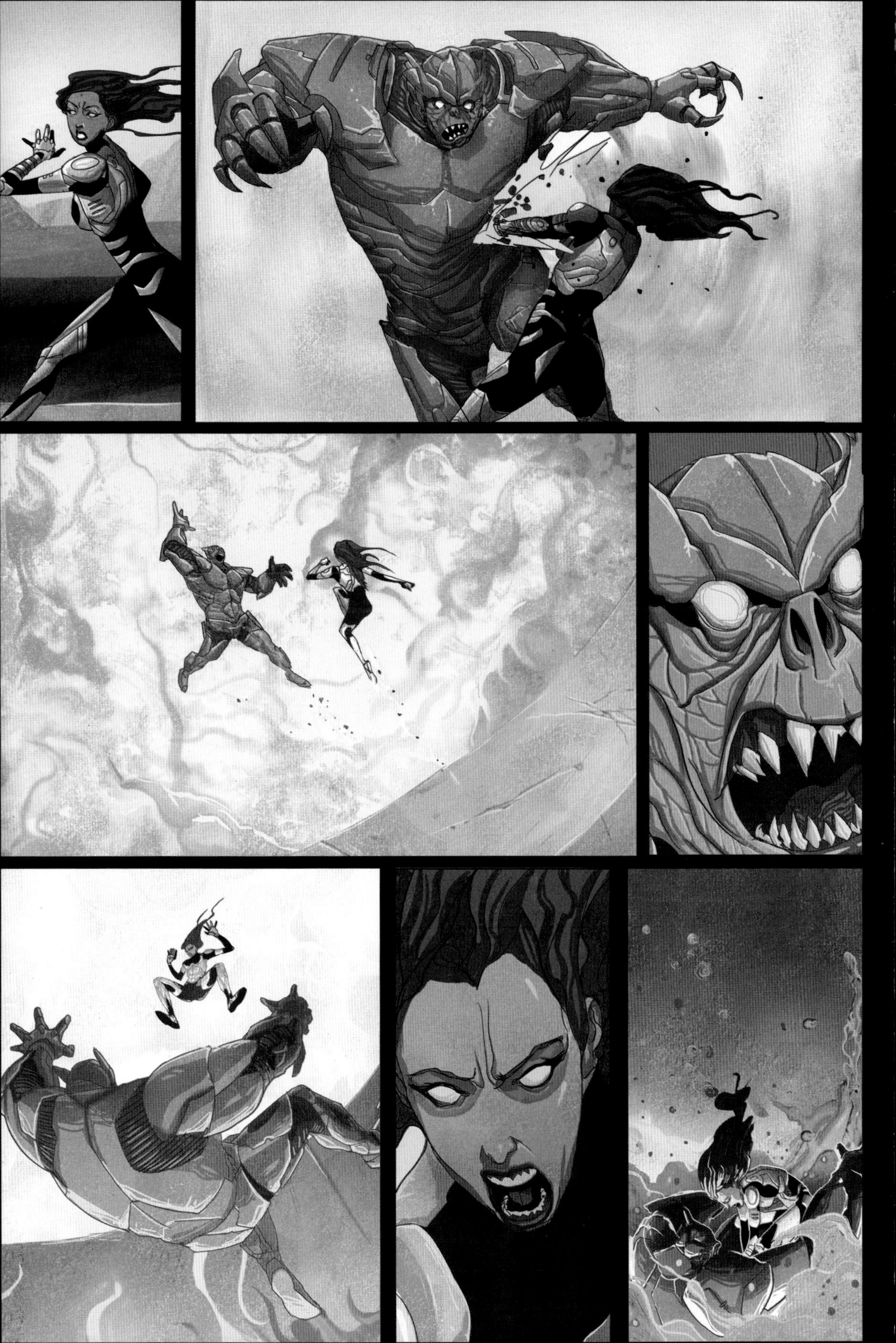

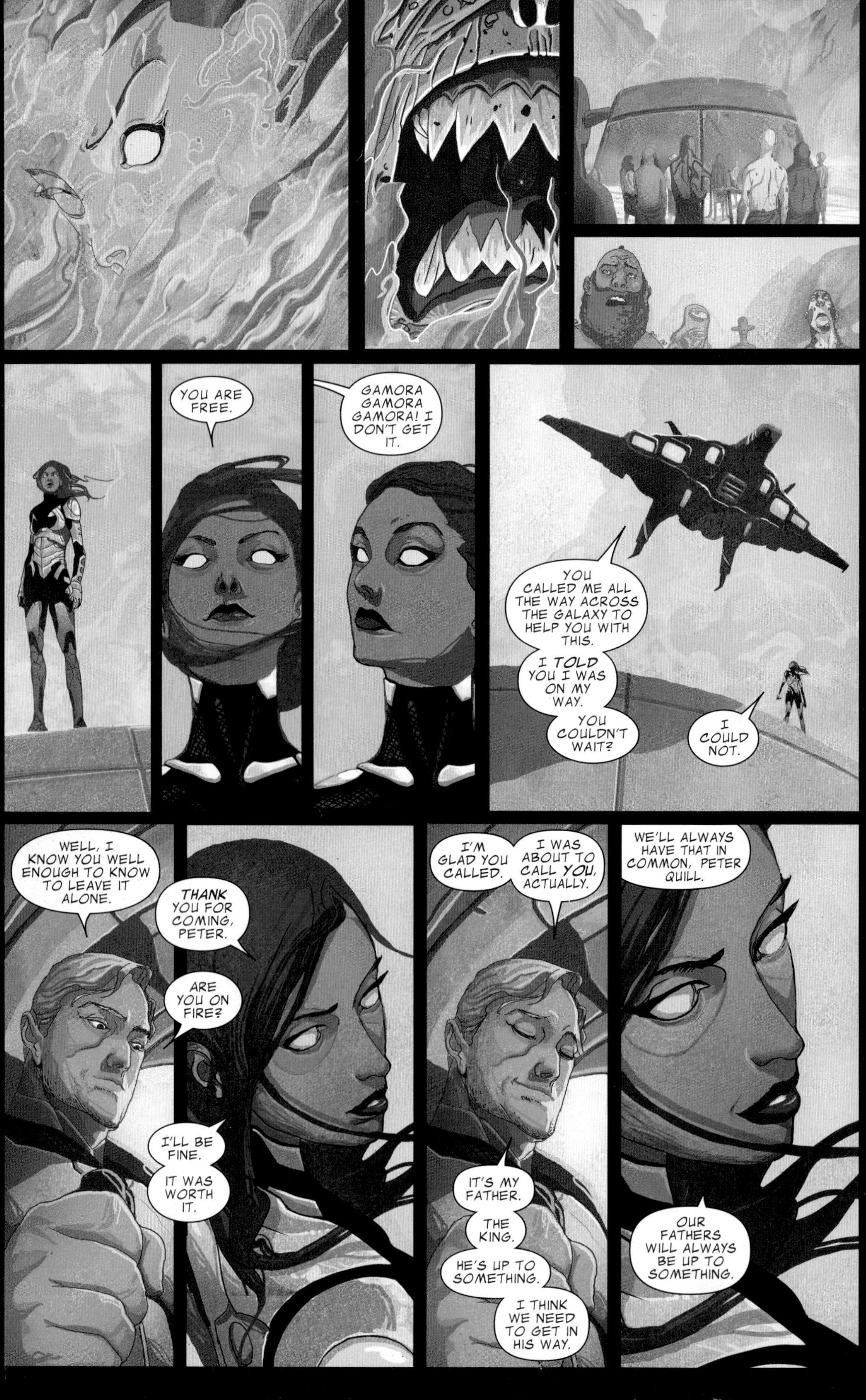
YOU ARE FREE.
GAMORA GAMORA GAMORA! I DON'T GET IT.
YOU CALLED ME ALL THE WAY ACROSS THE GALAXY TO HELP YOU WITH THIS.
I TOLD YOU I WAS ON MY WAY.
YOU COULDN'T WAIT?
I COULD NOT.
WELL, I KNOW YOU WELL ENOUGH TO KNOW TO LEAVE IT ALONE.
THANK YOU FOR COMING, PETER.
ARE YOU ON FIRE?
I'LL BE FINE.
IT WAS WORTH IT.
I'M GLAD YOU CALLED.
I WAS ABOUT TO CALL YOU, ACTUALLY.
IT'S MY FATHER.
THE KING.
HE'S UP TO SOMETHING.
I THINK WE NEED TO GET IN HIS WAY.
WE'LL ALWAYS HAVE THAT IN COMMON, PETER QUILL.
OUR FATHERS WILL ALWAYS BE UP TO SOMETHING.

MARVEL GRAPHIC NOVEL **GUARDIANS OF THE GALAXY #1**

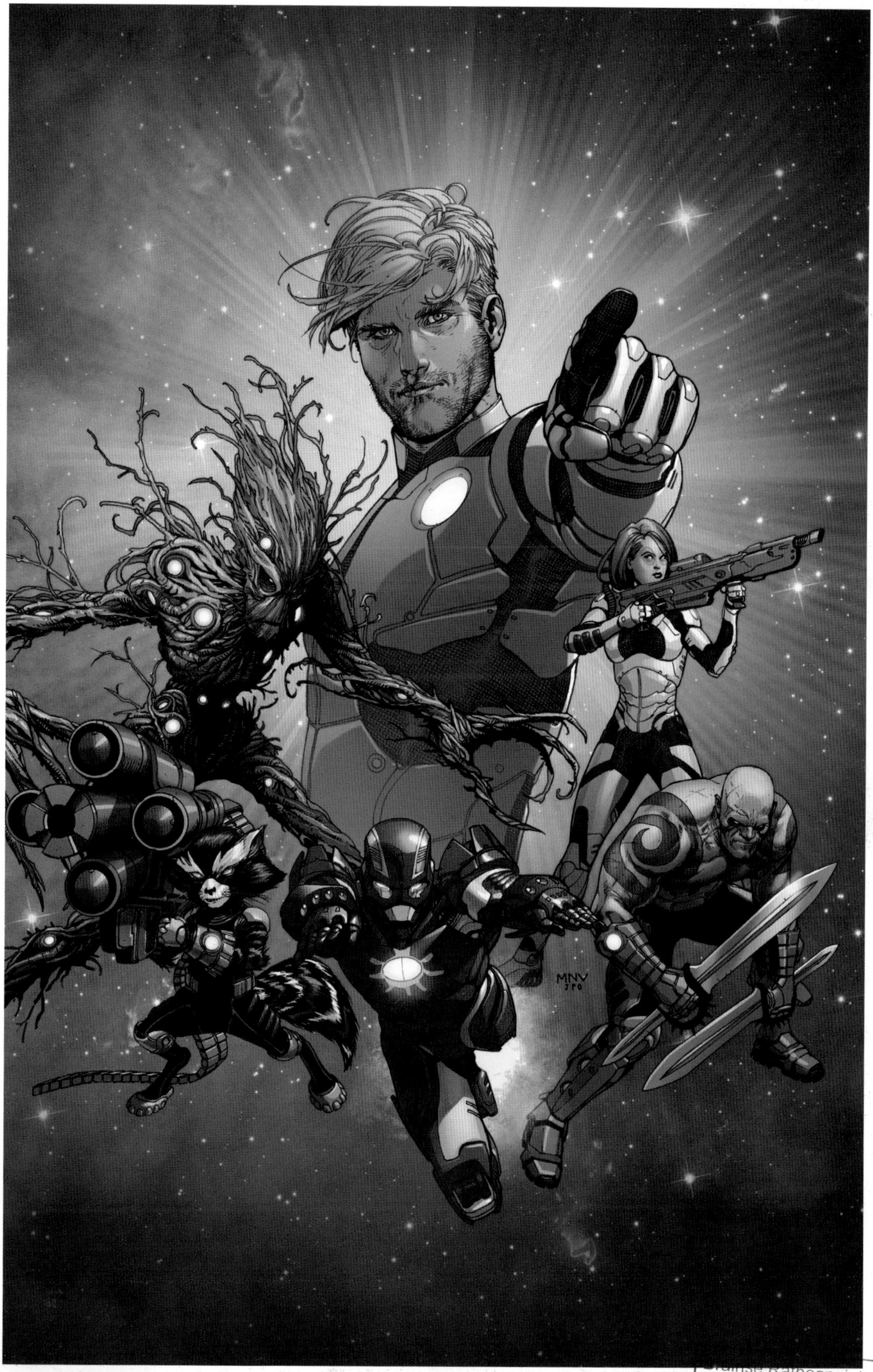

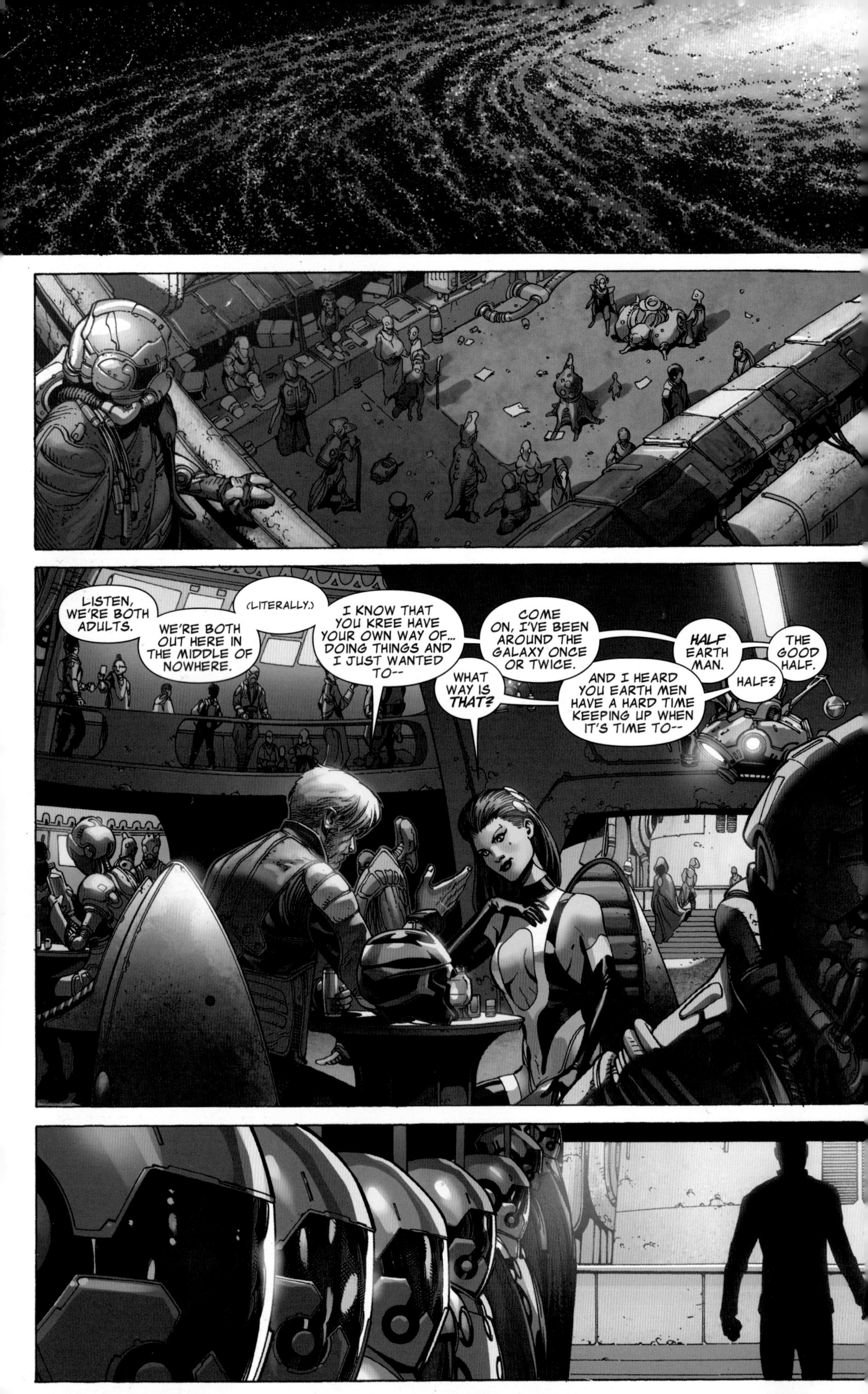
LISTEN, WE'RE BOTH ADULTS.
WE'RE BOTH OUT HERE IN THE MIDDLE OF NOWHERE.
(LITERALLY.)
I KNOW THAT YOU KREE HAVE YOUR OWN WAY OF... DOING THINGS AND I JUST WANTED TO--
WHAT WAY IS *THAT?*
COME ON, I'VE BEEN AROUND THE GALAXY ONCE OR TWICE.
AND I HEARD YOU EARTH MEN HAVE A HARD TIME KEEPING UP WHEN IT'S TIME TO--
HALF EARTH MAN.
HALF?
THE GOOD HALF.

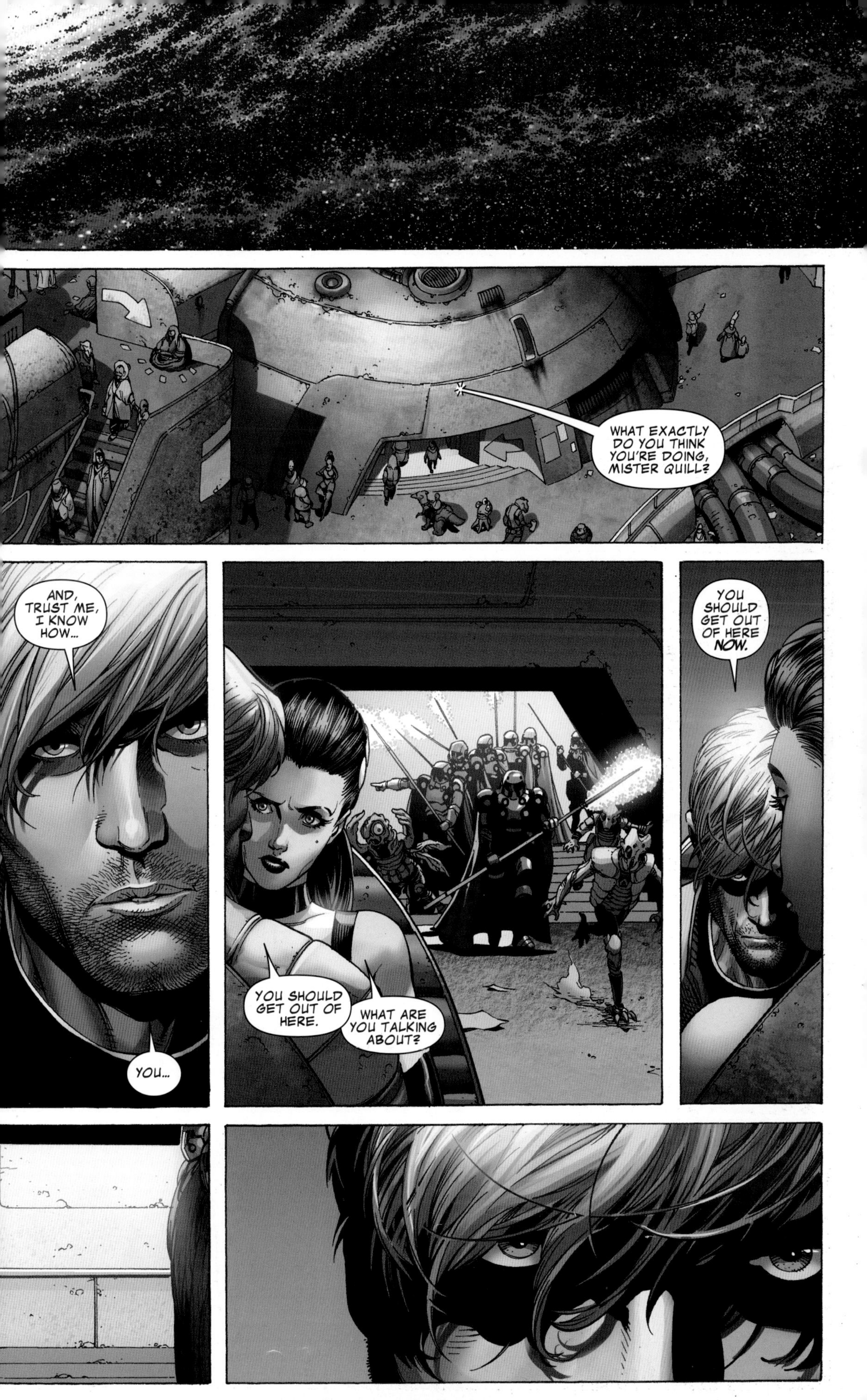
WHAT EXACTLY DO YOU THINK YOU'RE DOING, MISTER QUILL?
AND, TRUST ME, I KNOW HOW...
YOU...
YOU SHOULD GET OUT OF HERE.
WHAT ARE YOU TALKING ABOUT?
YOU SHOULD GET OUT OF HERE NOW.

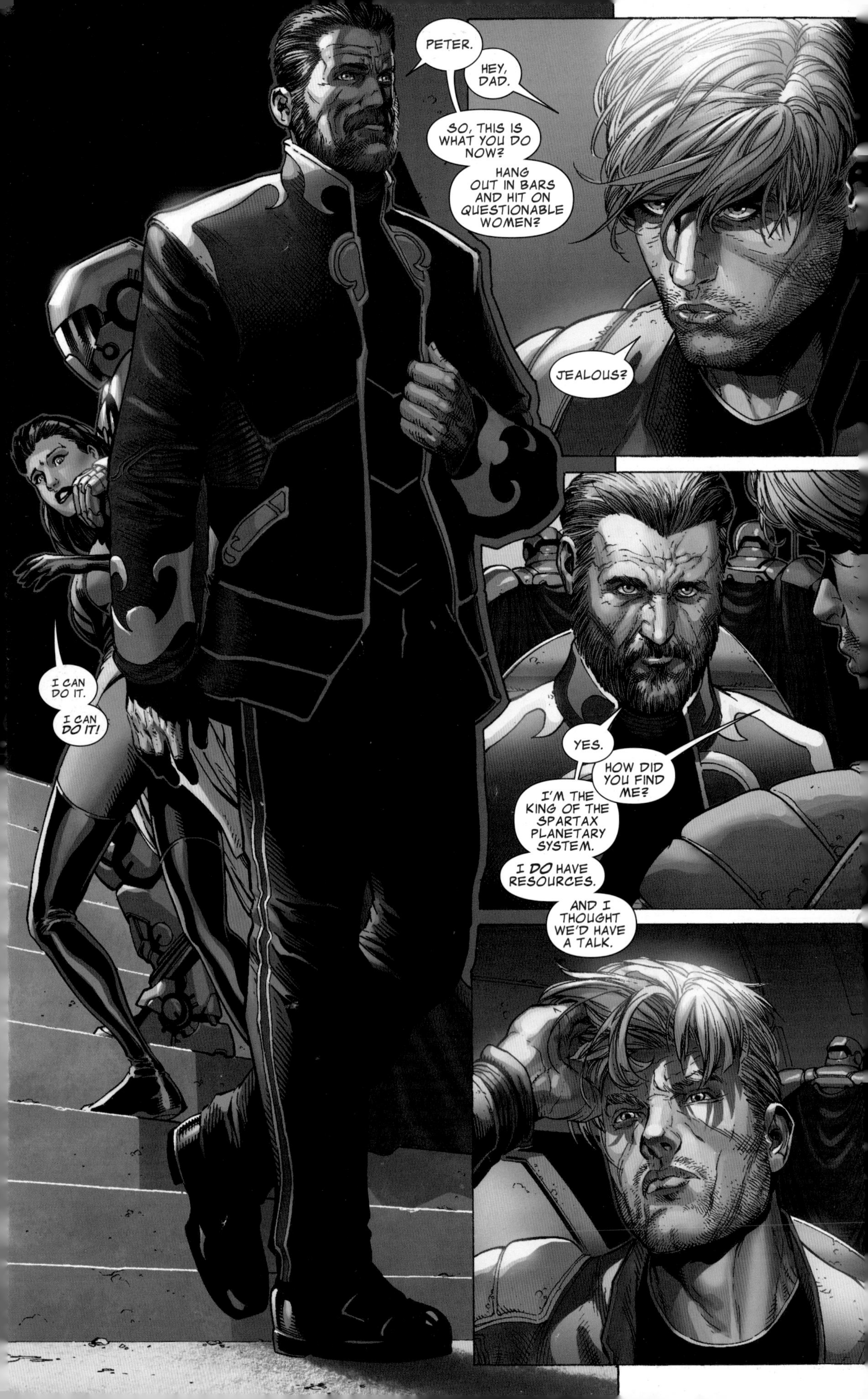
PETER.
HEY, DAD.
SO, THIS IS WHAT YOU DO NOW?
HANG OUT IN BARS AND HIT ON QUESTIONABLE WOMEN?
JEALOUS?
I CAN DO IT.
I CAN DO IT!
YES.
HOW DID YOU FIND ME?
I'M THE KING OF THE SPARTAX PLANETARY SYSTEM.
I DO HAVE RESOURCES.
AND I THOUGHT WE'D HAVE A TALK.

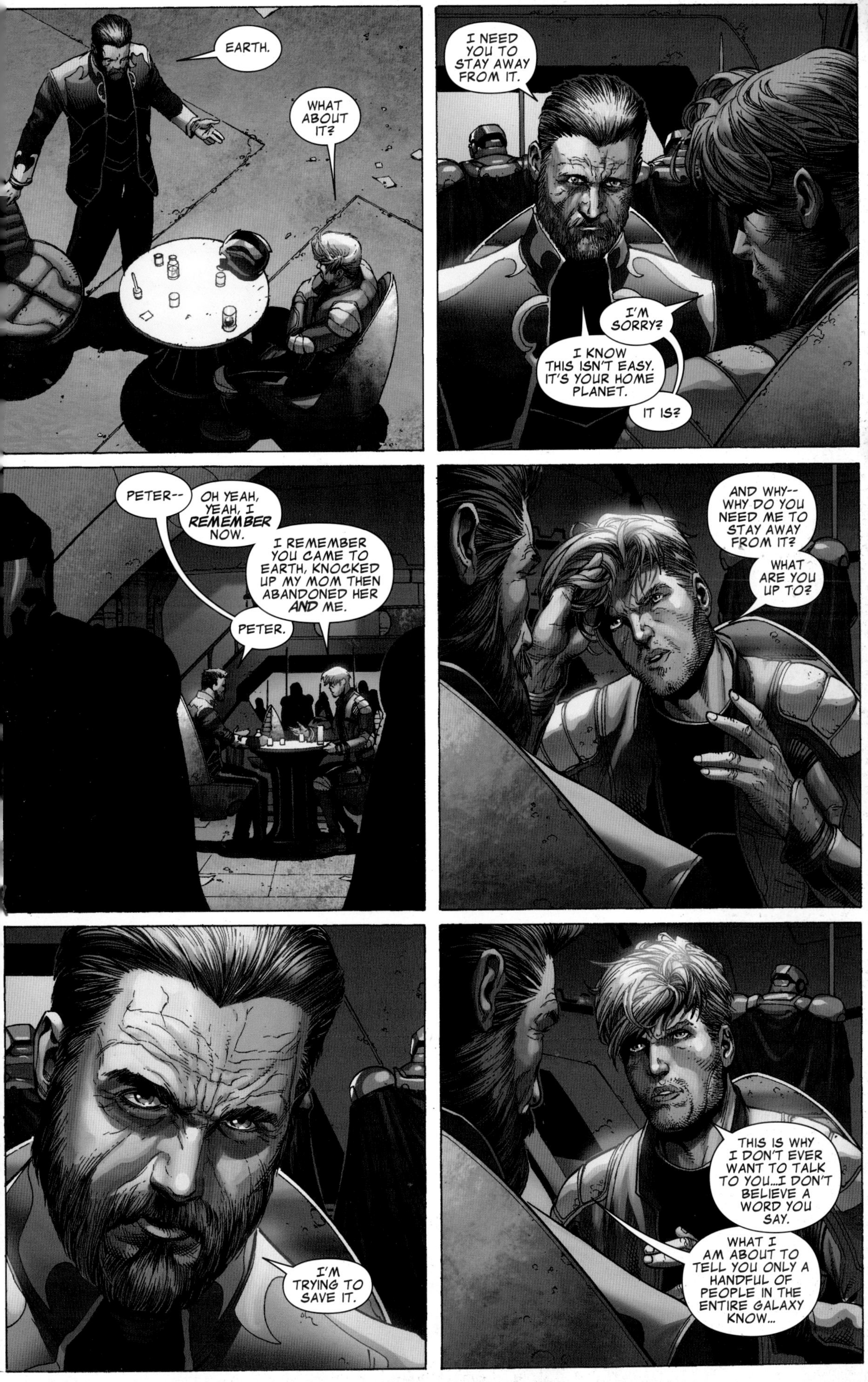
EARTH.
WHAT ABOUT IT?
I NEED YOU TO STAY AWAY FROM IT.
I'M SORRY?
I KNOW THIS ISN'T EASY. IT'S YOUR HOME PLANET.
IT IS?
PETER--
OH YEAH, YEAH, I REMEMBER NOW.
I REMEMBER YOU CAME TO EARTH, KNOCKED UP MY MOM THEN ABANDONED HER AND ME.
PETER.
AND WHY-- WHY DO YOU NEED ME TO STAY AWAY FROM IT?
WHAT ARE YOU UP TO?
I'M TRYING TO SAVE IT.
THIS IS WHY I DON'T EVER WANT TO TALK TO YOU...I DON'T BELIEVE A WORD YOU SAY.
WHAT I AM ABOUT TO TELL YOU ONLY A HANDFUL OF PEOPLE IN THE ENTIRE GALAXY KNOW...

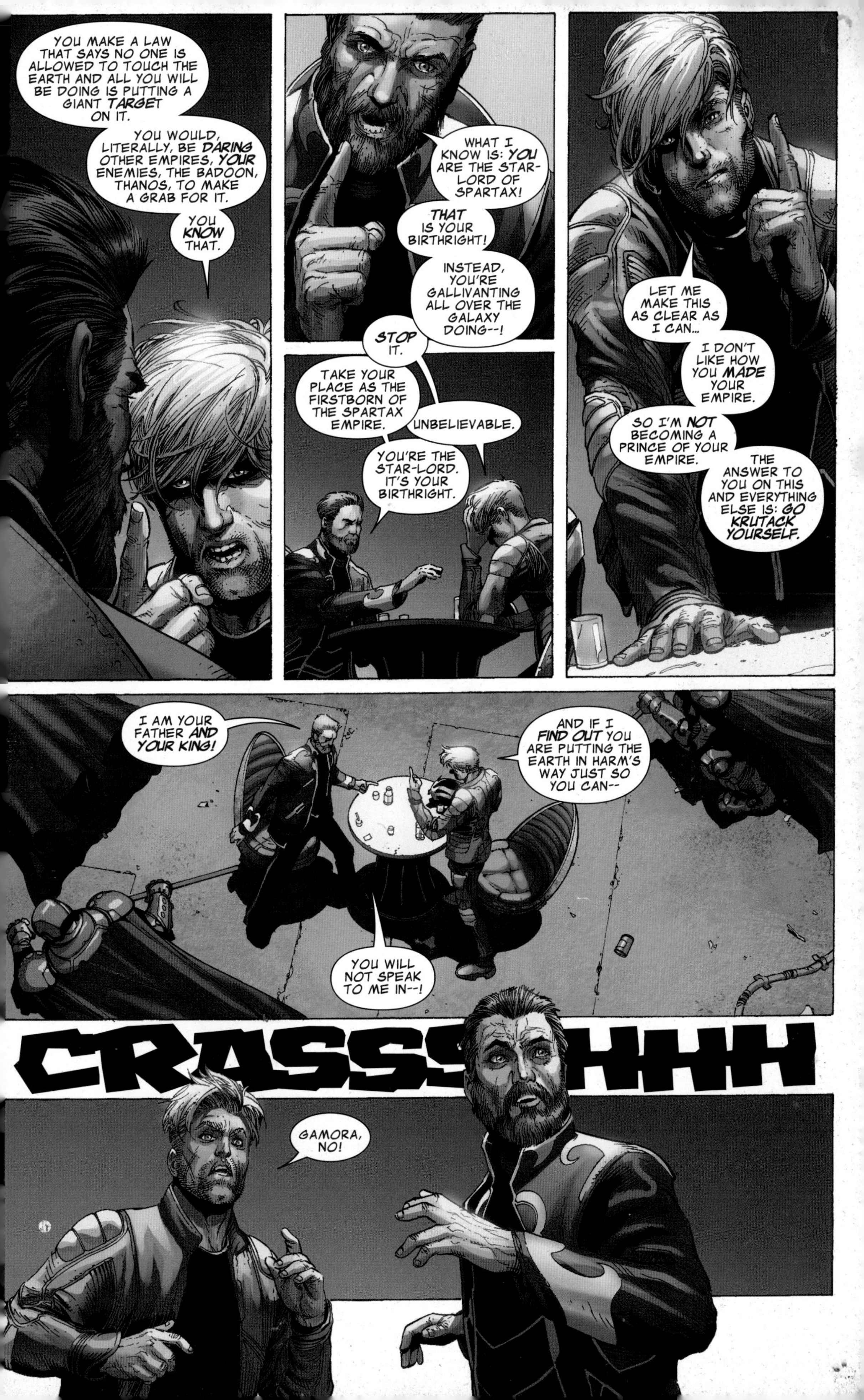
YOU MAKE A LAW THAT SAYS NO ONE IS ALLOWED TO TOUCH THE EARTH AND ALL YOU WILL BE DOING IS PUTTING A GIANT TARGET ON IT.
YOU WOULD, LITERALLY, BE DARING OTHER EMPIRES, YOUR ENEMIES, THE BADOON, THANOS, TO MAKE A GRAB FOR IT.
YOU KNOW THAT.
WHAT I KNOW IS: YOU ARE THE STAR-LORD OF SPARTAX!
THAT IS YOUR BIRTHRIGHT!
INSTEAD, YOU'RE GALLIVANTING ALL OVER THE GALAXY DOING--!
STOP IT.
TAKE YOUR PLACE AS THE FIRSTBORN OF THE SPARTAX EMPIRE.
UNBELIEVABLE.
YOU'RE THE STAR-LORD. IT'S YOUR BIRTHRIGHT.
LET ME MAKE THIS AS CLEAR AS I CAN...
I DON'T LIKE HOW YOU MADE YOUR EMPIRE.
SO I'M NOT BECOMING A PRINCE OF YOUR EMPIRE.
THE ANSWER TO YOU ON THIS AND EVERYTHING ELSE IS: GO KRUTACK YOURSELF.
I AM YOUR FATHER AND YOUR KING!
AND IF I FIND OUT YOU ARE PUTTING THE EARTH IN HARM'S WAY JUST SO YOU CAN--
YOU WILL NOT SPEAK TO ME IN--!
CRASSSHHHH
GAMORA, NO!

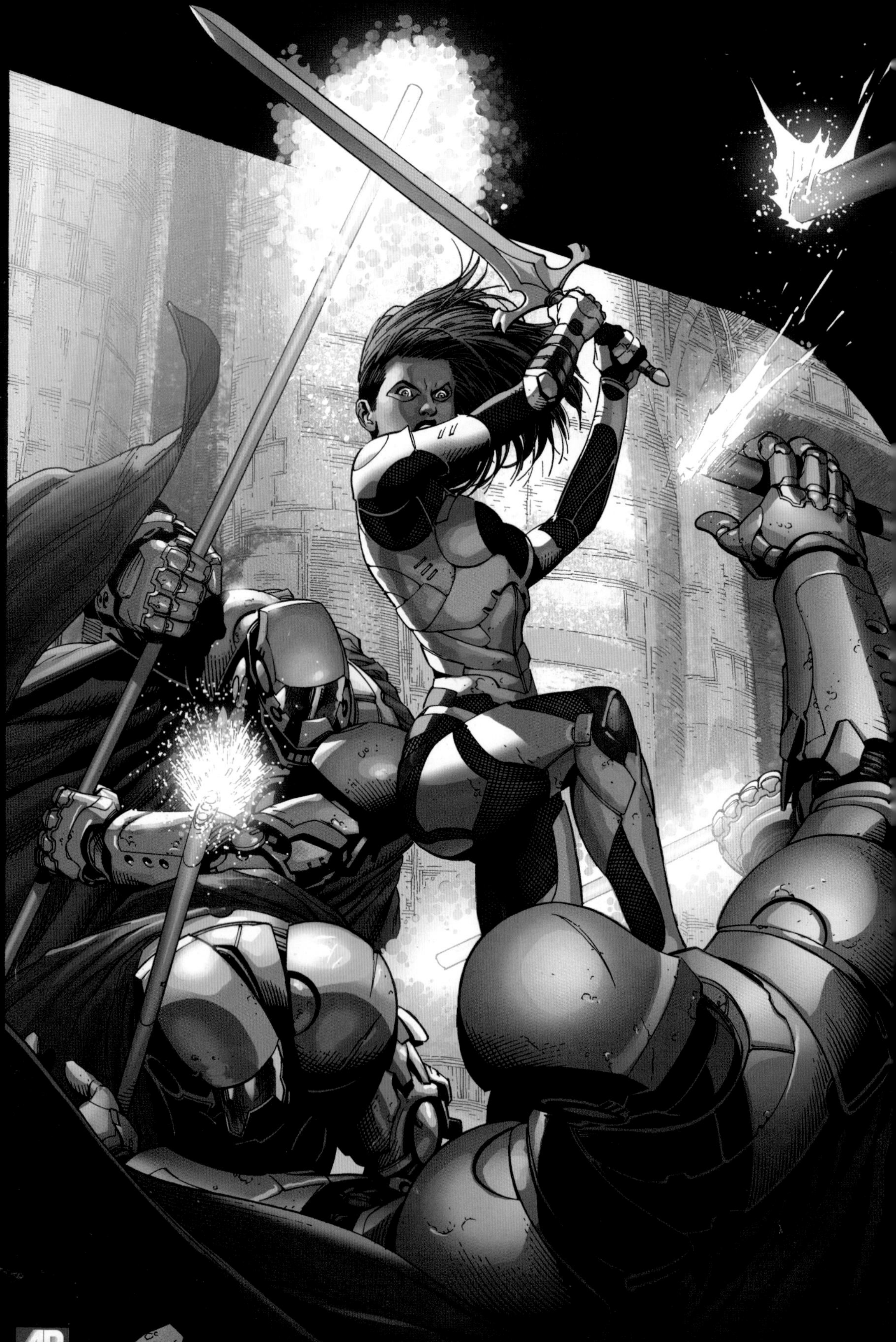

I SHOULD HAVE DONE THIS YEARS AGO.
I SHOULD HAVE OILED UP MY IRON MAN ARMOR AND-- AND JUST TAKEN OFF.
GET THE HELL AWAY FROM EVERYTHING.
GET AWAY FROM THE TEN TEAMS OF AVENGERS, GET AWAY FROM THE STARK BOARD OF DIRECTORS AND THE CHARITY BALLS AND THE REAL HOUSEWIVES OF WHATEVER THE HELL...
...AND JUST COME OUT HERE TO SEEK MY FORTUNE.
OR AT LEAST MY NEXT FORTUNE.
GO OUT INTO THE UNIVERSE AND SEE WHAT ELSE I HAVE TO OFFER.
JUST TAKE A STEP WAY BACK AND LOOK AT THE EARTH AS PART OF THE COSMIC TAPESTRY.
TONY!
YOU'VE BEEN TARGETED.
EVASIVE ACTION REQUIRED.
WHAT?
OH, COME ON!

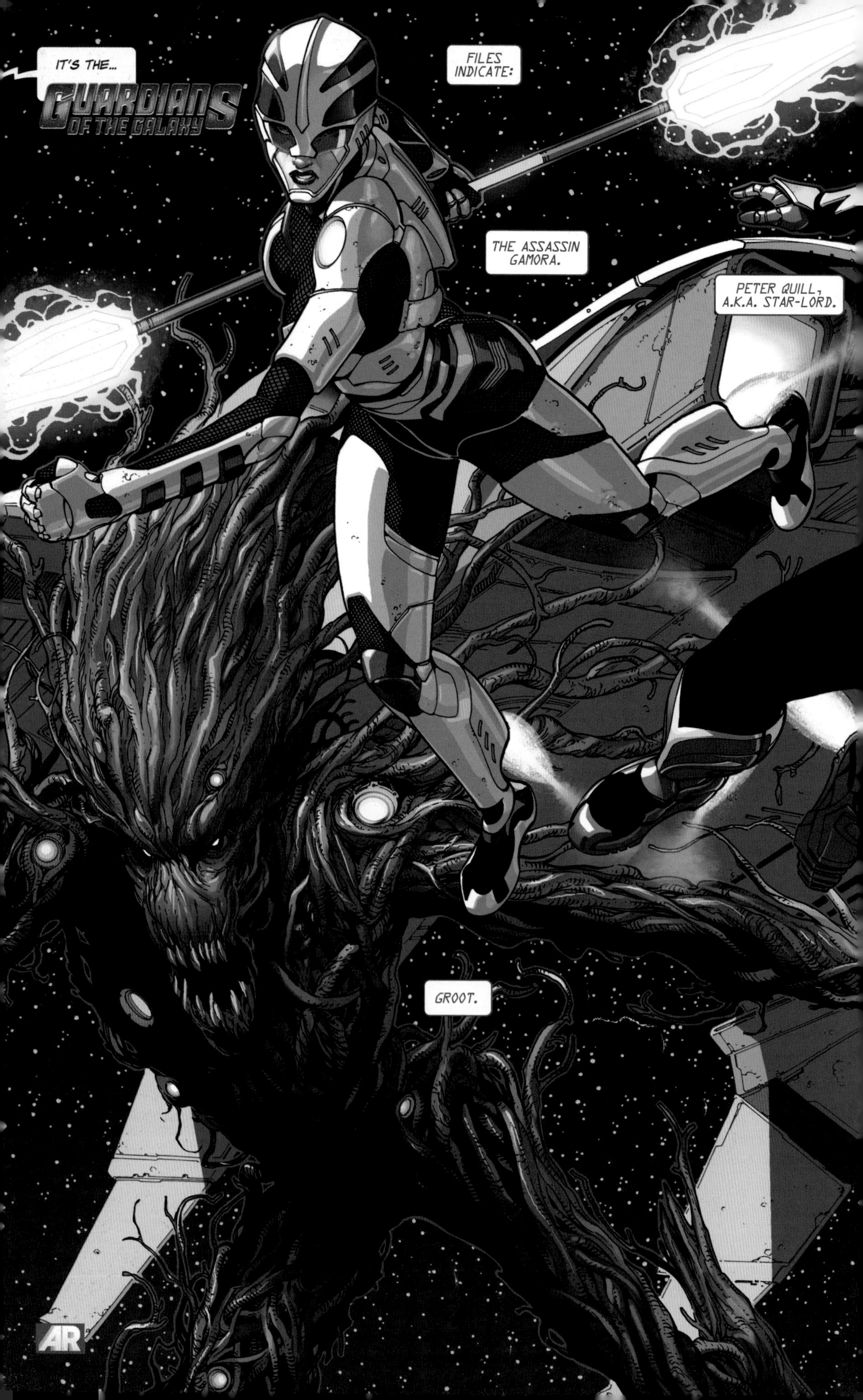
IT'S THE...
GUARDIANS OF THE GALAXY
FILES INDICATE:
THE ASSASSIN GAMORA.
PETER QUILL, A.K.A. STAR-LORD.
GROOT.

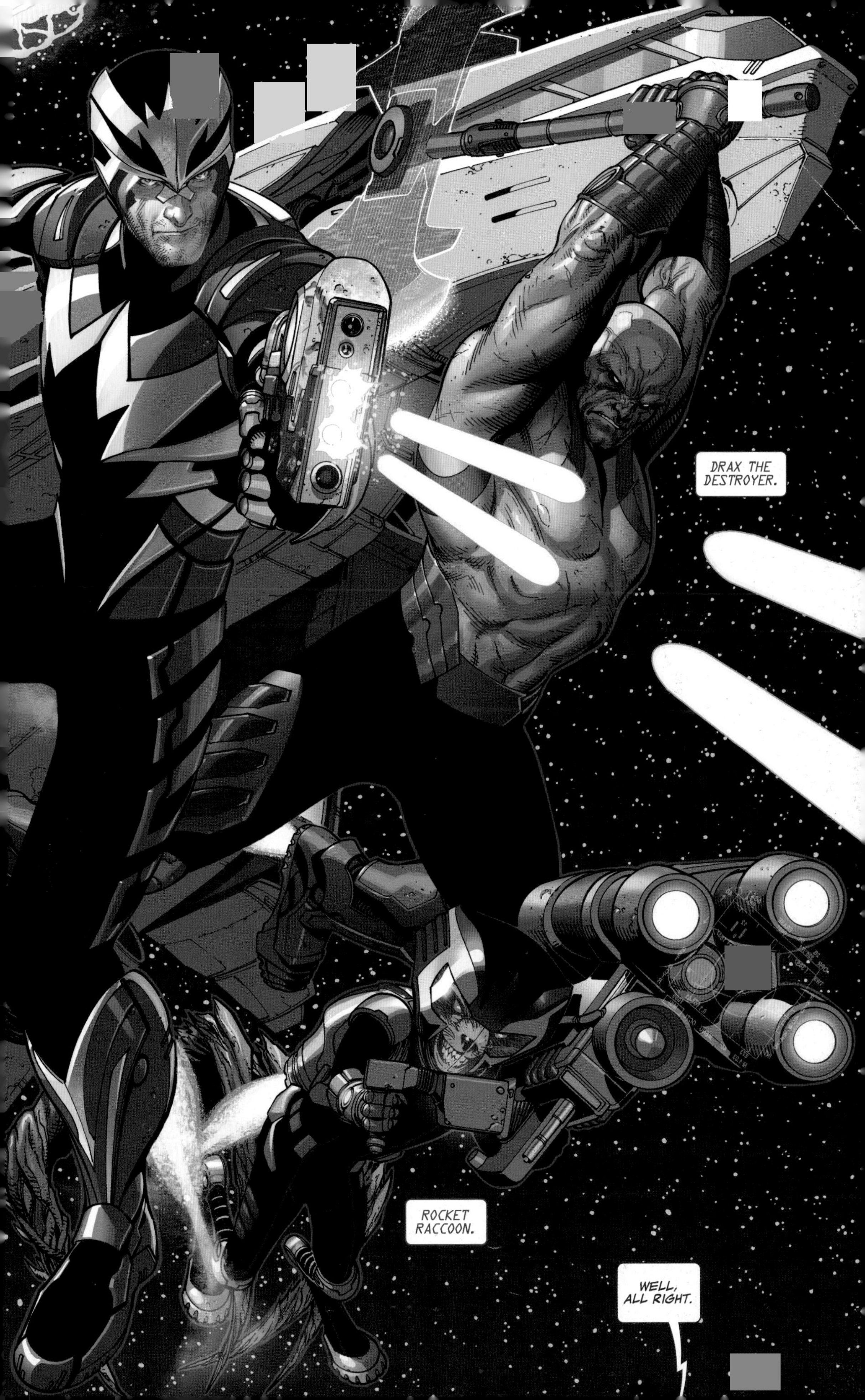
DRAX THE DESTROYER.
ROCKET RACCOON.
WELL, ALL RIGHT.

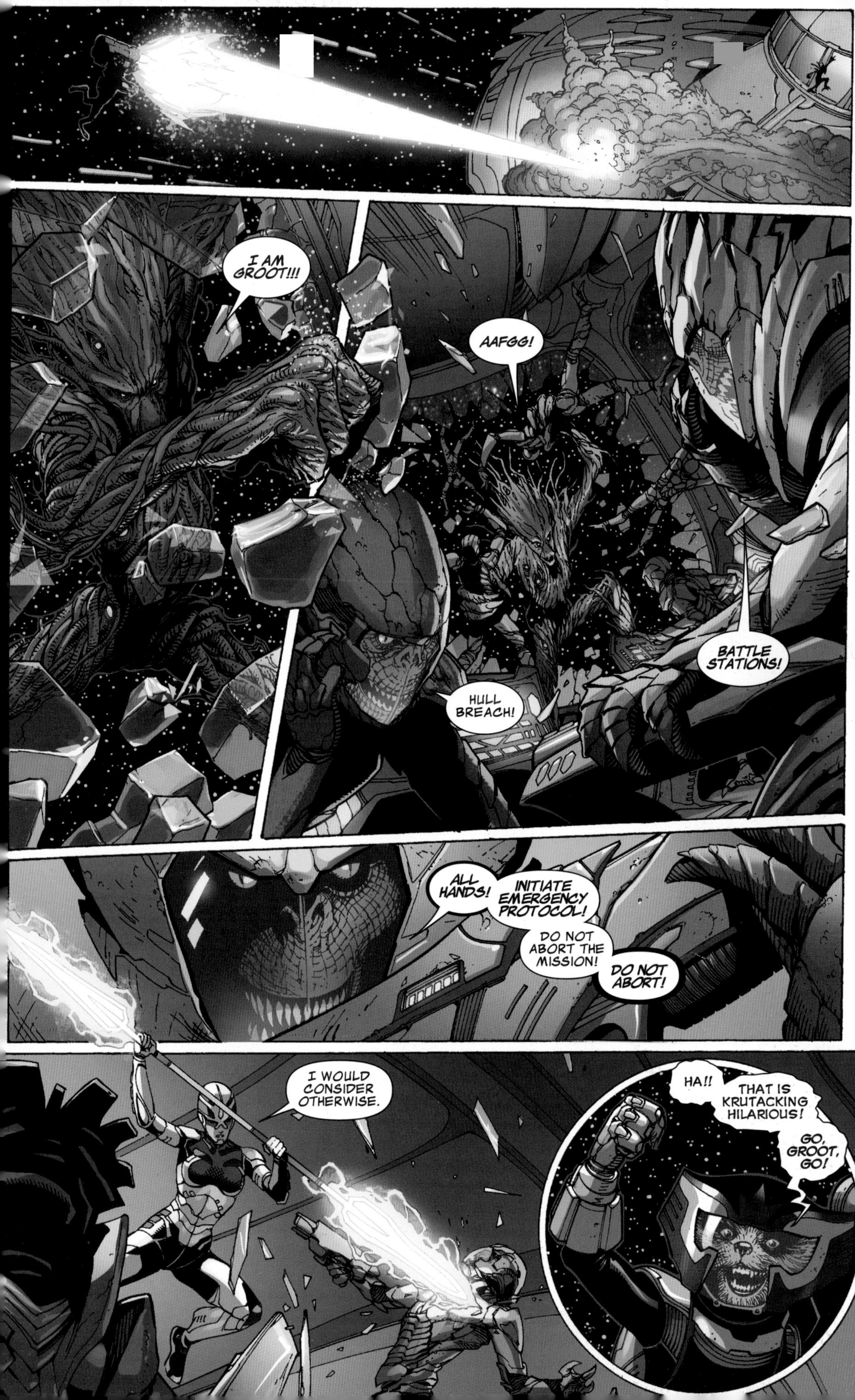
I AM GROOT!!!
AAFGG!
BATTLE STATIONS!
HULL BREACH!
ALL HANDS!
INITIATE EMERGENCY PROTOCOL!
DO NOT ABORT THE MISSION!
DO NOT ABORT!
I WOULD CONSIDER OTHERWISE.
HA!!
THAT IS KRUTACKING HILARIOUS!
GO, GROOT, GO!

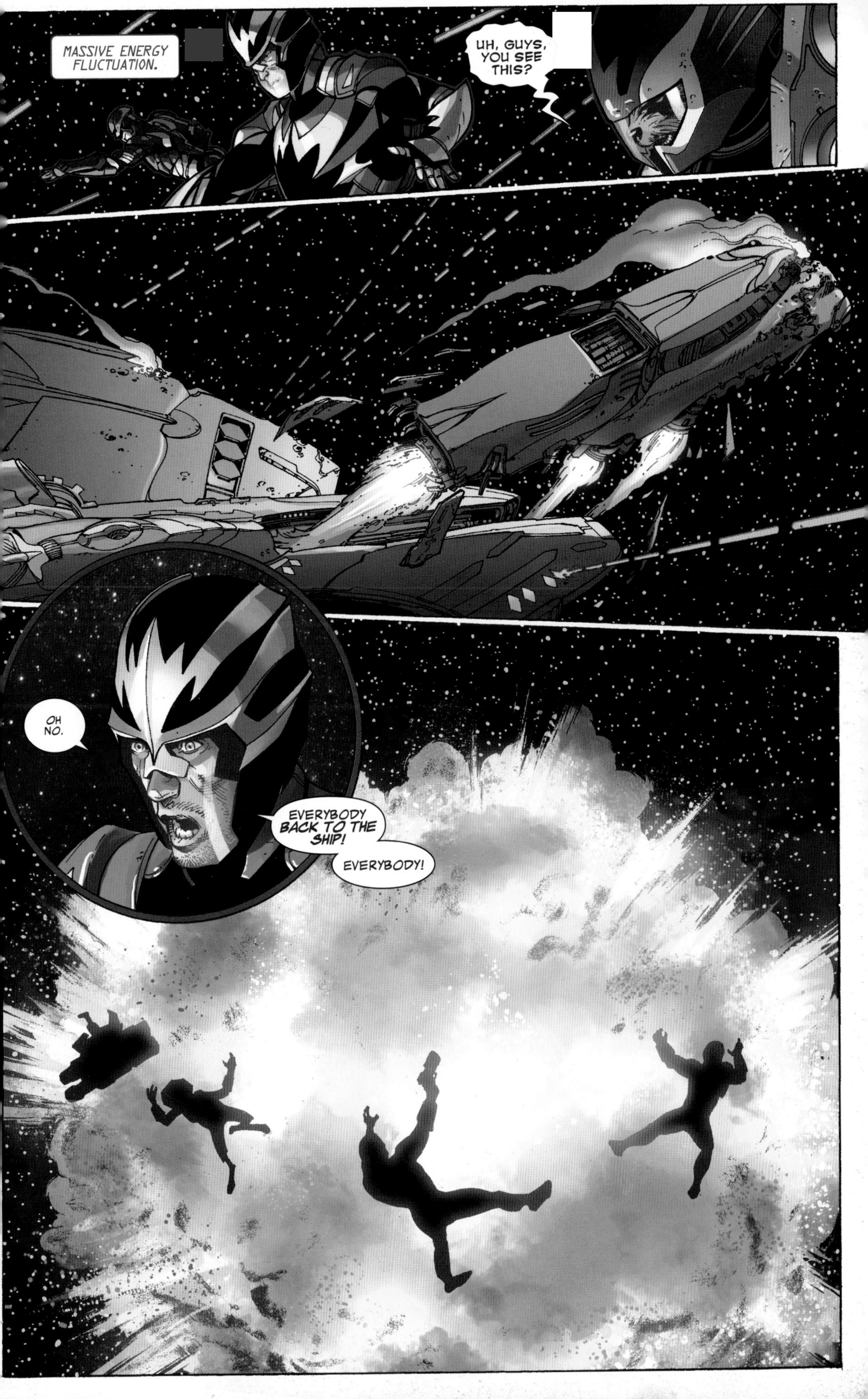
MASSIVE ENERGY FLUCTUATION.
UH, GUYS, YOU SEE THIS?
OH NO.
EVERYBODY BACK TO THE SHIP!
EVERYBODY!

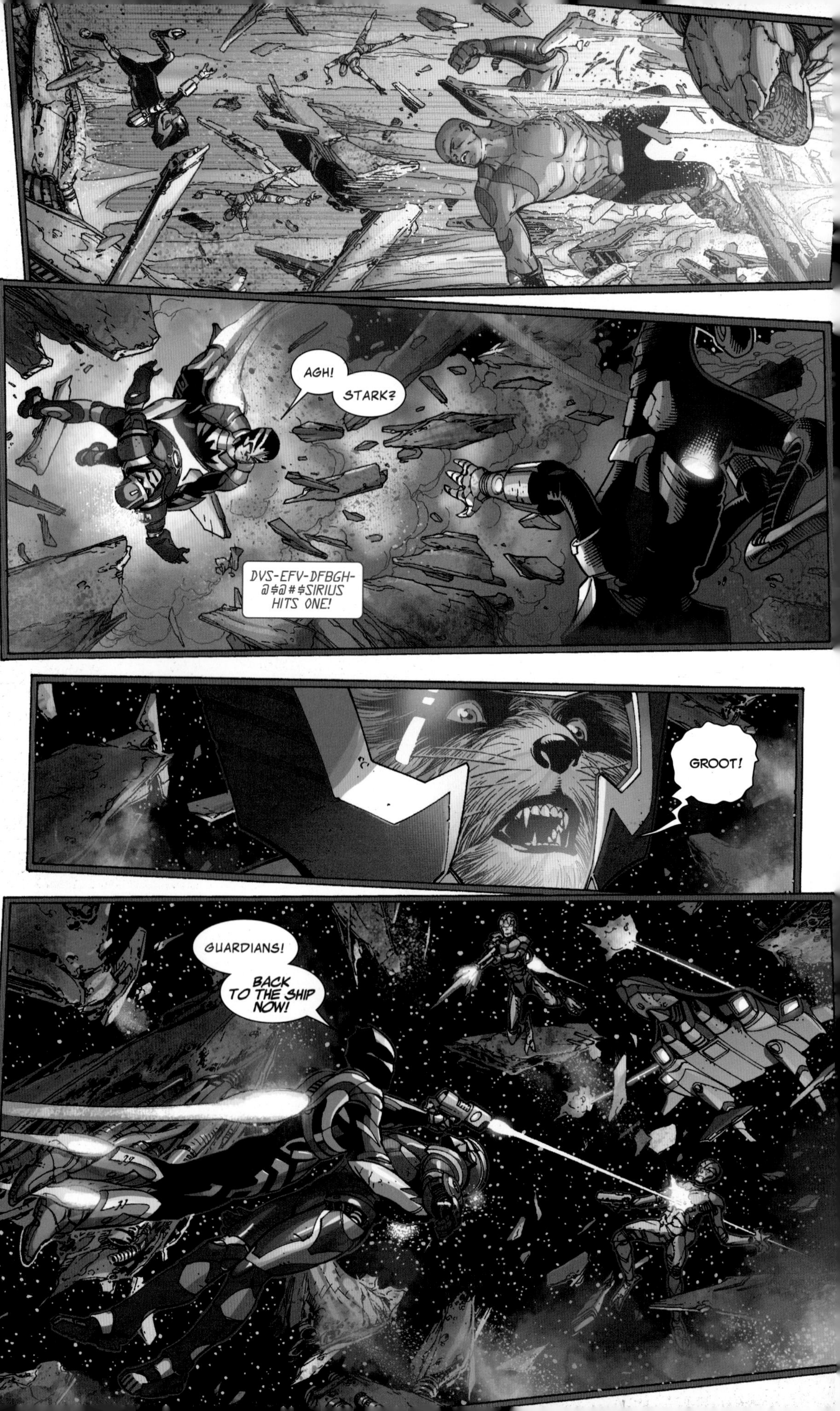
AGH!
STARK?
DVS-EFV-DFBGH-@$@#$SIRIUS HITS ONE!
GROOT!
GUARDIANS!
BACK TO THE SHIP NOW!

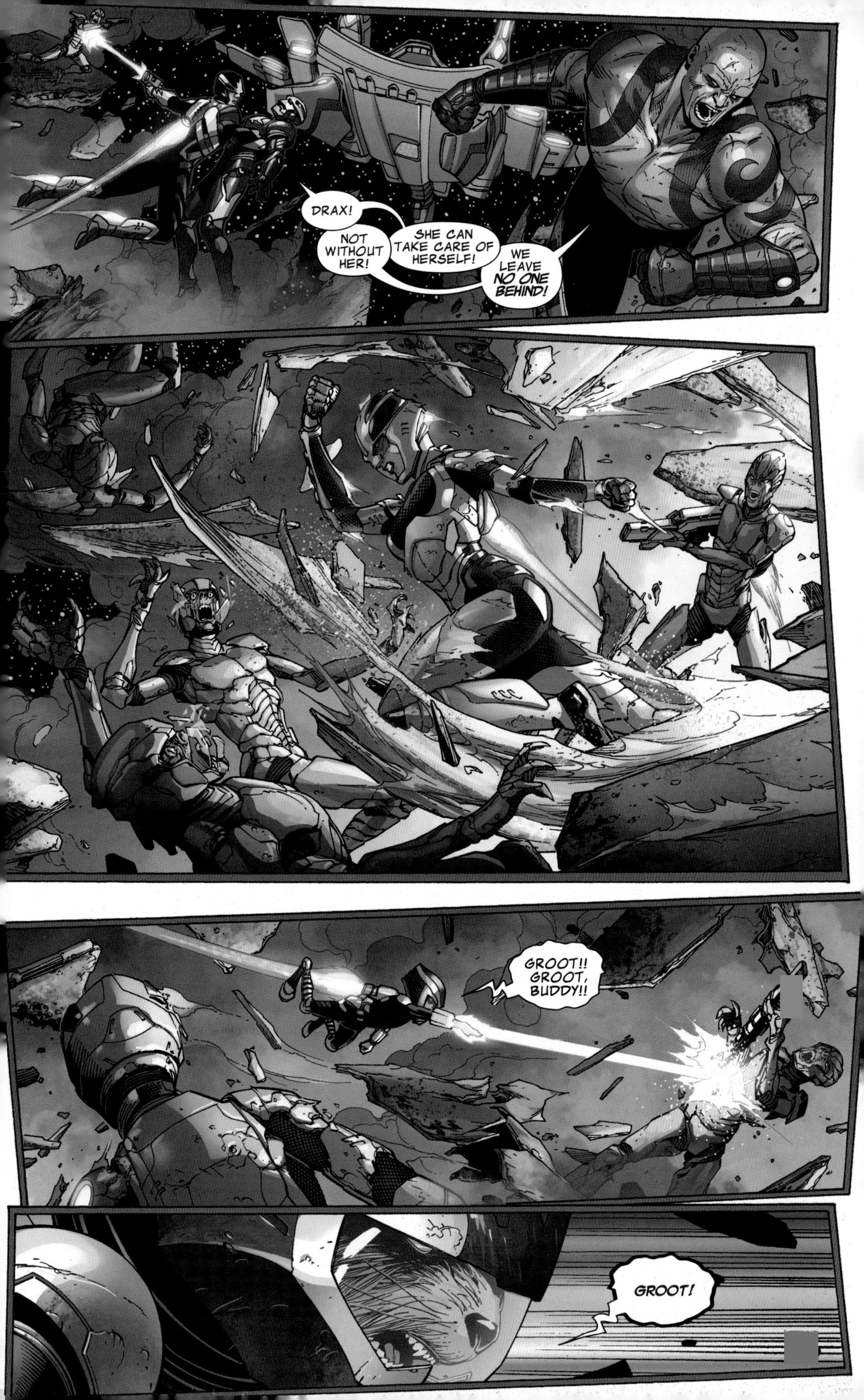
DRAX!
NOT WITHOUT HER!
SHE CAN TAKE CARE OF HERSELF!
WE LEAVE NO ONE BEHIND!
GROOT!! GROOT, BUDDY!!
GROOT!

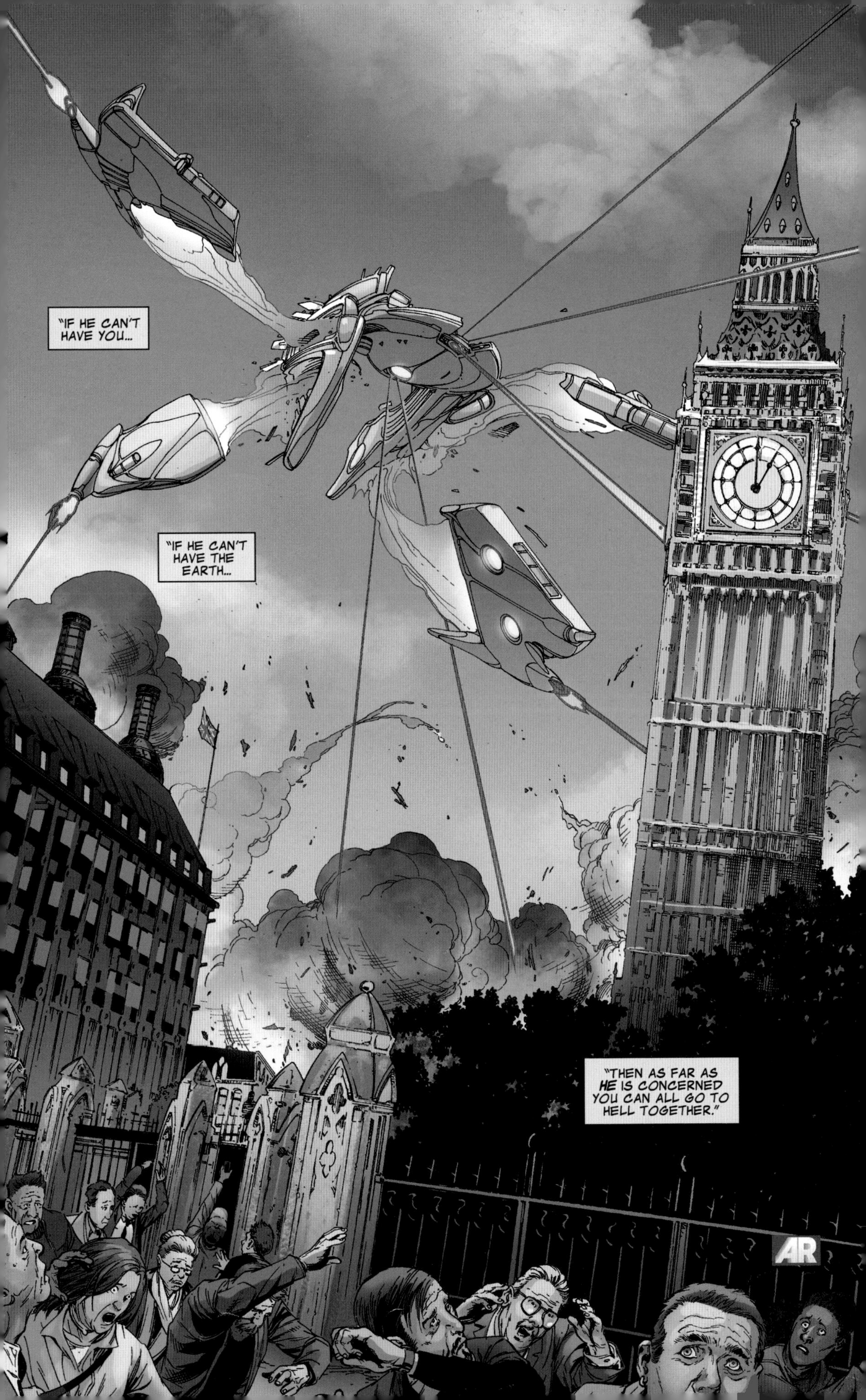
"IF HE CAN'T HAVE YOU...
"IF HE CAN'T HAVE THE EARTH...
"THEN AS FAR AS HE IS CONCERNED YOU CAN ALL GO TO HELL TOGETHER."
AR

Variant Covers

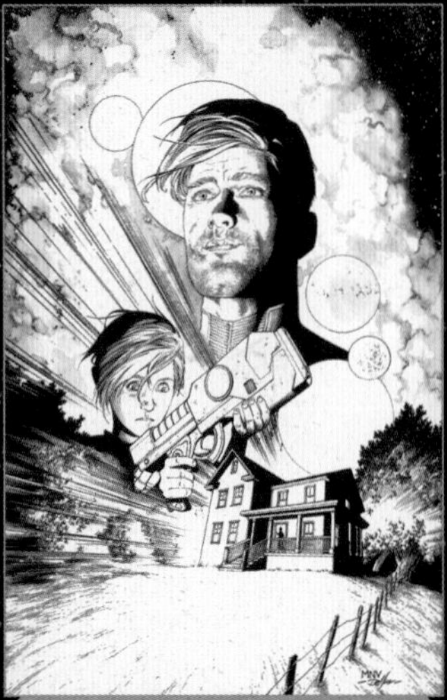

Guardians of the Galaxy #0.1
Variant by Steve McNiven

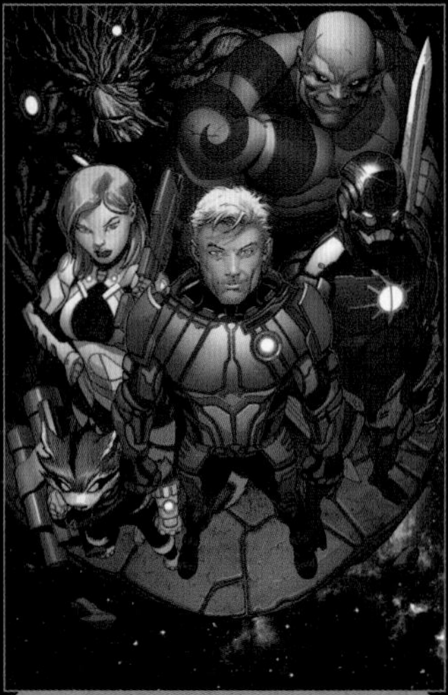

Guardians of the Galaxy #0.1
Variant by Ed McGuinness

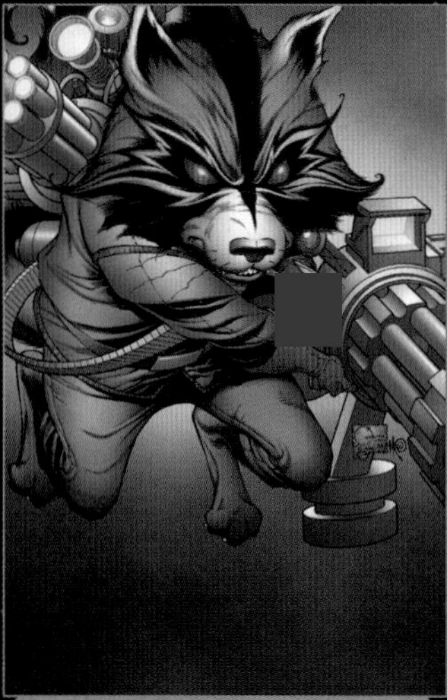

Guardians of the Galaxy #1
Variant by Joe Quesada

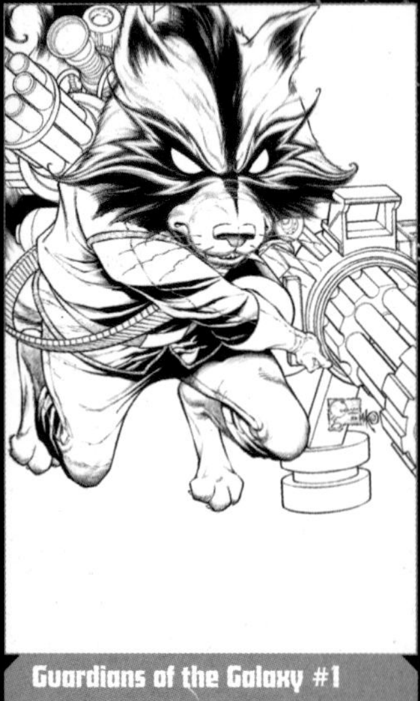

Guardians of the Galaxy #1
Variant by Joe Quesada

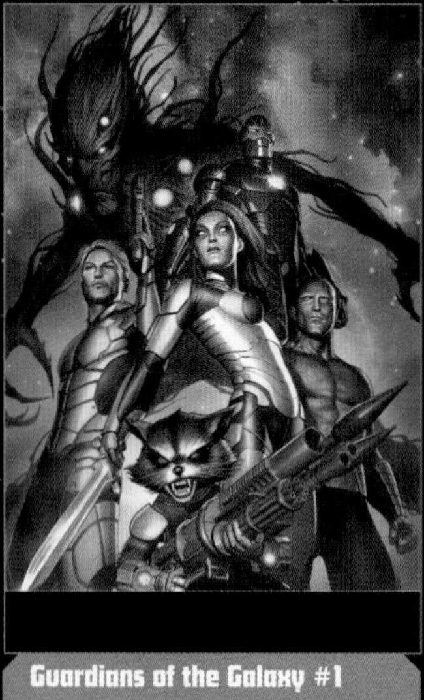

Guardians of the Galaxy #1
Variant by Adi Granov

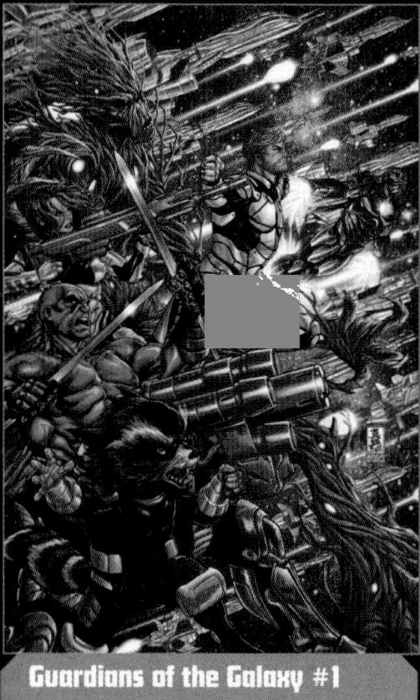

Guardians of the Galaxy #1
Variant by Mark Brooks

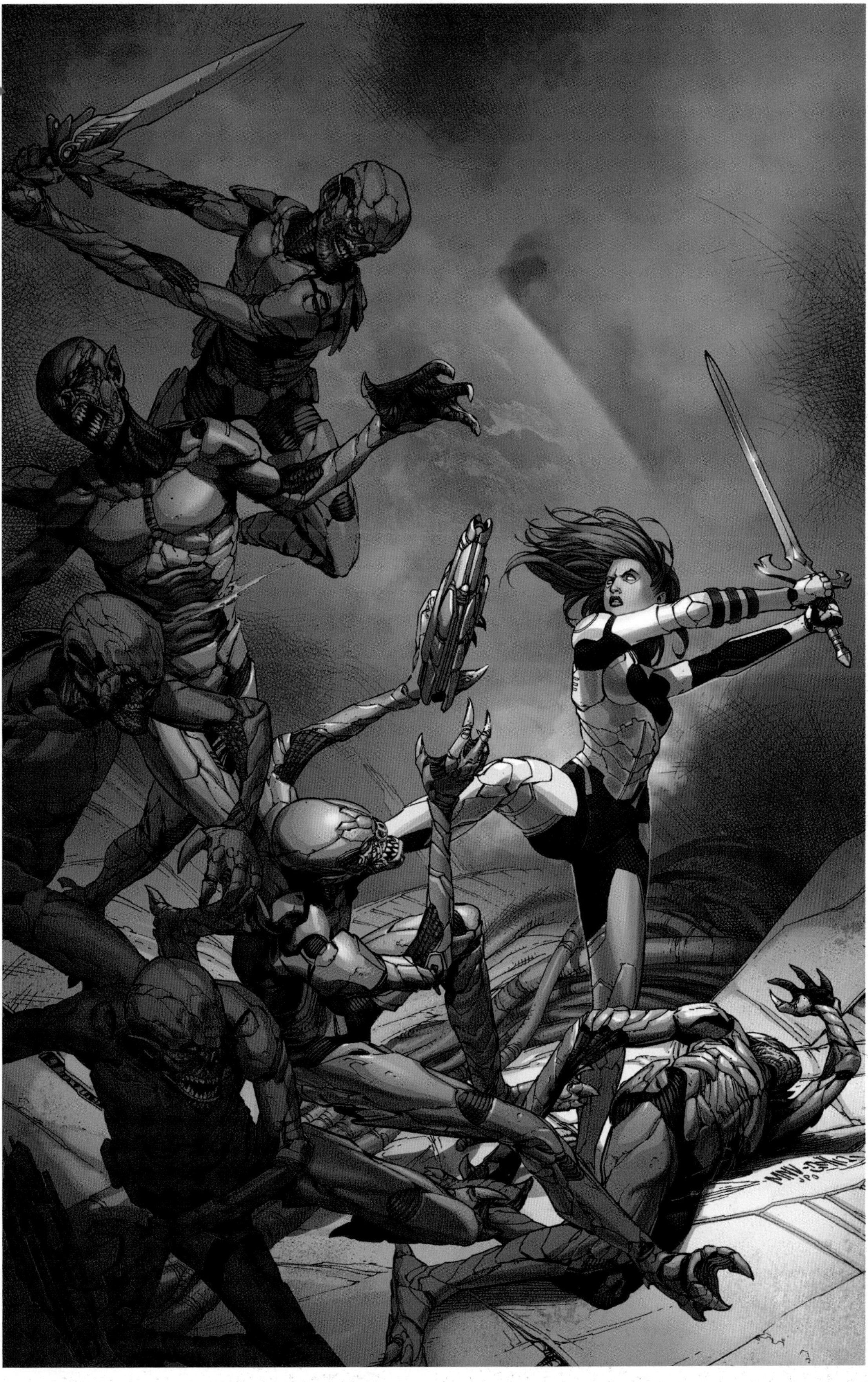

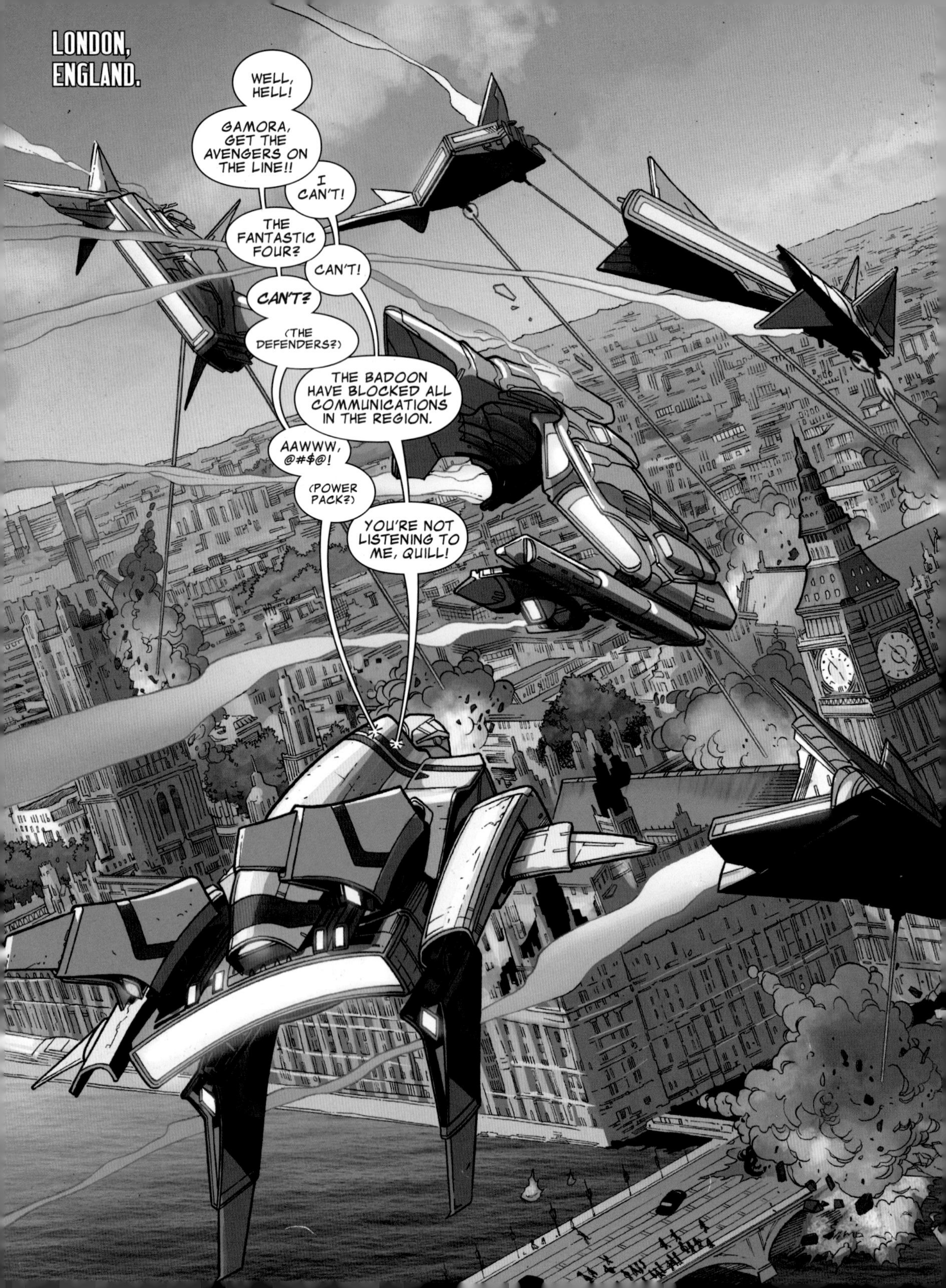

LONDON, ENGLAND.
WELL, HELL!
GAMORA, GET THE AVENGERS ON THE LINE!!
I CAN'T!
THE FANTASTIC FOUR?
CAN'T!
CAN'T?
(THE DEFENDERS?)
THE BADOON HAVE BLOCKED ALL COMMUNICATIONS IN THE REGION.
AAWWW, @#$@!
(POWER PACK?)
YOU'RE NOT LISTENING TO ME, QUILL!

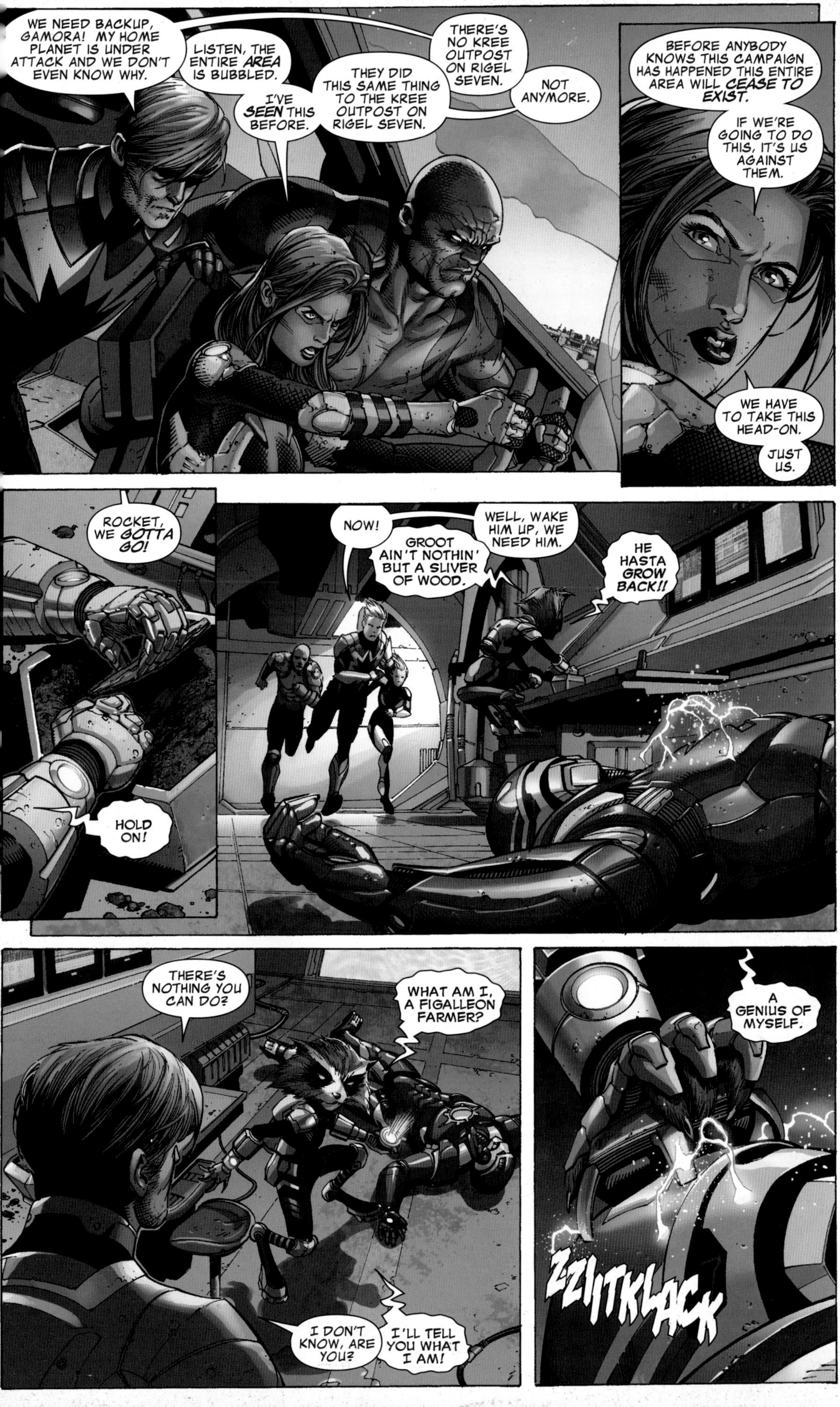
WE NEED BACKUP, GAMORA! MY HOME PLANET IS UNDER ATTACK AND WE DON'T EVEN KNOW WHY.
LISTEN, THE ENTIRE AREA IS BUBBLED.
I'VE SEEN THIS BEFORE.
THEY DID THIS SAME THING TO THE KREE OUTPOST ON RIGEL SEVEN.
THERE'S NO KREE OUTPOST ON RIGEL SEVEN.
NOT ANYMORE.
BEFORE ANYBODY KNOWS THIS CAMPAIGN HAS HAPPENED THIS ENTIRE AREA WILL CEASE TO EXIST.
IF WE'RE GOING TO DO THIS, IT'S US AGAINST THEM.
WE HAVE TO TAKE THIS HEAD-ON.
JUST US.
ROCKET, WE GOTTA GO!
HOLD ON!
NOW!
GROOT AIN'T NOTHIN' BUT A SLIVER OF WOOD.
WELL, WAKE HIM UP, WE NEED HIM.
HE HASTA GROW BACK!!
THERE'S NOTHING YOU CAN DO?
WHAT AM I, A FIGALLEON FARMER?
I DON'T KNOW, ARE YOU?
I'LL TELL YOU WHAT I AM!
A GENIUS OF MYSELF.
ZZITKLACK

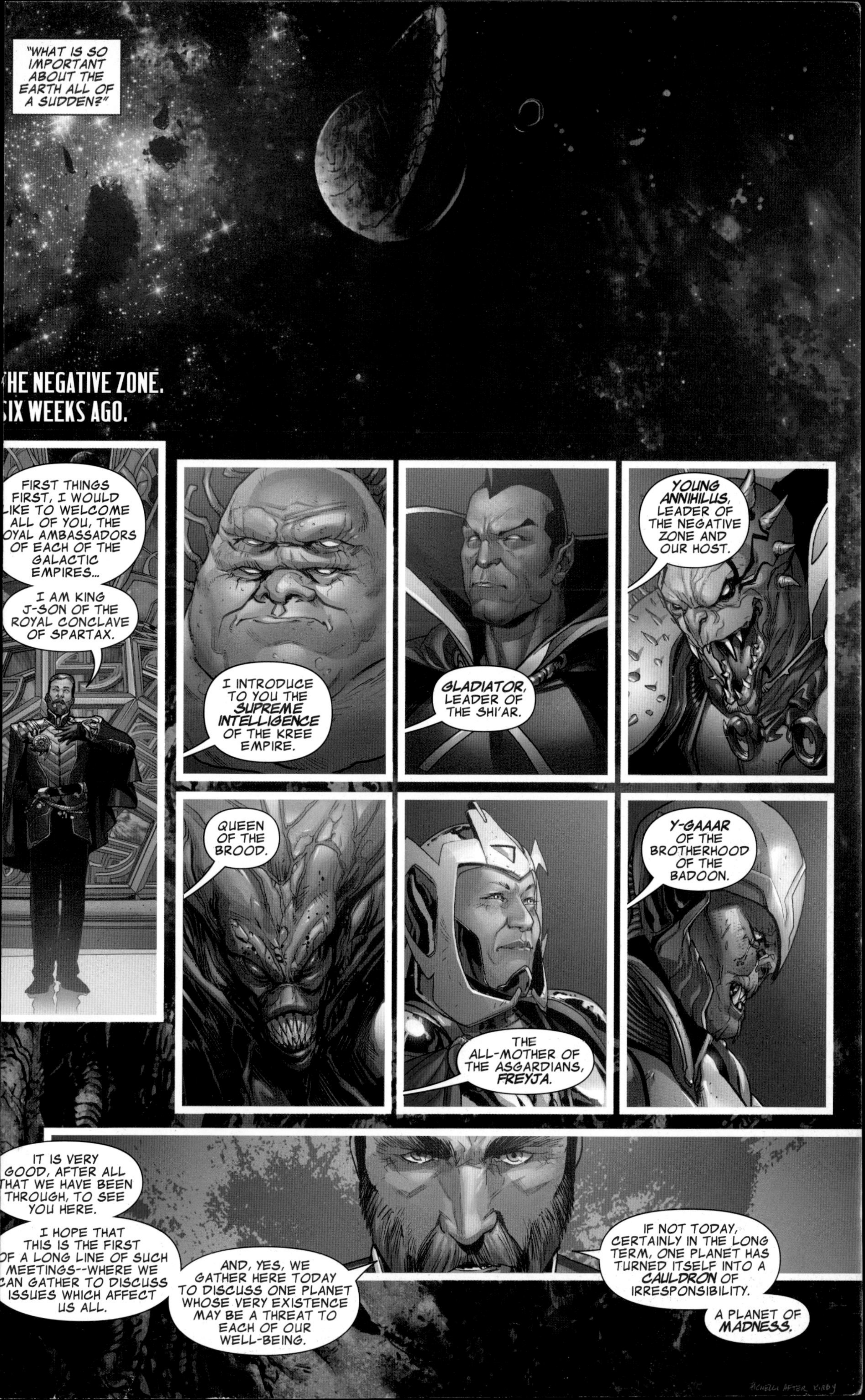

"WHAT IS SO IMPORTANT ABOUT THE EARTH ALL OF A SUDDEN?"
HE NEGATIVE ZONE.
IX WEEKS AGO.
FIRST THINGS FIRST, I WOULD LIKE TO WELCOME ALL OF YOU, THE OYAL AMBASSADORS OF EACH OF THE GALACTIC EMPIRES...
I AM KING J-SON OF THE ROYAL CONCLAVE OF SPARTAX.
I INTRODUCE TO YOU THE SUPREME INTELLIGENCE OF THE KREE EMPIRE.
GLADIATOR, LEADER OF THE SHI'AR.
YOUNG ANNIHILUS, LEADER OF THE NEGATIVE ZONE AND OUR HOST.
QUEEN OF THE BROOD.
THE ALL-MOTHER OF THE ASGARDIANS, FREYJA.
Y-GAAAR OF THE BROTHERHOOD OF THE BADOON.
IT IS VERY GOOD, AFTER ALL THAT WE HAVE BEEN THROUGH, TO SEE YOU HERE.
I HOPE THAT THIS IS THE FIRST OF A LONG LINE OF SUCH MEETINGS--WHERE WE CAN GATHER TO DISCUSS ISSUES WHICH AFFECT US ALL.
AND, YES, WE GATHER HERE TODAY TO DISCUSS ONE PLANET WHOSE VERY EXISTENCE MAY BE A THREAT TO EACH OF OUR WELL-BEING.
IF NOT TODAY, CERTAINLY IN THE LONG TERM, ONE PLANET HAS TURNED ITSELF INTO A CAULDRON OF IRRESPONSIBILITY.
A PLANET OF MADNESS.

LONDON, ENGLAND.

GUYS, FAST AND FURIOUS AND STAY IN CONTACT.

I HAVE THE SHOT.

IF YOU DON'T THINK YOU HAVE THE SHOT, DON'T TAKE IT.

SYNCHRONIZED ATTACK ON TARGET. STAY WITH THE OTHER SHIPS. WE OUTNUMBER THEM.

BY YOUR COMMAND.

BUT THE GUARDIANS?

THE STARLORD IS BUT ONE SHIP.

MOTHER COMMAND WILL TAKE CARE OF THEM.

BOOM

AGH!

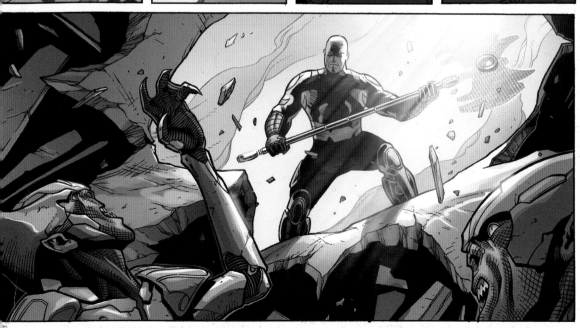

HEY, STARK,
ARE THERE ANY
LONDON-BASED
SUPER HERO
INITIATIVES?

ANY
BRITISH
X-MEN?

THERE IS
A CAPTAIN
BRITAIN.

IS
HE ANY
GOOD?

NOT
REALLY.

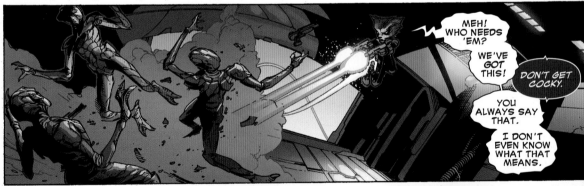

MEH!
WHO NEEDS
'EM?

WE'VE
GOT THIS!

DON'T GET
COCKY.

YOU
ALWAYS SAY
THAT.

I DON'T
EVEN KNOW
WHAT THAT
MEANS.

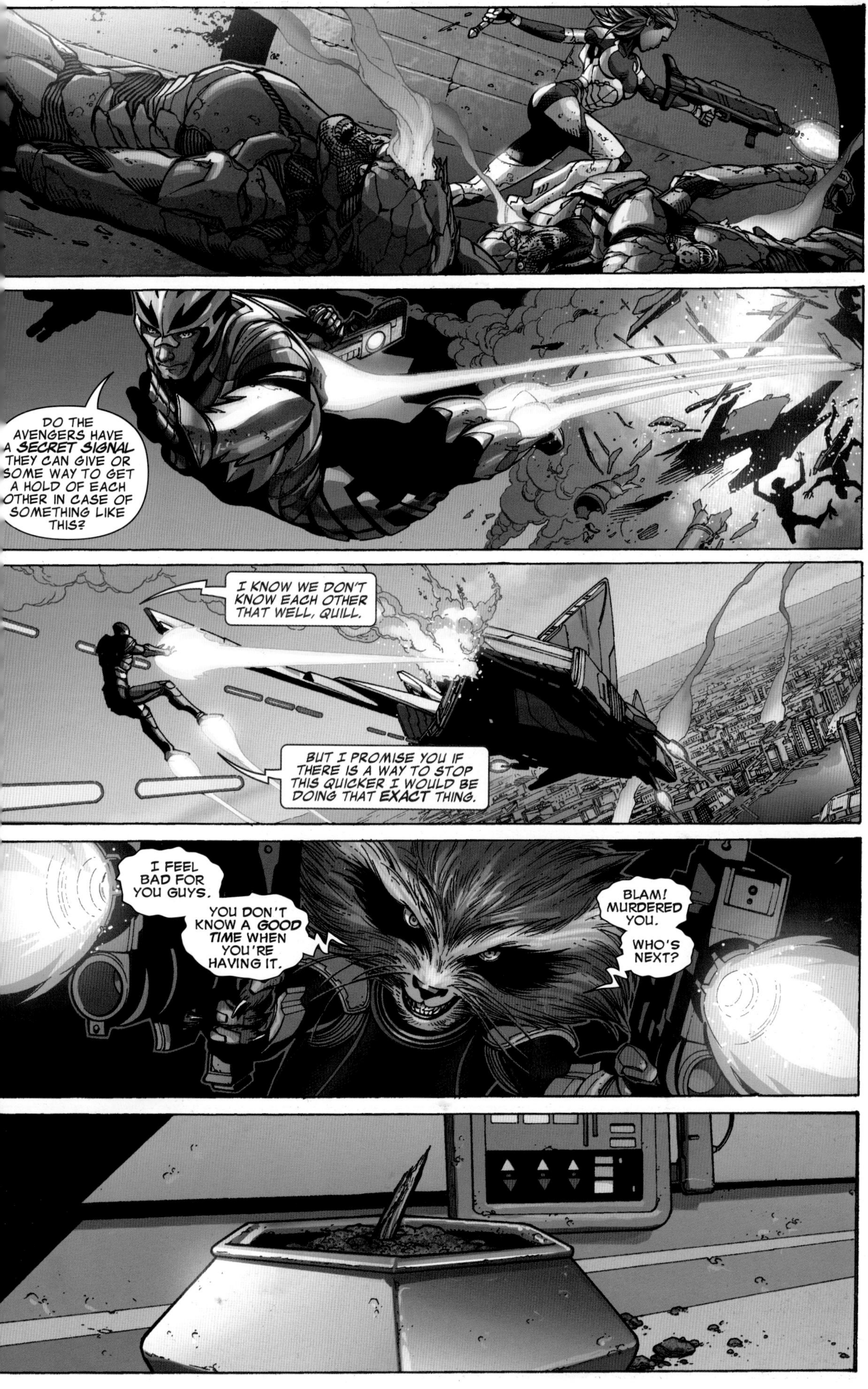
DO THE AVENGERS HAVE A SECRET SIGNAL THEY CAN GIVE OR SOME WAY TO GET A HOLD OF EACH OTHER IN CASE OF SOMETHING LIKE THIS?
I KNOW WE DON'T KNOW EACH OTHER THAT WELL, QUILL.
BUT I PROMISE YOU IF THERE IS A WAY TO STOP THIS QUICKER I WOULD BE DOING THAT EXACT THING.
I FEEL BAD FOR YOU GUYS.
YOU DON'T KNOW A GOOD TIME WHEN YOU'RE HAVING IT.
BLAM! MURDERED YOU.
WHO'S NEXT?

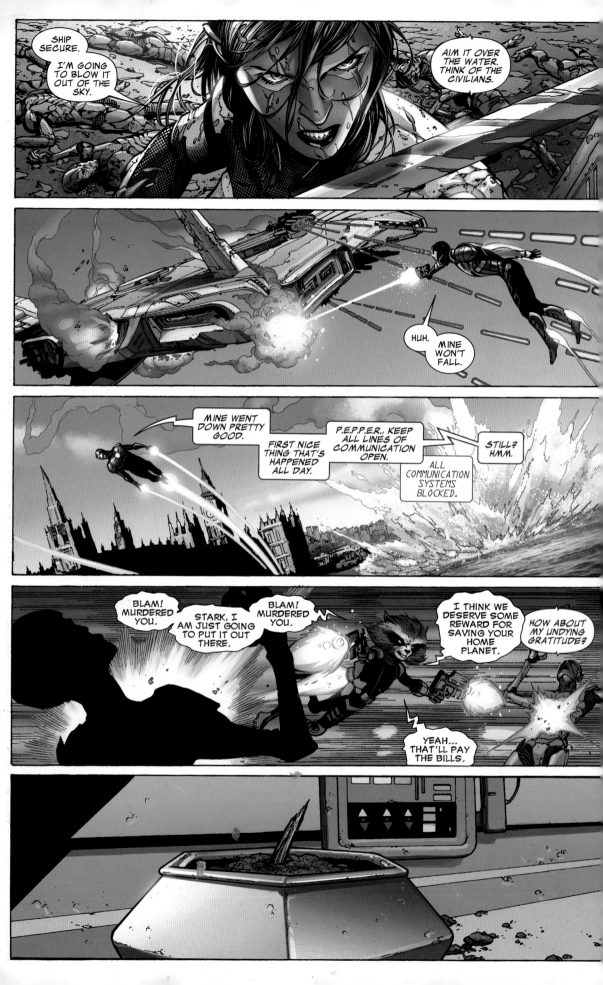

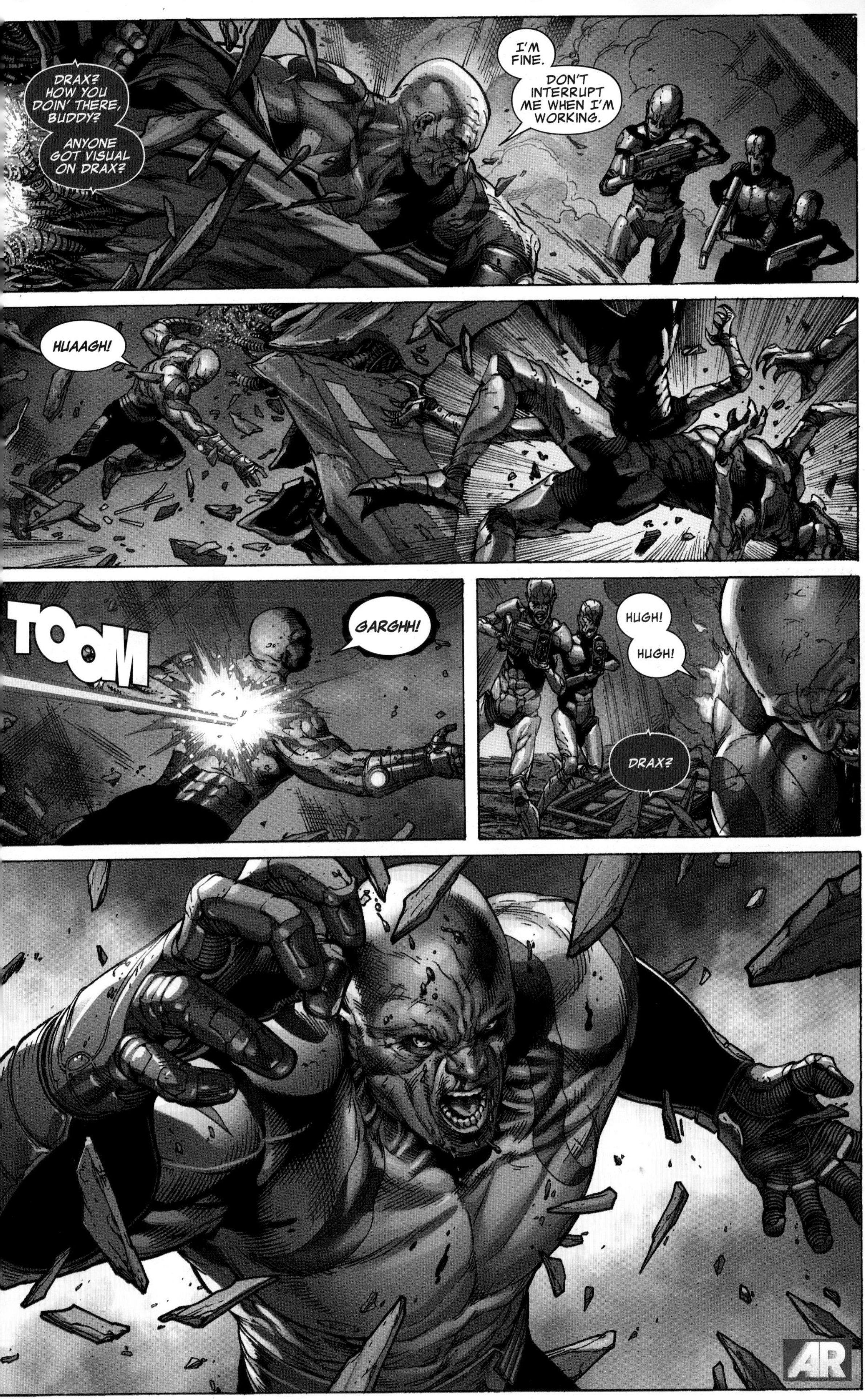
DRAX? HOW YOU DOIN' THERE, BUDDY?
ANYONE GOT VISUAL ON DRAX?
I'M FINE.
DON'T INTERRUPT ME WHEN I'M WORKING.
HUAAGH!
TOOM
GARGHH!
HUGH!
HUGH!
DRAX?
AR

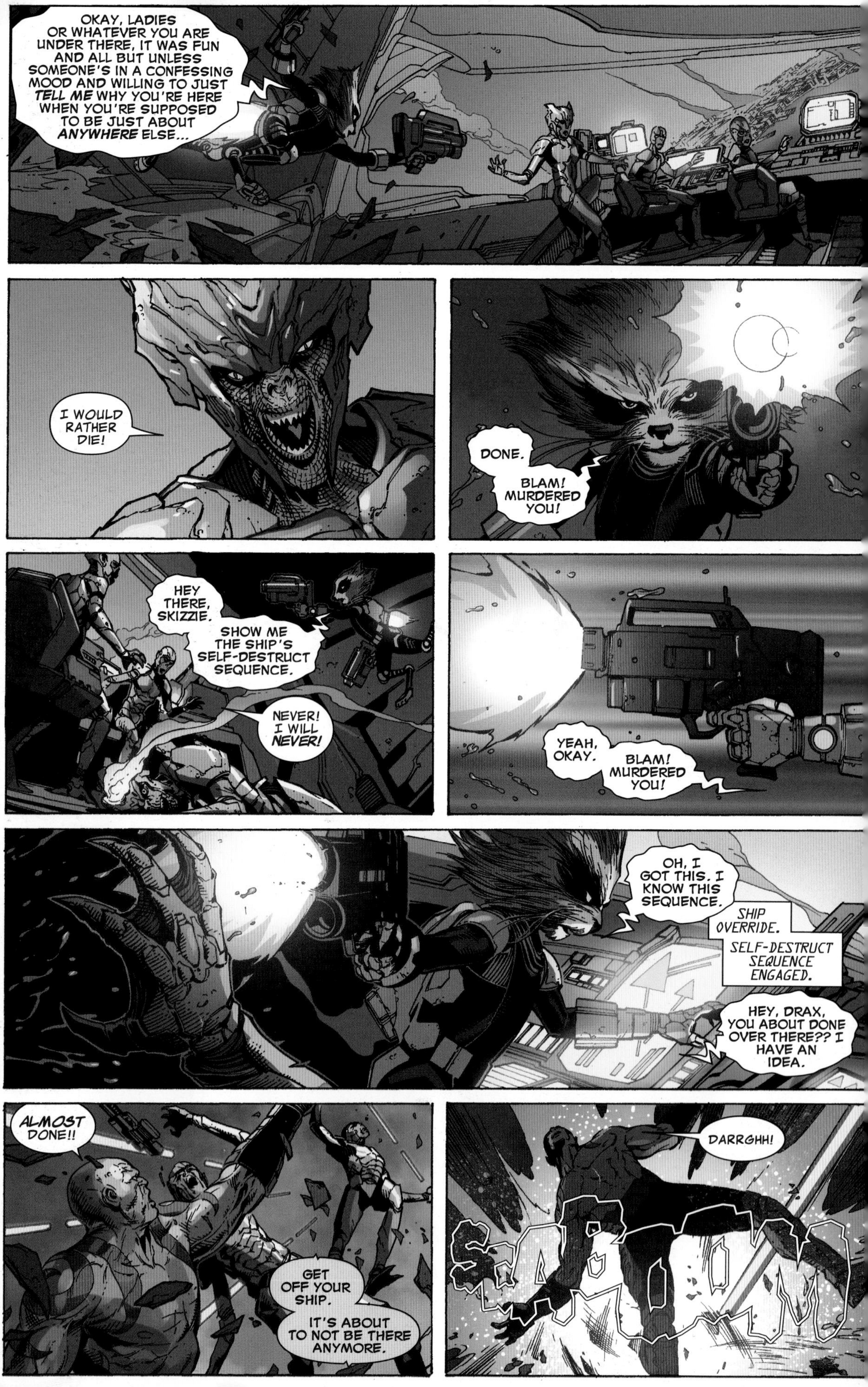
OKAY, LADIES OR WHATEVER YOU ARE UNDER THERE, IT WAS FUN AND ALL BUT UNLESS SOMEONE'S IN A CONFESSING MOOD AND WILLING TO JUST TELL ME WHY YOU'RE HERE WHEN YOU'RE SUPPOSED TO BE JUST ABOUT ANYWHERE ELSE...
I WOULD RATHER DIE!
DONE.
BLAM! MURDERED YOU!
HEY THERE, SKIZZIE.
SHOW ME THE SHIP'S SELF-DESTRUCT SEQUENCE.
NEVER! I WILL NEVER!
YEAH, OKAY.
BLAM! MURDERED YOU!
OH, I GOT THIS. I KNOW THIS SEQUENCE.
SHIP OVERRIDE.
SELF-DESTRUCT SEQUENCE ENGAGED.
HEY, DRAX, YOU ABOUT DONE OVER THERE?? I HAVE AN IDEA.
ALMOST DONE!!
GET OFF YOUR SHIP.
IT'S ABOUT TO NOT BE THERE ANYMORE.
DARRGHH!
SKA-BOOM

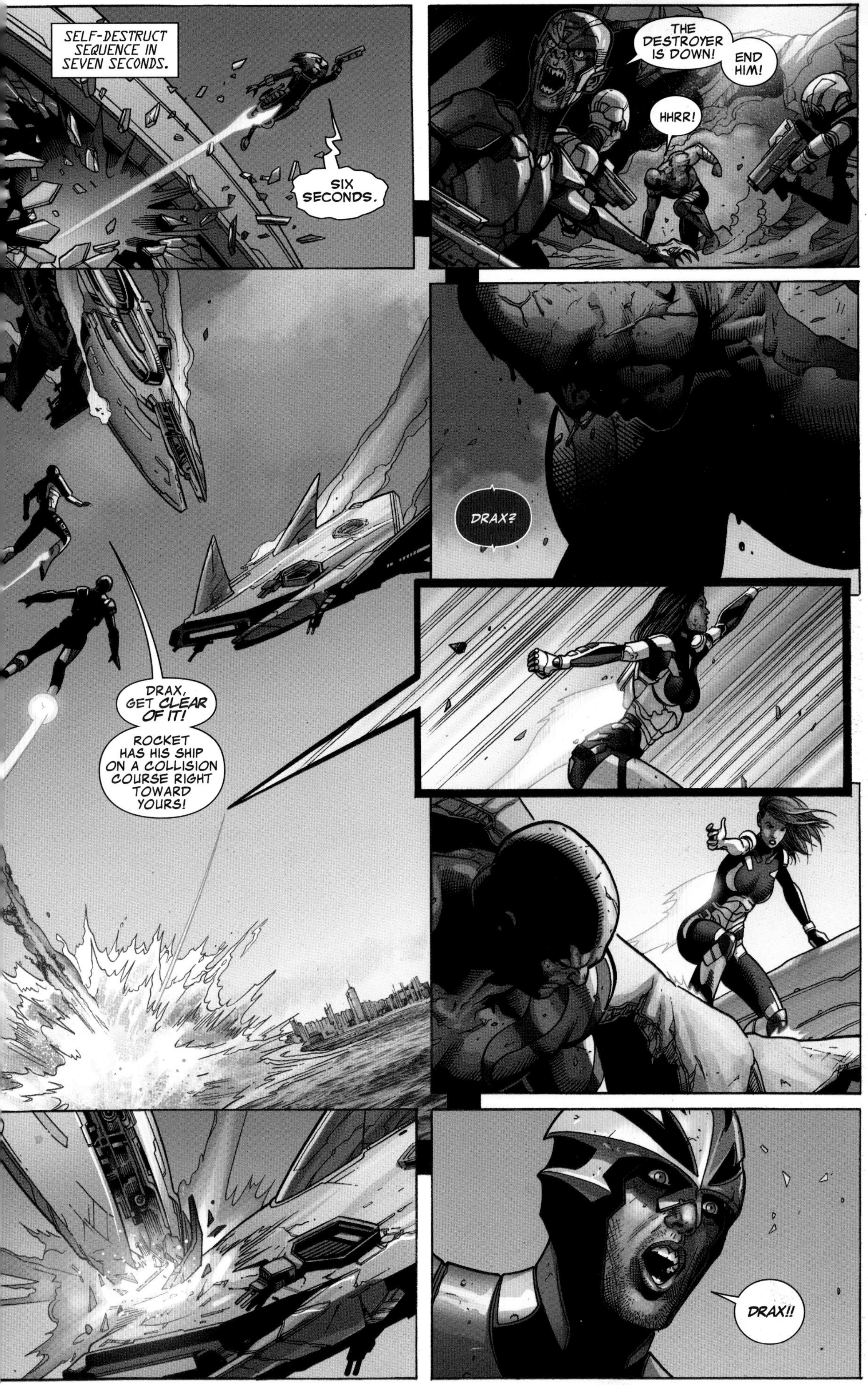
SELF-DESTRUCT SEQUENCE IN SEVEN SECONDS.
SIX SECONDS.
THE DESTROYER IS DOWN!
END HIM!
HHRR!
DRAX?
DRAX, GET CLEAR OF IT!
ROCKET HAS HIS SHIP ON A COLLISION COURSE RIGHT TOWARD YOURS!
DRAX!!

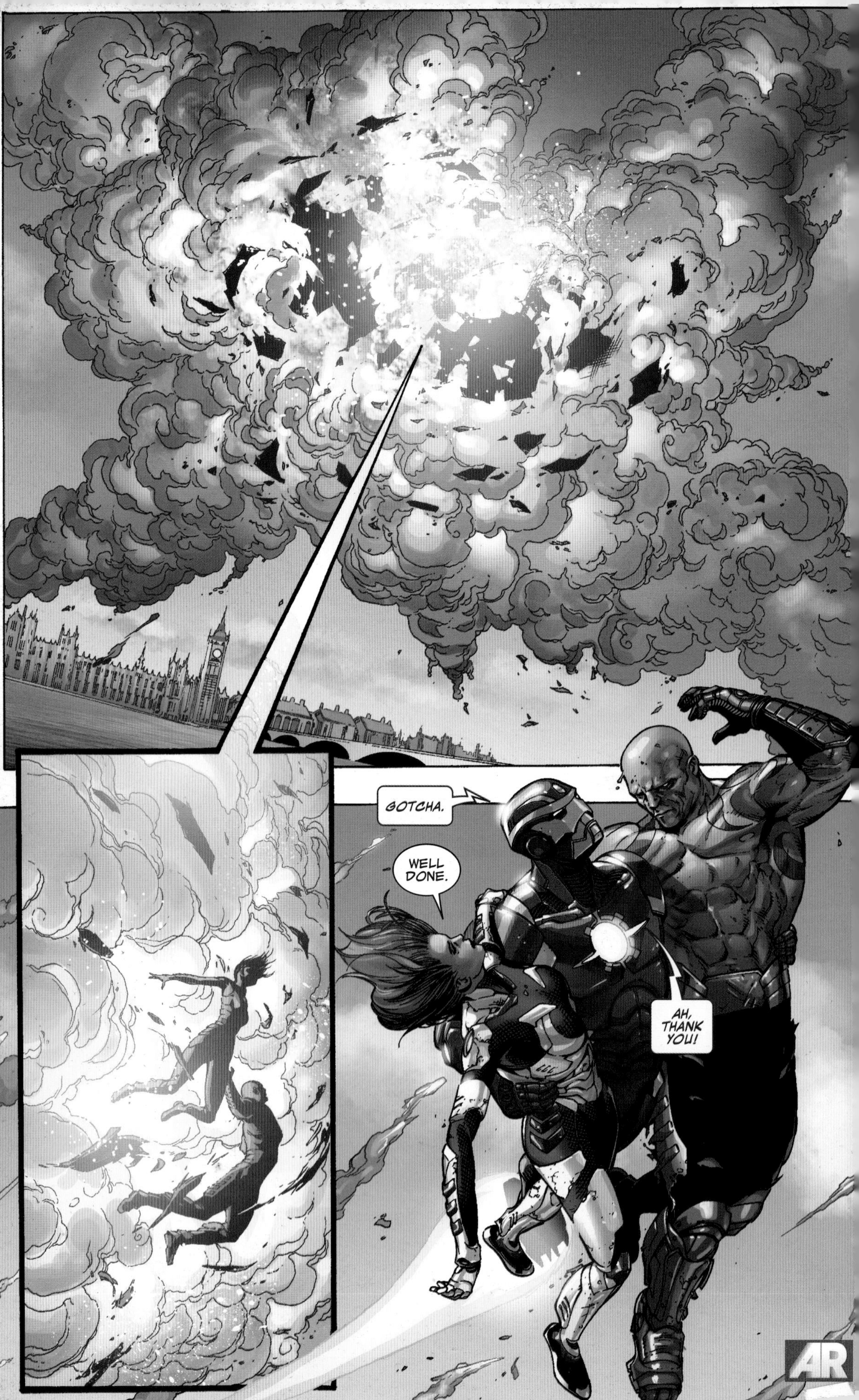
GOTCHA.
WELL DONE.
AH, THANK YOU!

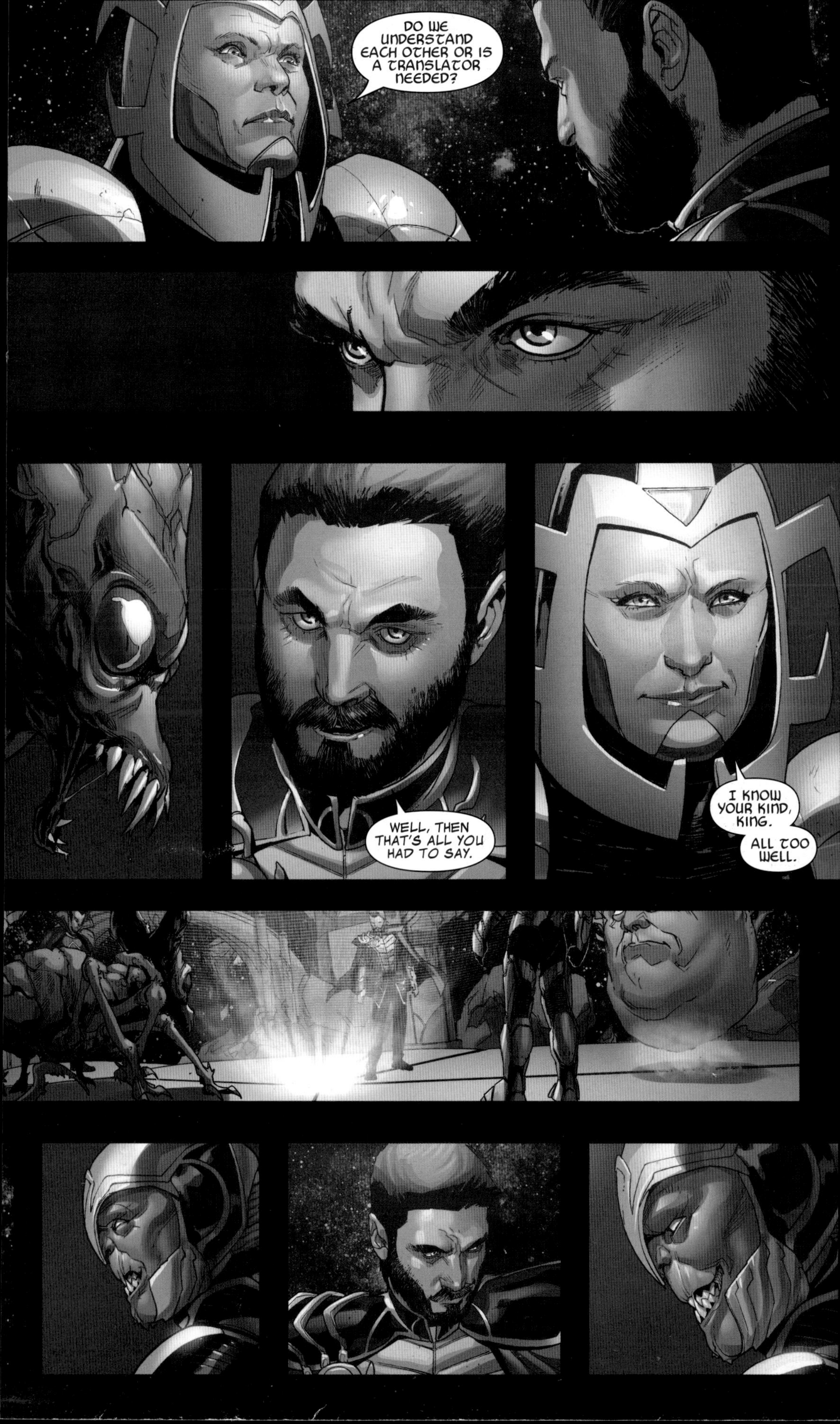
DO WE UNDERSTAND EACH OTHER OR IS A TRANSLATOR NEEDED?
WELL, THEN THAT'S ALL YOU HAD TO SAY.
I KNOW YOUR KIND, KING.
ALL TOO WELL.

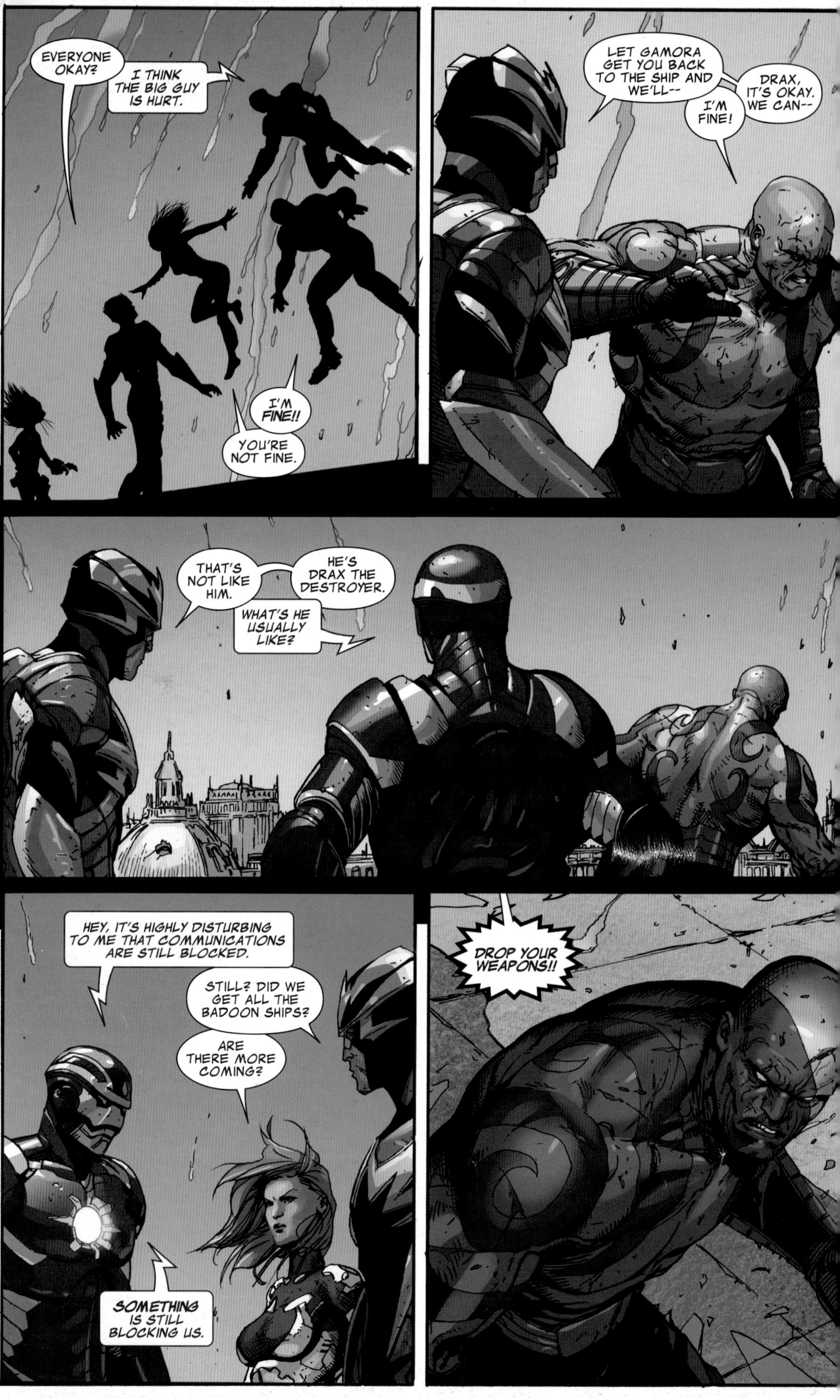
EVERYONE OKAY?
I THINK THE BIG GUY IS HURT.
I'M FINE!!
YOU'RE NOT FINE.
LET GAMORA GET YOU BACK TO THE SHIP AND WE'LL--
I'M FINE!
DRAX, IT'S OKAY. WE CAN--
THAT'S NOT LIKE HIM.
HE'S DRAX THE DESTROYER.
WHAT'S HE USUALLY LIKE?
HEY, IT'S HIGHLY DISTURBING TO ME THAT COMMUNICATIONS ARE STILL BLOCKED.
STILL? DID WE GET ALL THE BADOON SHIPS?
ARE THERE MORE COMING?
SOMETHING IS STILL BLOCKING US.
DROP YOUR WEAPONS!!

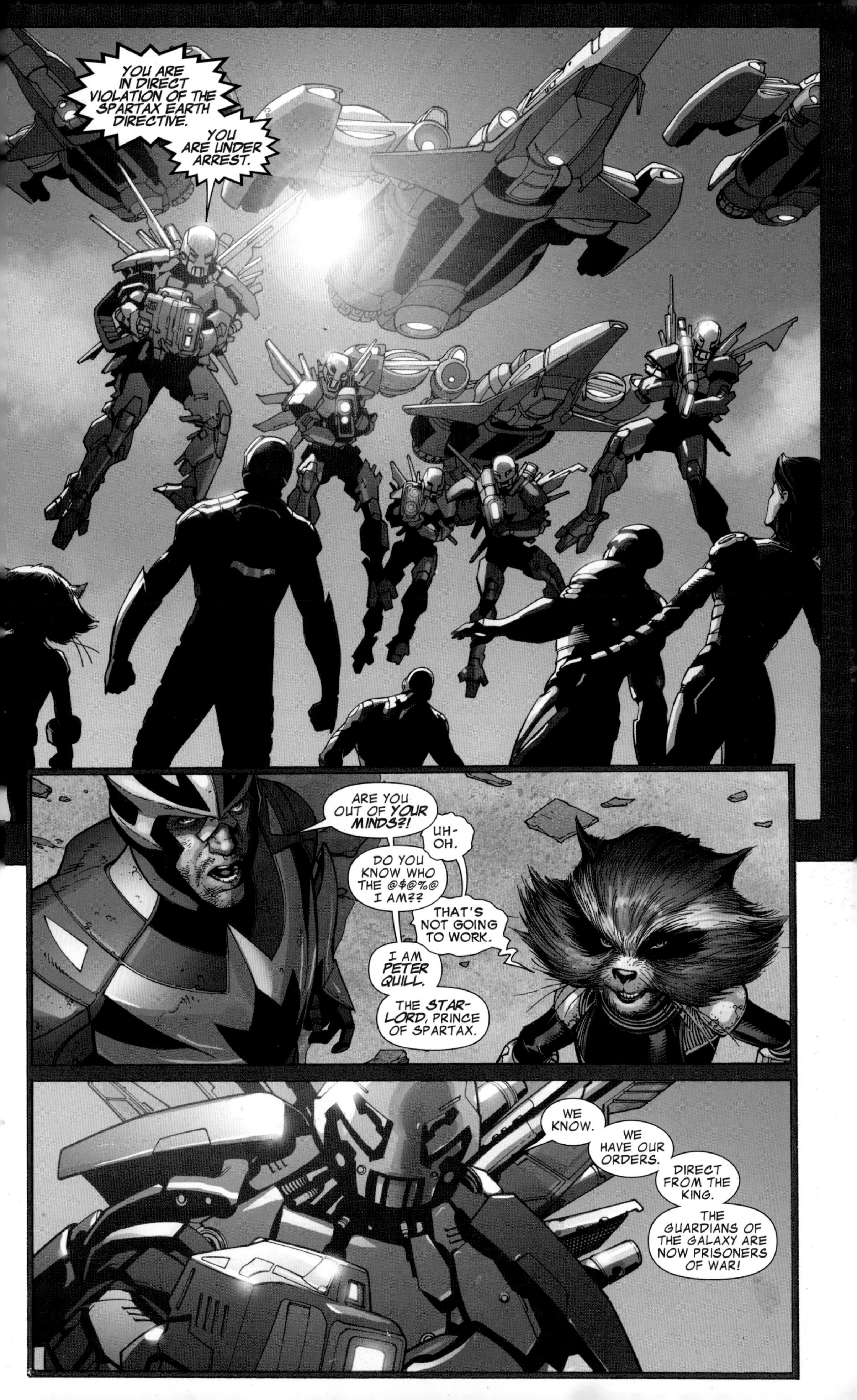
YOU ARE IN DIRECT VIOLATION OF THE SPARTAX EARTH DIRECTIVE.
YOU ARE UNDER ARREST.
ARE YOU OUT OF YOUR MINDS?!
UH-OH.
DO YOU KNOW WHO THE @$@%@ I AM??
THAT'S NOT GOING TO WORK.
I AM PETER QUILL.
THE STAR-LORD, PRINCE OF SPARTAX.
WE KNOW.
WE HAVE OUR ORDERS.
DIRECT FROM THE KING.
THE GUARDIANS OF THE GALAXY ARE NOW PRISONERS OF WAR!

Variant Covers

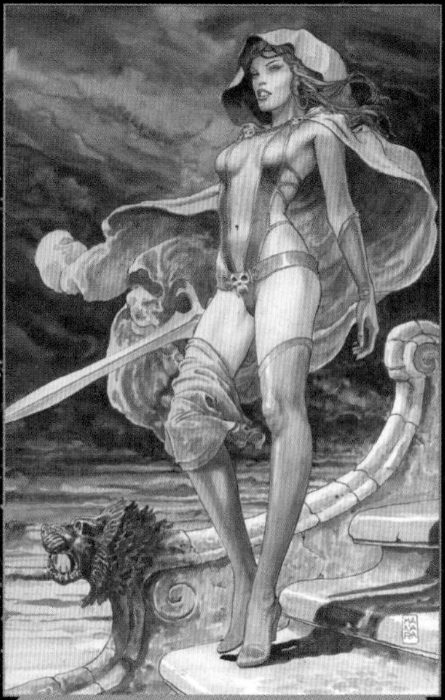

Guardians of the Galaxy #1
Variant by Milo Manara

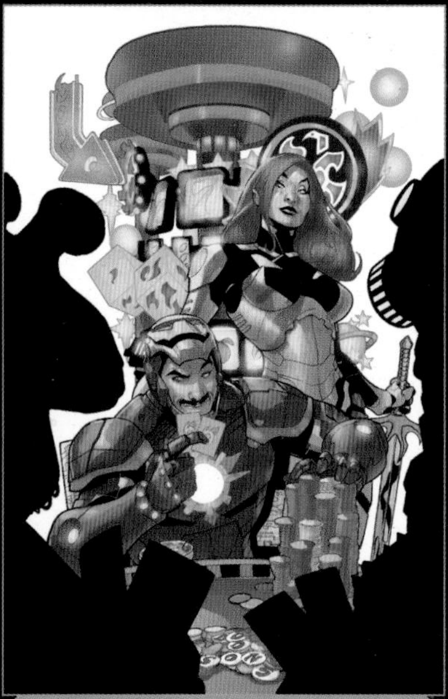

Guardians of the Galaxy #1
Variant by Terry Dodson

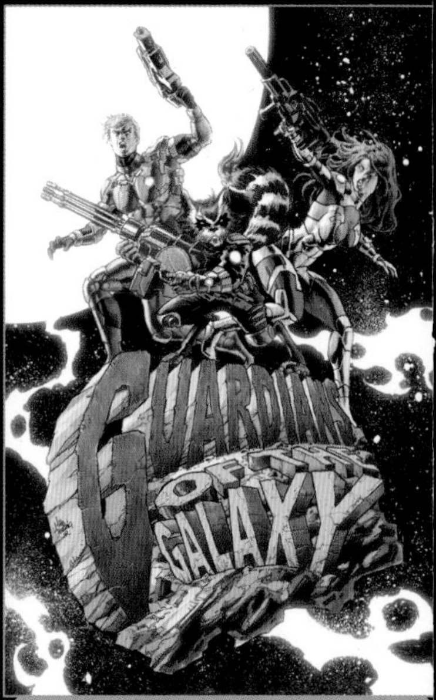
GUARDIANS
OF THE
GALAXY

Guardians of the Galaxy #1
Variant by Mike Deodato Jr.

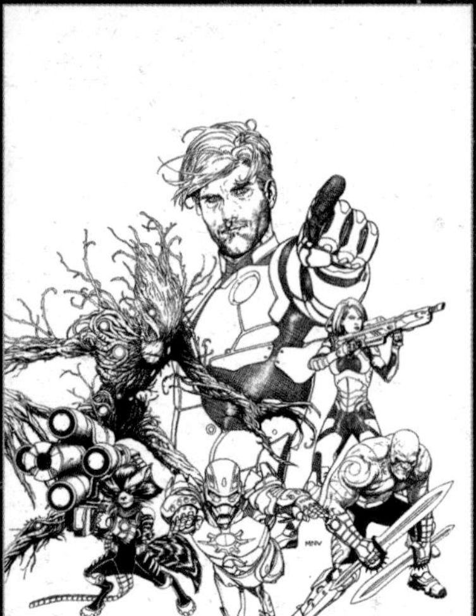

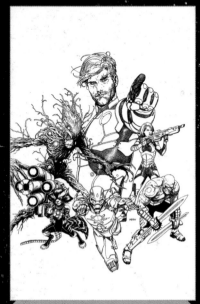

Guardians of the Galaxy #1
Variant by Steve McNiven

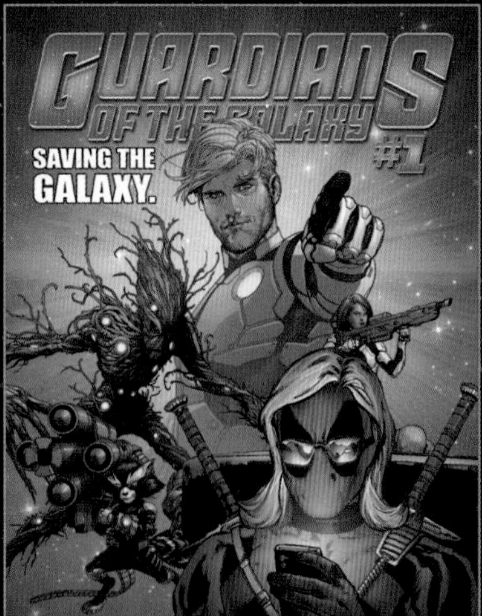
GUARDIANS
OF THE GALAXY
#1
SAVING THE
GALAXY.

Guardians of the Galaxy #1
Variant by Phil Jimenez

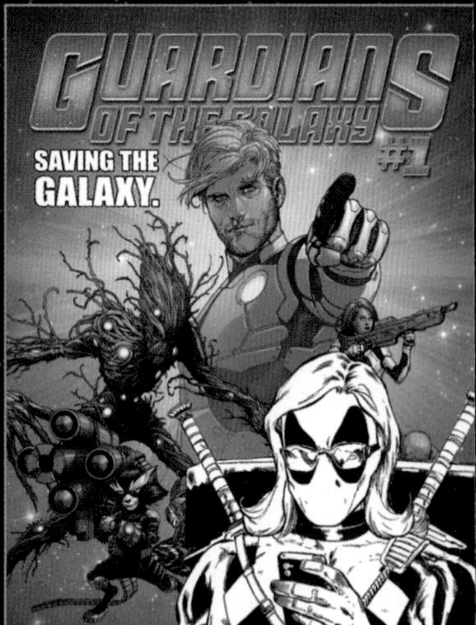
GUARDIANS
OF THE GALAXY
#1
SAVING THE
GALAXY.
GET IN LINE.

Guardians of the Galaxy #1
Variant by Phil Jimenez

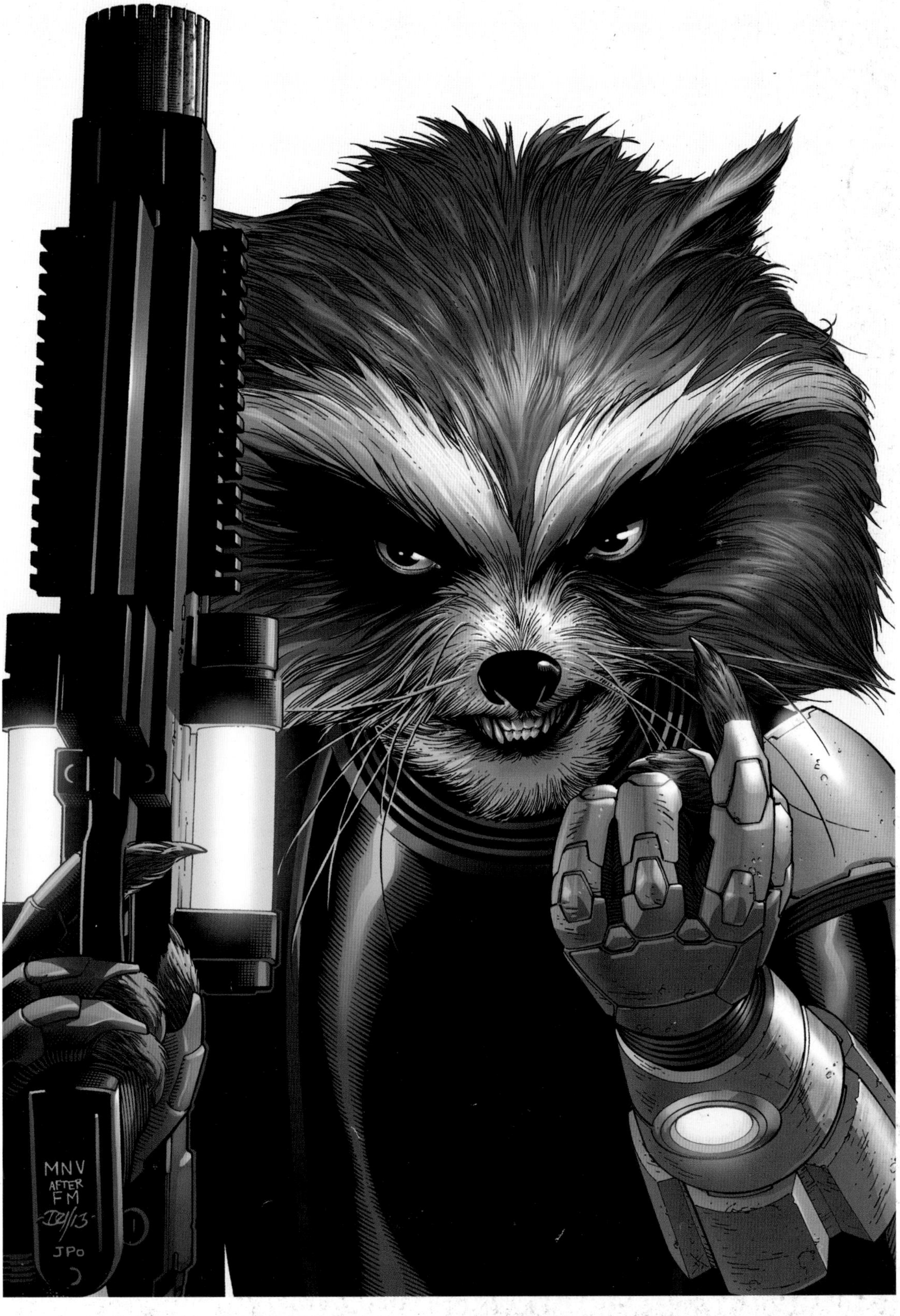
MNV
AFTER
FM
JPo

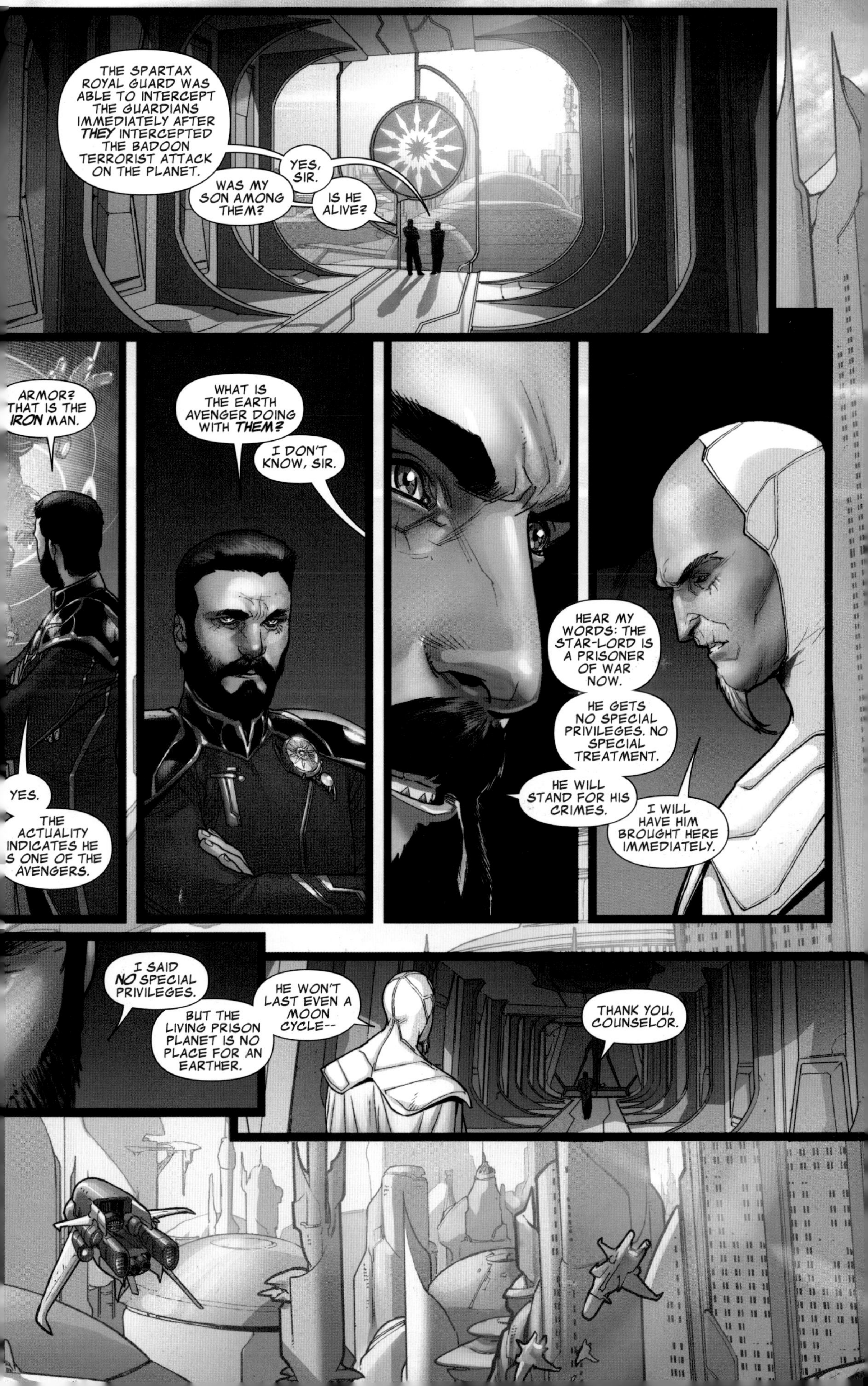
THE SPARTAX ROYAL GUARD WAS ABLE TO INTERCEPT THE GUARDIANS IMMEDIATELY AFTER *THEY* INTERCEPTED THE BADOON TERRORIST ATTACK ON THE PLANET.
WAS MY SON AMONG THEM?
YES, SIR.
IS HE ALIVE?
ARMOR? THAT IS THE *IRON* MAN.
YES.
THE ACTUALITY INDICATES HE S ONE OF THE AVENGERS.
WHAT IS THE EARTH AVENGER DOING WITH *THEM?*
I DON'T KNOW, SIR.
HEAR MY WORDS: THE STAR-LORD IS A PRISONER OF WAR NOW.
HE GETS NO SPECIAL PRIVILEGES. NO SPECIAL TREATMENT.
HE WILL STAND FOR HIS CRIMES.
I WILL HAVE HIM BROUGHT HERE IMMEDIATELY.
I SAID *NO* SPECIAL PRIVILEGES.
BUT THE LIVING PRISON PLANET IS NO PLACE FOR AN EARTHER.
HE WON'T LAST EVEN A MOON CYCLE--
THANK YOU, COUNSELOR.

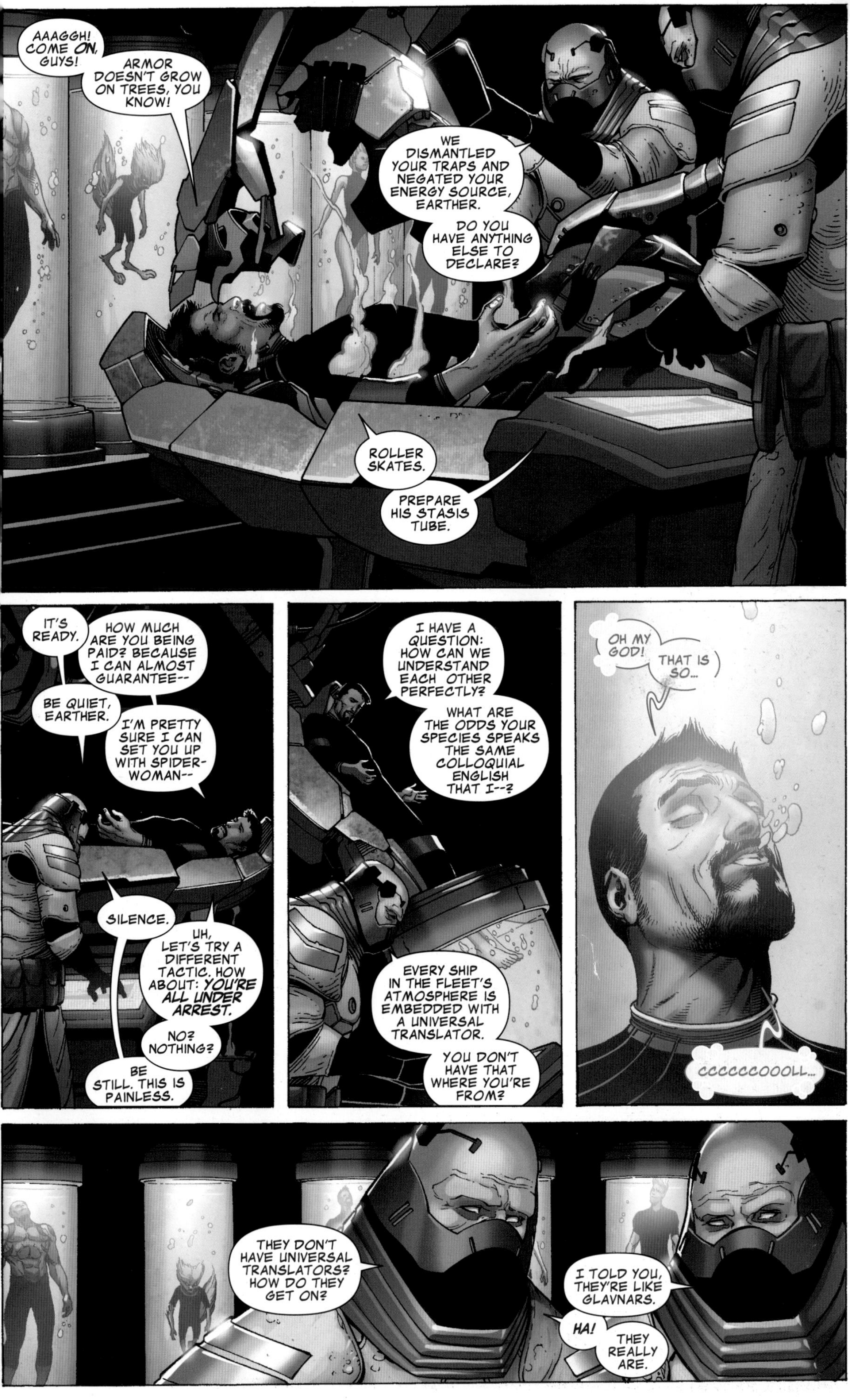
AAAGGH! COME ON, GUYS!
ARMOR DOESN'T GROW ON TREES, YOU KNOW!
WE DISMANTLED YOUR TRAPS AND NEGATED YOUR ENERGY SOURCE, EARTHER.
DO YOU HAVE ANYTHING ELSE TO DECLARE?
ROLLER SKATES.
PREPARE HIS STASIS TUBE.
IT'S READY.
HOW MUCH ARE YOU BEING PAID? BECAUSE I CAN ALMOST GUARANTEE--
BE QUIET, EARTHER.
I'M PRETTY SURE I CAN SET YOU UP WITH SPIDER-WOMAN--
SILENCE.
UH, LET'S TRY A DIFFERENT TACTIC. HOW ABOUT: YOU'RE ALL UNDER ARREST.
NO? NOTHING?
BE STILL. THIS IS PAINLESS.
I HAVE A QUESTION: HOW CAN WE UNDERSTAND EACH OTHER PERFECTLY?
WHAT ARE THE ODDS YOUR SPECIES SPEAKS THE SAME COLLOQUIAL ENGLISH THAT I--?
EVERY SHIP IN THE FLEET'S ATMOSPHERE IS EMBEDDED WITH A UNIVERSAL TRANSLATOR.
YOU DON'T HAVE THAT WHERE YOU'RE FROM?
OH MY GOD!
THAT IS SO...
CCCCCCOOOLL...
THEY DON'T HAVE UNIVERSAL TRANSLATORS? HOW DO THEY GET ON?
I TOLD YOU, THEY'RE LIKE GLAVNARS.
HA!
THEY REALLY ARE.

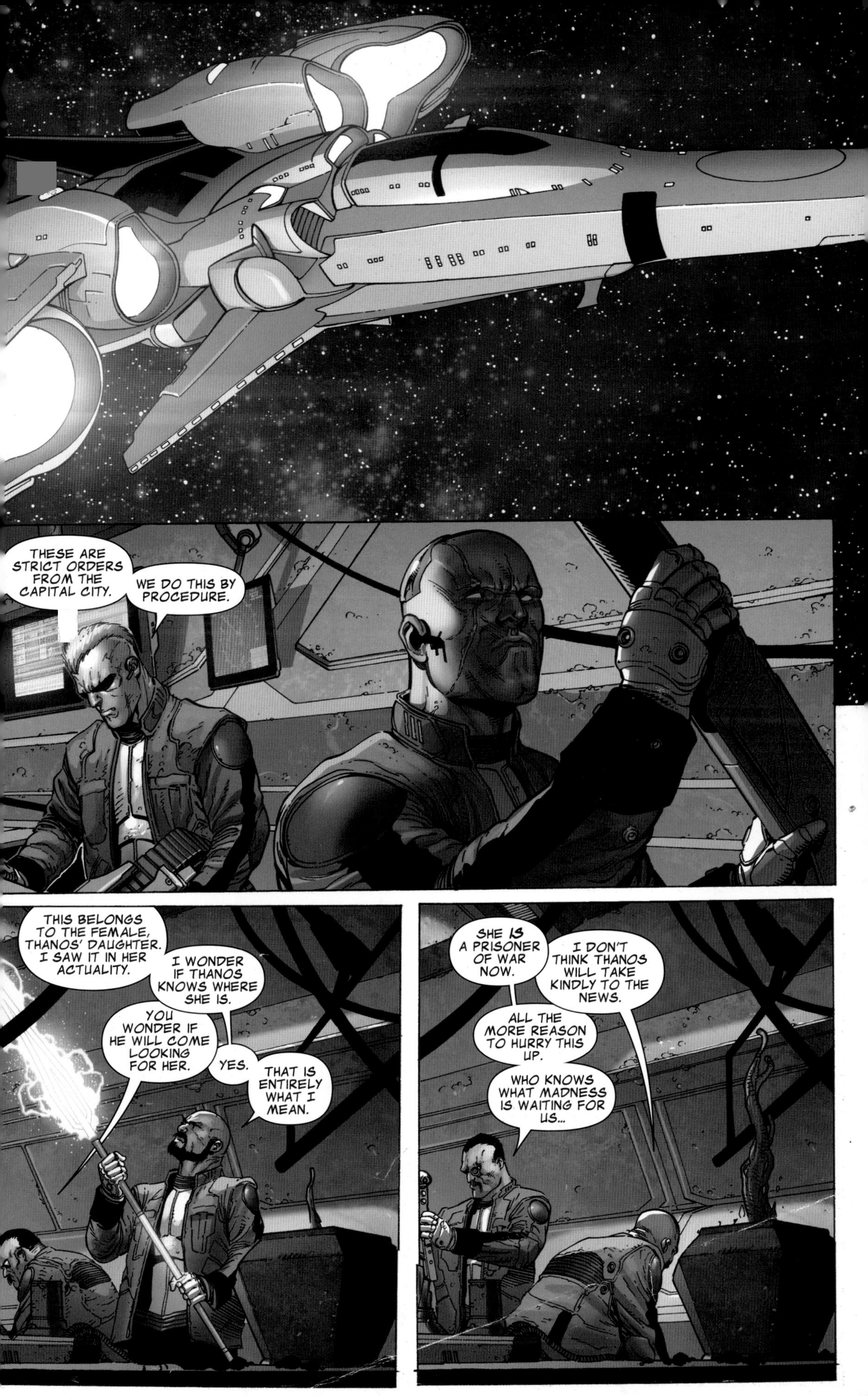
THESE ARE STRICT ORDERS FROM THE CAPITAL CITY.
WE DO THIS BY PROCEDURE.
THIS BELONGS TO THE FEMALE, THANOS' DAUGHTER. I SAW IT IN HER ACTUALITY.
I WONDER IF THANOS KNOWS WHERE SHE IS.
YOU WONDER IF HE WILL COME LOOKING FOR HER.
YES.
THAT IS ENTIRELY WHAT I MEAN.
SHE *IS* A PRISONER OF WAR NOW.
I DON'T THINK THANOS WILL TAKE KINDLY TO THE NEWS.
ALL THE MORE REASON TO HURRY THIS UP.
WHO KNOWS WHAT MADNESS IS WAITING FOR US...

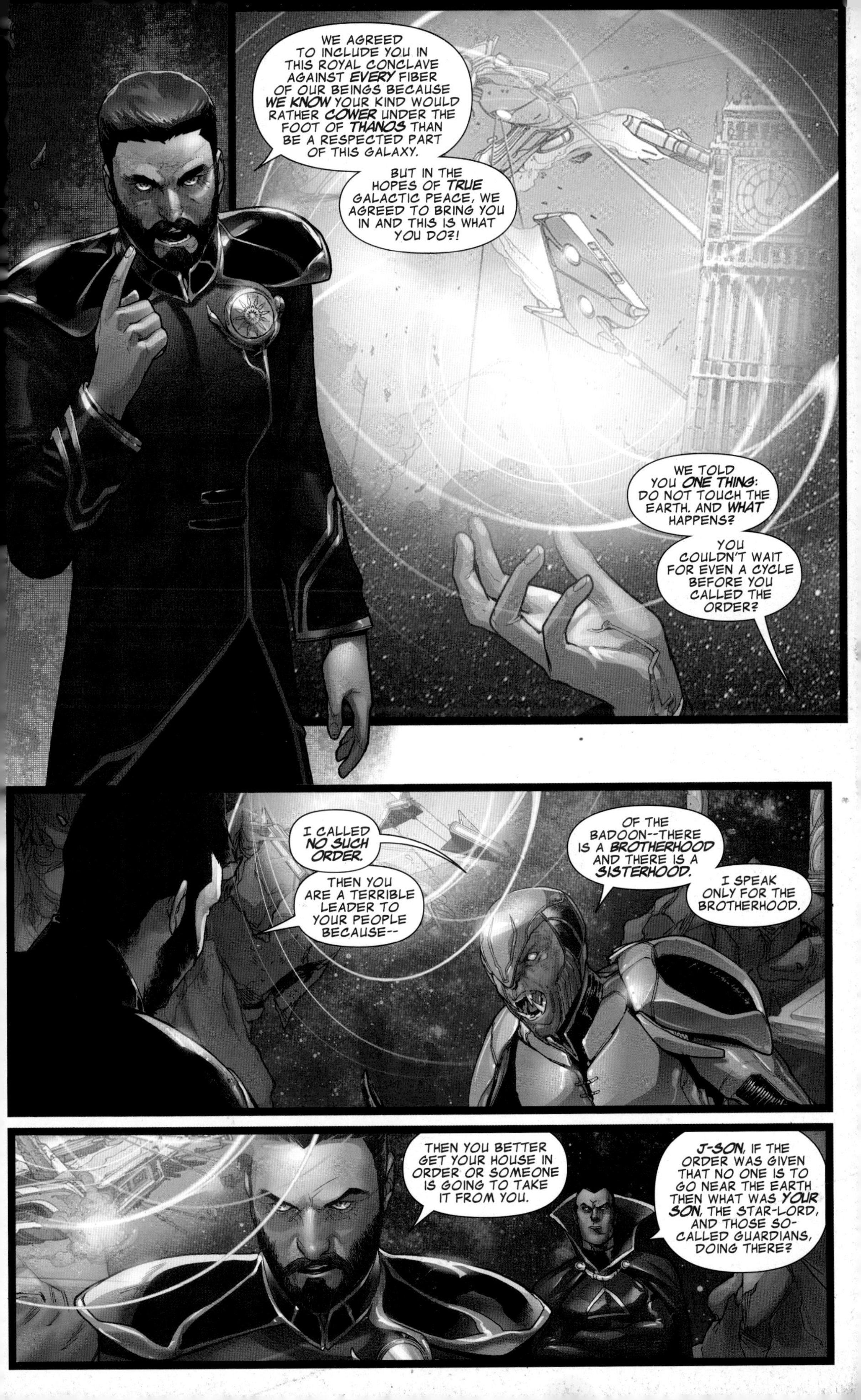
WE AGREED TO INCLUDE YOU IN THIS ROYAL CONCLAVE AGAINST EVERY FIBER OF OUR BEINGS BECAUSE WE KNOW YOUR KIND WOULD RATHER COWER UNDER THE FOOT OF THANOS THAN BE A RESPECTED PART OF THIS GALAXY.
BUT IN THE HOPES OF TRUE GALACTIC PEACE, WE AGREED TO BRING YOU IN AND THIS IS WHAT YOU DO?!
WE TOLD YOU ONE THING: DO NOT TOUCH THE EARTH. AND WHAT HAPPENS?
YOU COULDN'T WAIT FOR EVEN A CYCLE BEFORE YOU CALLED THE ORDER?
I CALLED NO SUCH ORDER.
THEN YOU ARE A TERRIBLE LEADER TO YOUR PEOPLE BECAUSE--
OF THE BADOON--THERE IS A BROTHERHOOD AND THERE IS A SISTERHOOD.
I SPEAK ONLY FOR THE BROTHERHOOD.
THEN YOU BETTER GET YOUR HOUSE IN ORDER OR SOMEONE IS GOING TO TAKE IT FROM YOU.
J-SON, IF THE ORDER WAS GIVEN THAT NO ONE IS TO GO NEAR THE EARTH THEN WHAT WAS YOUR SON, THE STAR-LORD, AND THOSE SO-CALLED GUARDIANS, DOING THERE?

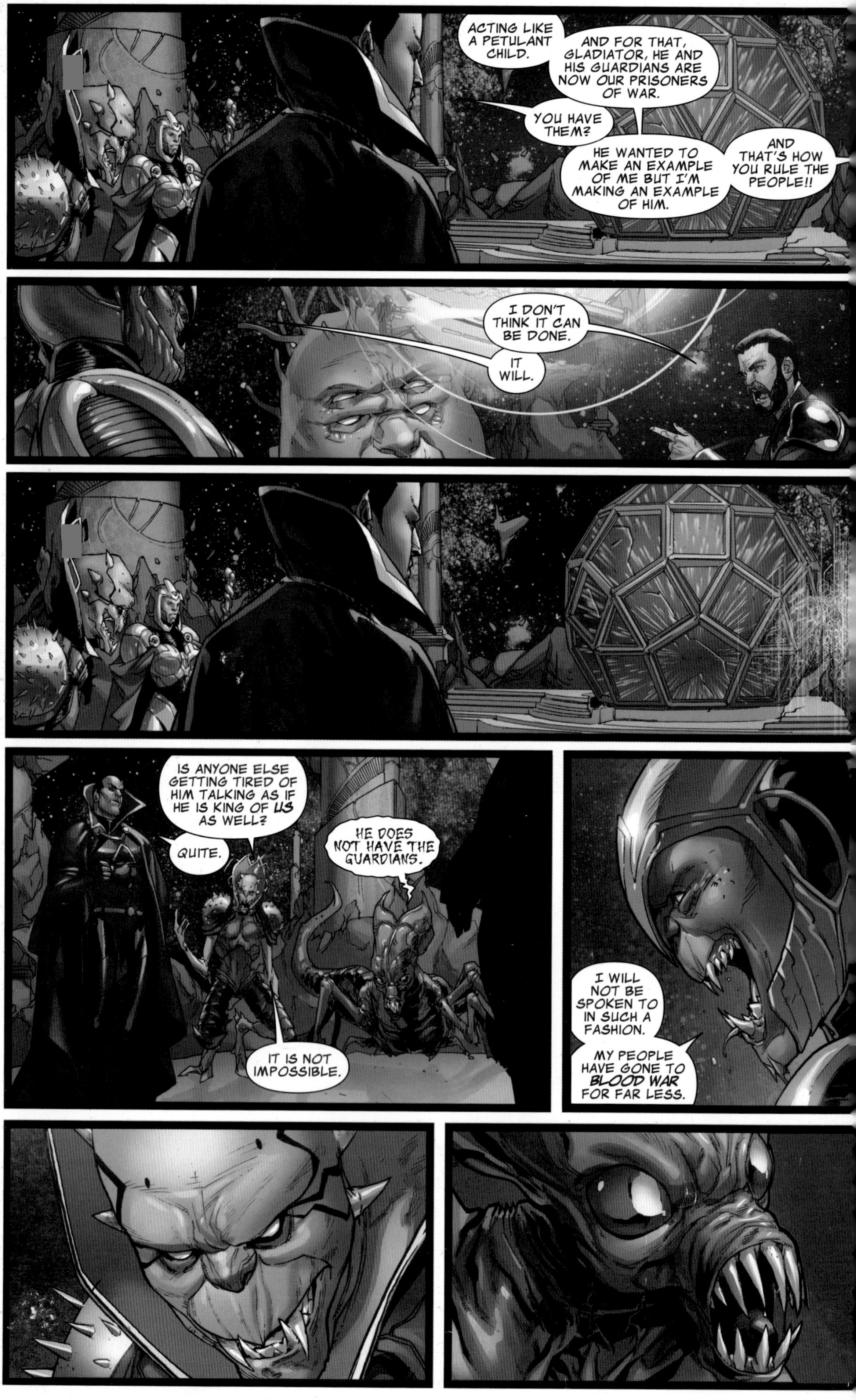
ACTING LIKE A PETULANT CHILD.
AND FOR THAT, GLADIATOR, HE AND HIS GUARDIANS ARE NOW OUR PRISONERS OF WAR.
YOU HAVE THEM?
HE WANTED TO MAKE AN EXAMPLE OF ME BUT I'M MAKING AN EXAMPLE OF HIM.
AND THAT'S HOW YOU RULE THE PEOPLE!!
I DON'T THINK IT CAN BE DONE.
IT WILL.
IS ANYONE ELSE GETTING TIRED OF HIM TALKING AS IF HE IS KING OF US AS WELL?
QUITE.
HE DOES NOT HAVE THE GUARDIANS.
IT IS NOT IMPOSSIBLE.
I WILL NOT BE SPOKEN TO IN SUCH A FASHION.
MY PEOPLE HAVE GONE TO BLOOD WAR FOR FAR LESS.

MAYBE WE NEED TO BROKER AN EXCHANGE BETWEEN THE BROTHERHOOD AND SISTERHOOD OF THE BADOON?

IF YOU WOULD LIKE TO DO THAT, SUPREME INTELLIGENCE, GO RIGHT AHEAD...

I WILL TAKE THAT AS A PROMISE.

AND THE NEXT TIME WE MEET, THAT PROMISE *WILL* BE KEPT.

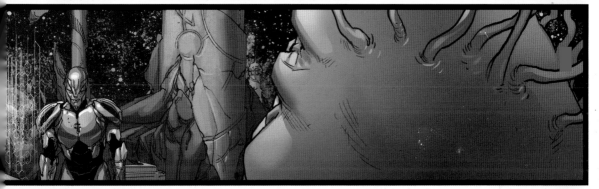

PROVE YOURSELF, Y-GAAAR.

AND PROVE J-SON WRONG...

...AND YOU WILL HAVE *ALL OUR* RESPECT.

I BELIEVE KING J-SON IS PLAYING A MORE COMPLICATED GAME THAN WE FIRST REALIZED.

I AM ALMOST CERTAIN OF IT.

I FEEL LIKE WE'RE MISSING SOMETHING.

THE SHIP HAS BEEN STRIPPED BARE.

THAT IS QUITE AN IMPRESSIVE ASSORTMENT.

THEY EVEN HAD A RIGELLIAN SELF-DUPLICATING MINE.

SPARTAX WARSHIP.

THIS WAS ALL OF THEM?

YES.

DID THEY NOT TRAVEL WITH A KALIKLAKIAN?

I DON'T RECALL.

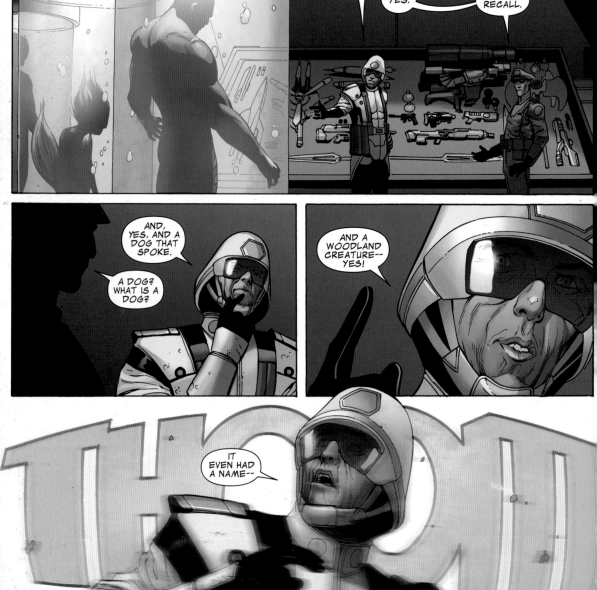

AND, YES, AND A DOG THAT SPOKE.

A DOG? WHAT IS A DOG?

AND A WOODLAND CREATURE-- YES!

IT EVEN HAD A NAME--

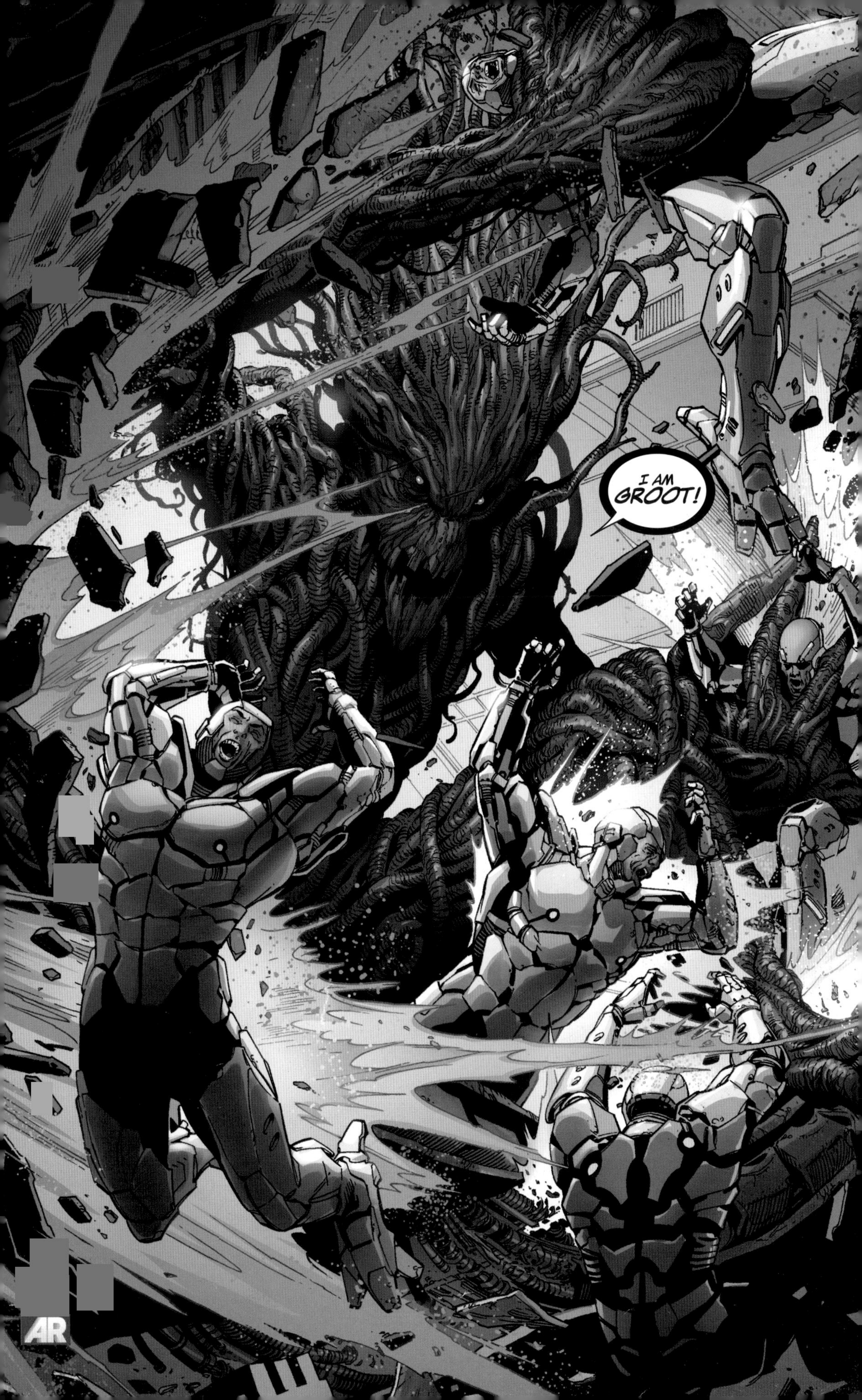
I AM GROOT!

I AM GROOT!

I AM GROOT.

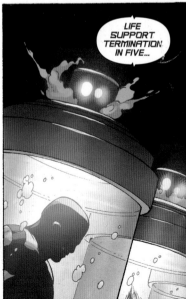

LIFE SUPPORT TERMINATION IN FIVE...

...I AM GROOT!

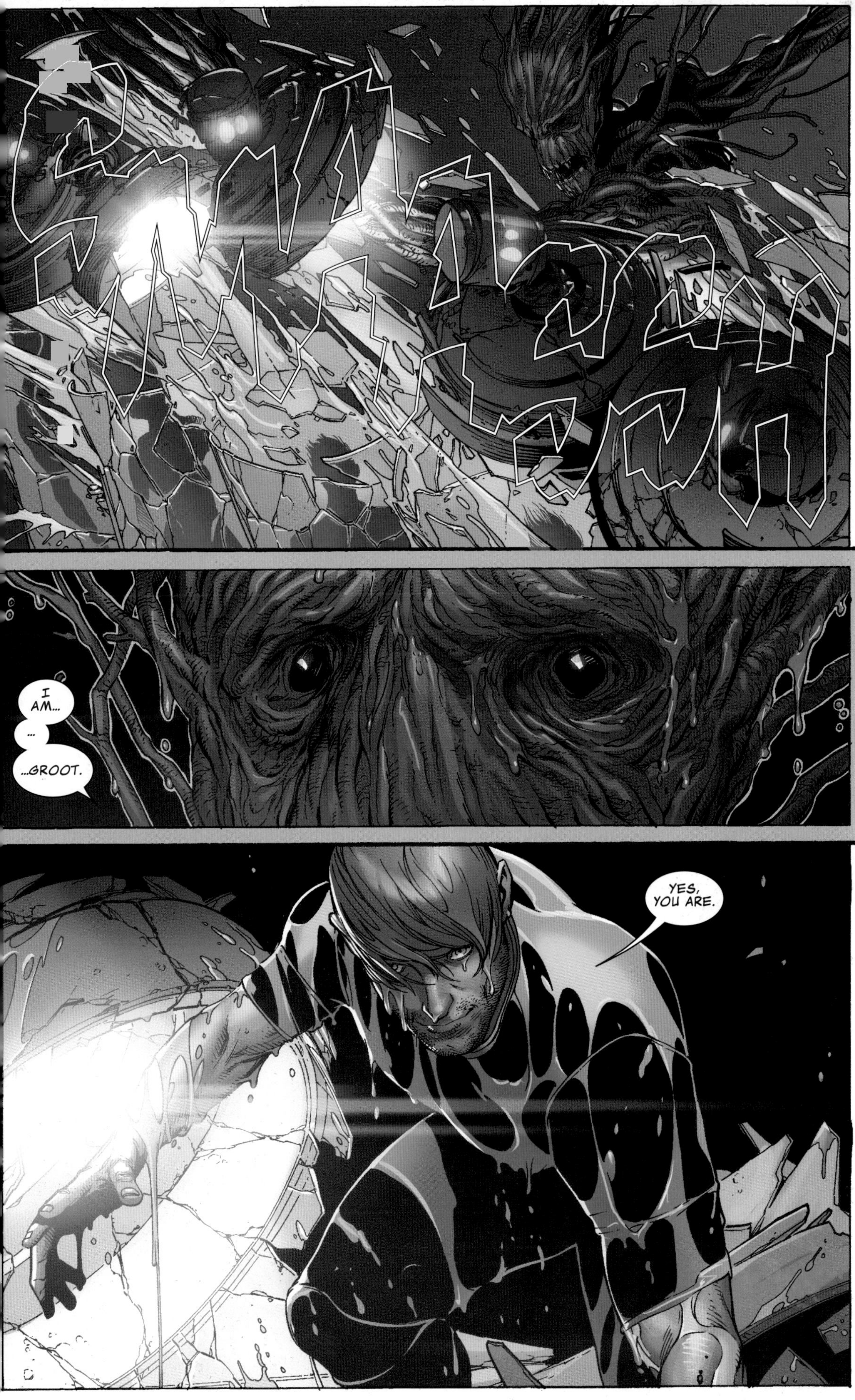
I AM...
...
...GROOT.
YES, YOU ARE.

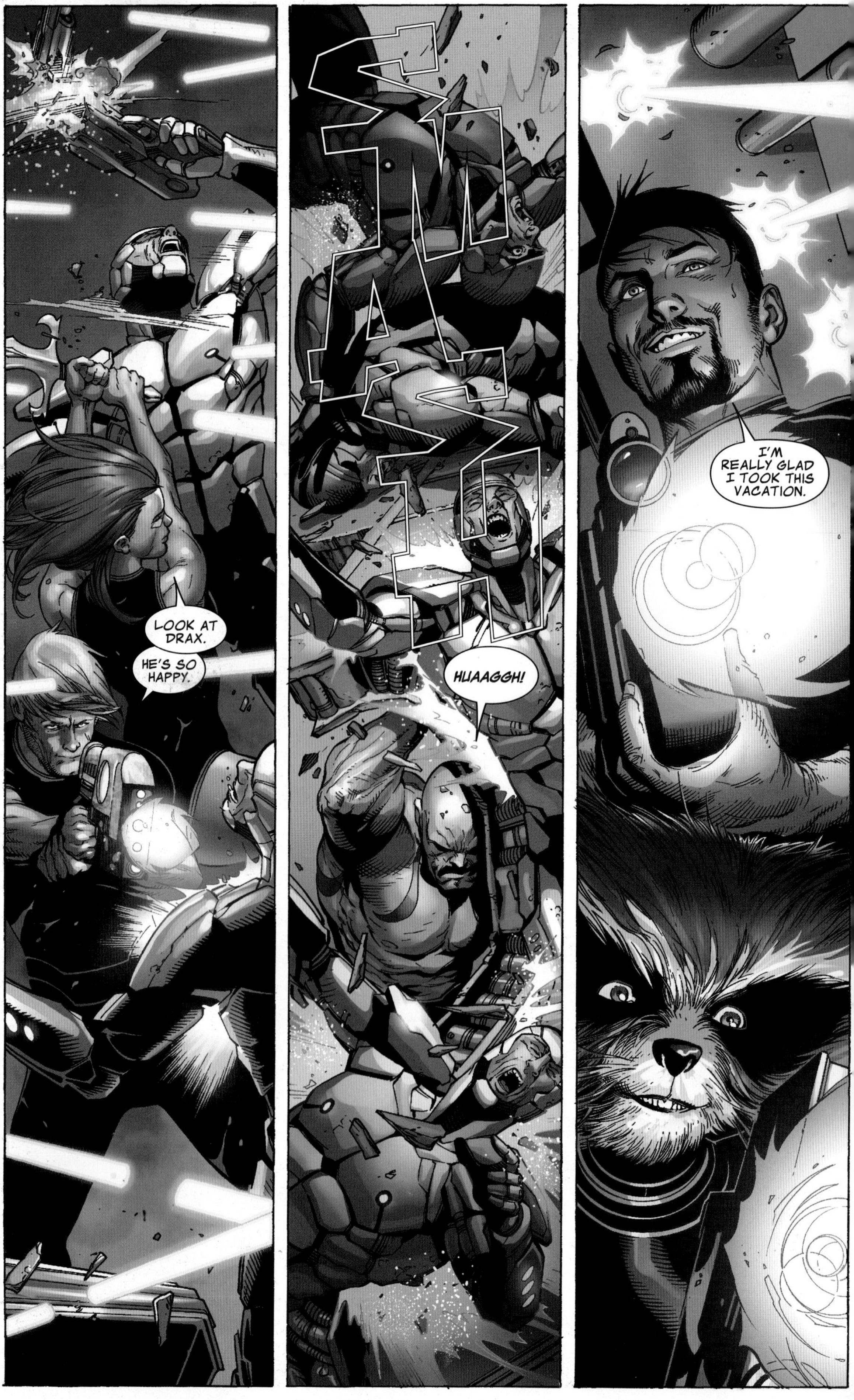
LOOK AT DRAX.
HE'S SO HAPPY.
SMASH
HUAAGGH!
I'M REALLY GLAD I TOOK THIS VACATION.

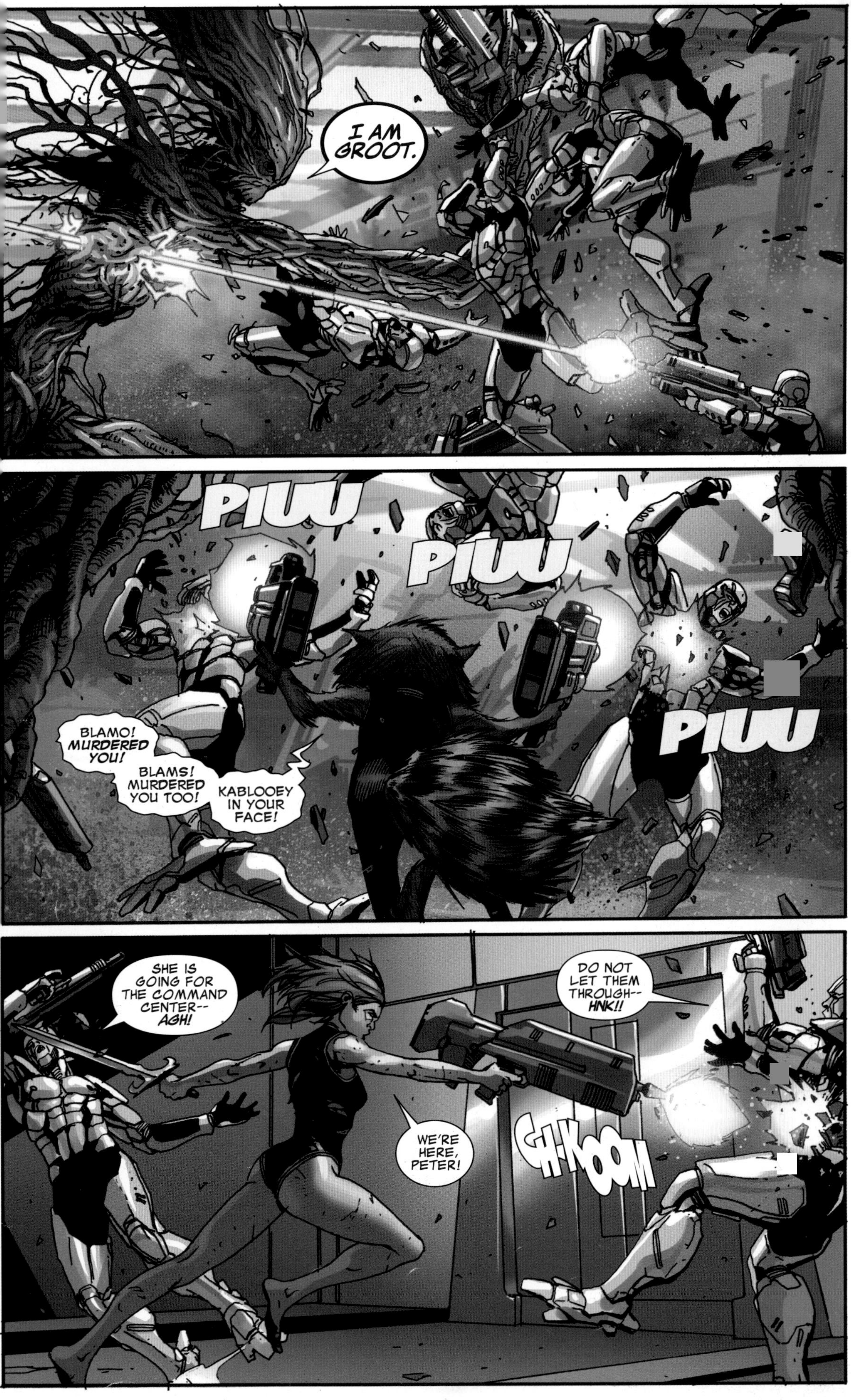
I AM GROOT.
PIUU
PIUU
PIUU
BLAMO! MURDERED YOU!
BLAMS! MURDERED YOU TOO!
KABLOOEY IN YOUR FACE!
SHE IS GOING FOR THE COMMAND CENTER-- AGH!
WE'RE HERE, PETER!
DO NOT LET THEM THROUGH-- HNK!!
CH-KOOM

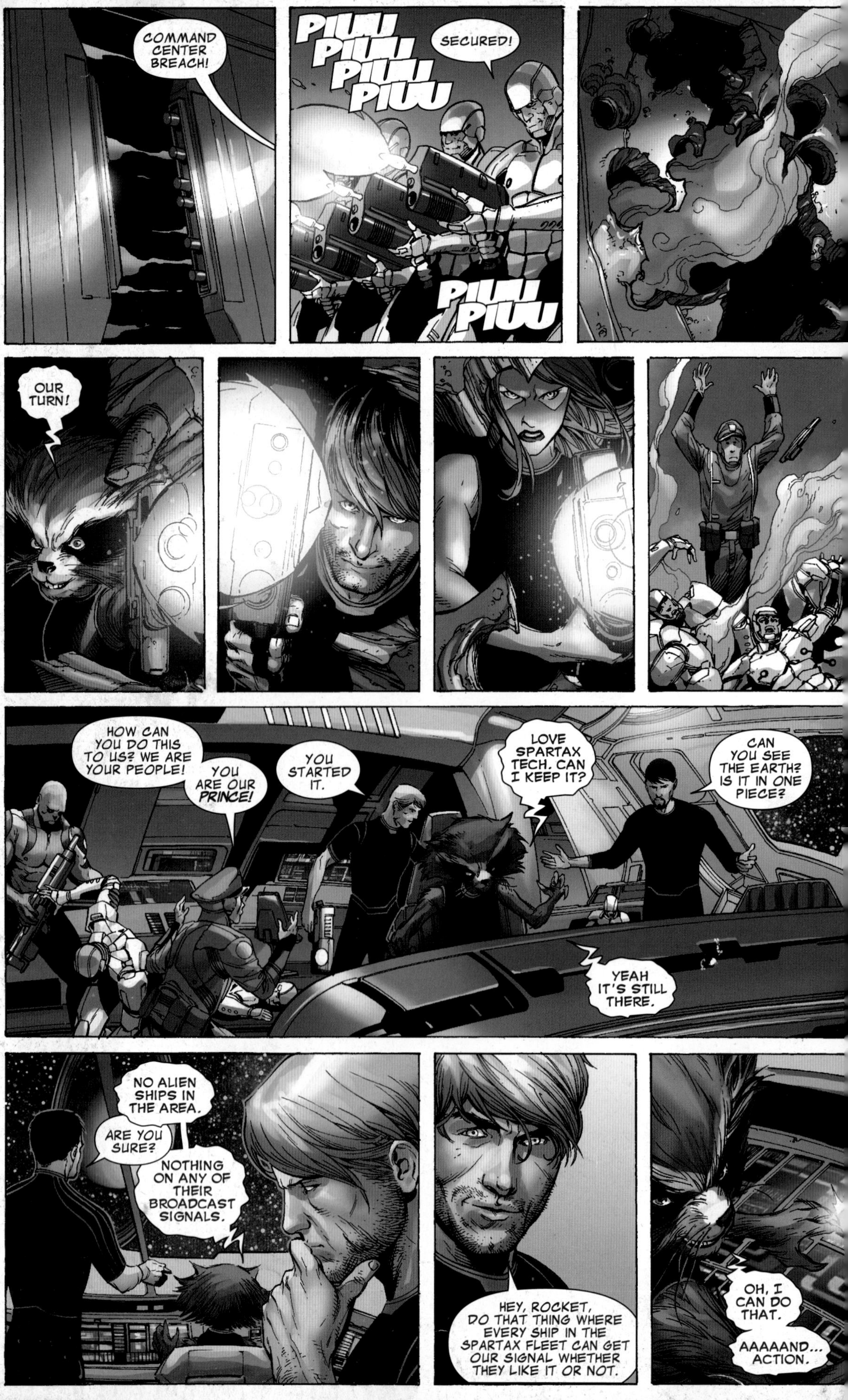
COMMAND CENTER BREACH!
PIUU PIUU PIUU PIUU
SECURED!
PIUU PIUU
OUR TURN!
HOW CAN YOU DO THIS TO US? WE ARE YOUR PEOPLE!
YOU ARE OUR PRINCE!
YOU STARTED IT.
LOVE SPARTAX TECH. CAN I KEEP IT?
CAN YOU SEE THE EARTH? IS IT IN ONE PIECE?
YEAH IT'S STILL THERE.
NO ALIEN SHIPS IN THE AREA.
ARE YOU SURE?
NOTHING ON ANY OF THEIR BROADCAST SIGNALS.
HEY, ROCKET, DO THAT THING WHERE EVERY SHIP IN THE SPARTAX FLEET CAN GET OUR SIGNAL WHETHER THEY LIKE IT OR NOT.
OH, I CAN DO THAT.
AAAAAND... ACTION.

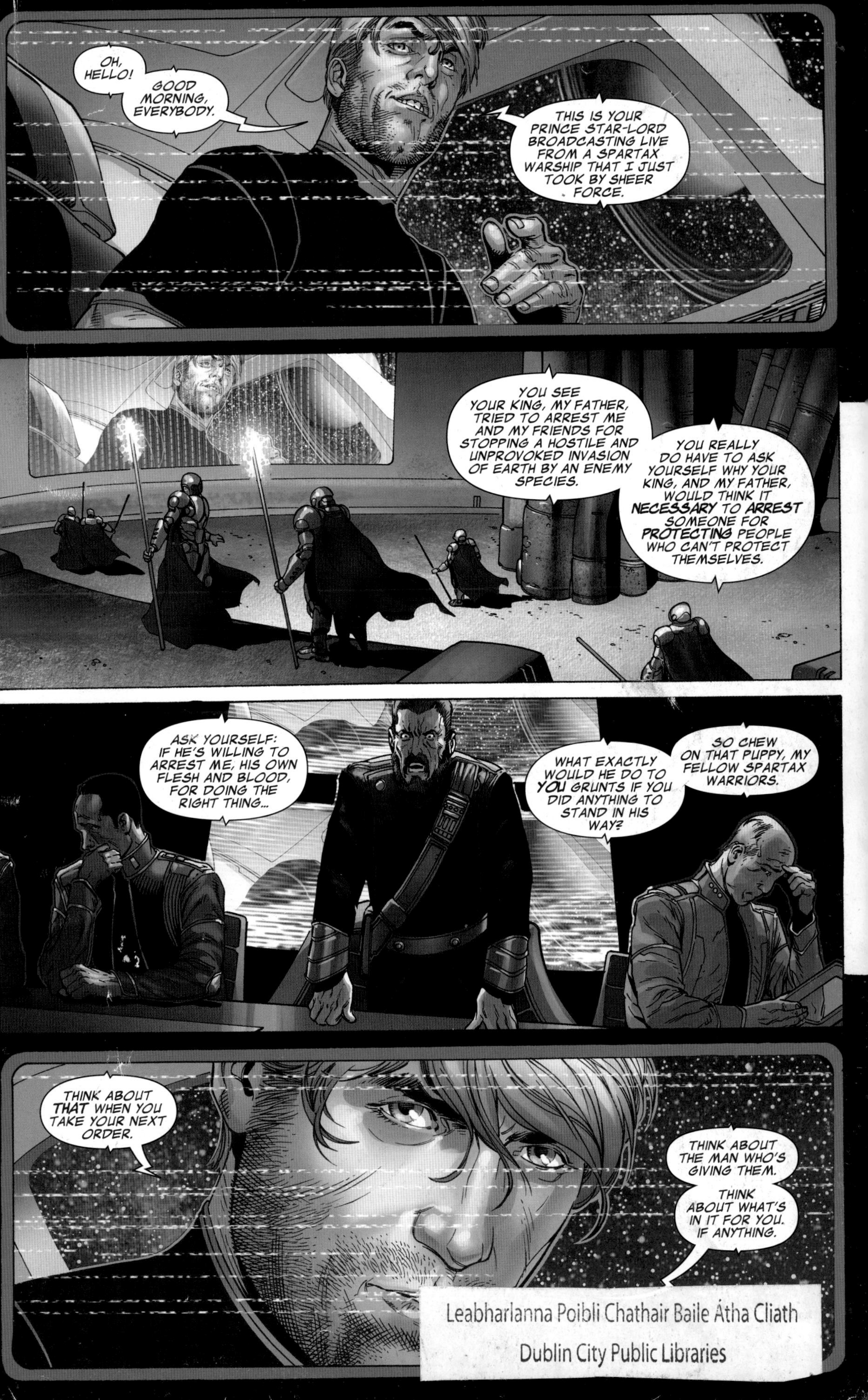
OH, HELLO!
GOOD MORNING, EVERYBODY.
THIS IS YOUR PRINCE STAR-LORD BROADCASTING LIVE FROM A SPARTAX WARSHIP THAT I JUST TOOK BY SHEER FORCE.
YOU SEE YOUR KING, MY FATHER, TRIED TO ARREST ME AND MY FRIENDS FOR STOPPING A HOSTILE AND UNPROVOKED INVASION OF EARTH BY AN ENEMY SPECIES.
YOU REALLY DO HAVE TO ASK YOURSELF WHY YOUR KING, AND MY FATHER, WOULD THINK IT NECESSARY TO ARREST SOMEONE FOR PROTECTING PEOPLE WHO CAN'T PROTECT THEMSELVES.
ASK YOURSELF: IF HE'S WILLING TO ARREST ME, HIS OWN FLESH AND BLOOD, FOR DOING THE RIGHT THING...
WHAT EXACTLY WOULD HE DO TO YOU GRUNTS IF YOU DID ANYTHING TO STAND IN HIS WAY?
SO CHEW ON THAT PUPPY, MY FELLOW SPARTAX WARRIORS.
THINK ABOUT THAT WHEN YOU TAKE YOUR NEXT ORDER.
THINK ABOUT THE MAN WHO'S GIVING THEM.
THINK ABOUT WHAT'S IN IT FOR YOU. IF ANYTHING.

Variant Covers

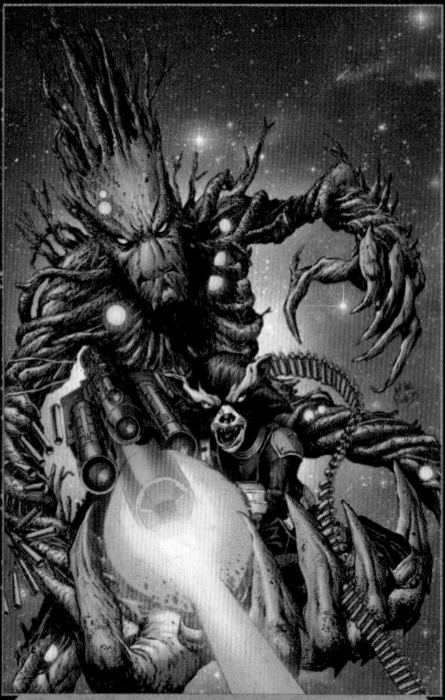

Guardians of the Galaxy #1
Variant by Mike Perkins

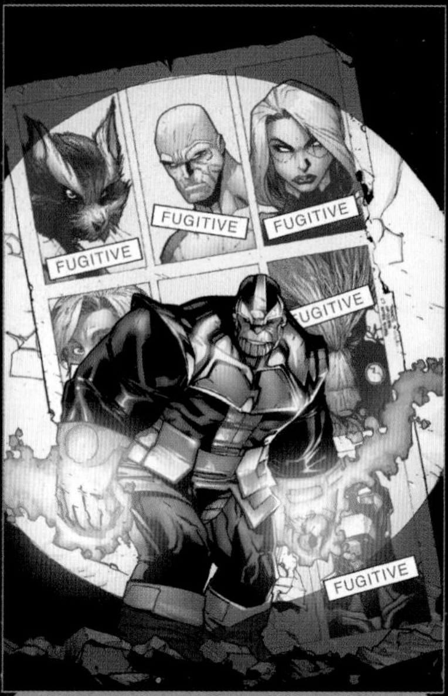
FUGITIVE
FUGITIVE
FUGITIVE
FUGITIVE

Guardians of the Galaxy #1
Variant by Humberto Ramos

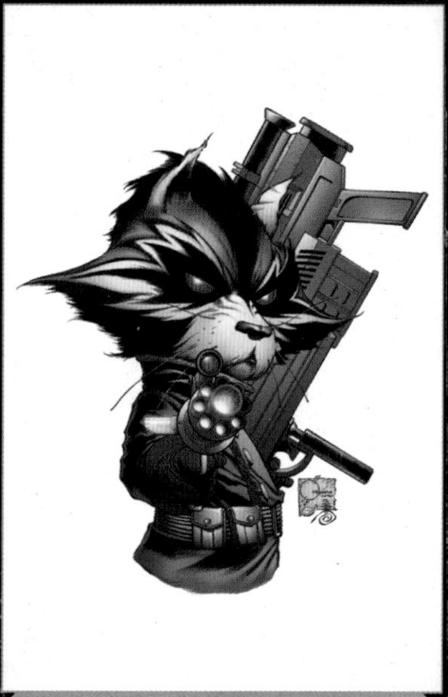

Guardians of the Galaxy #2
Variant by Joe Quesada

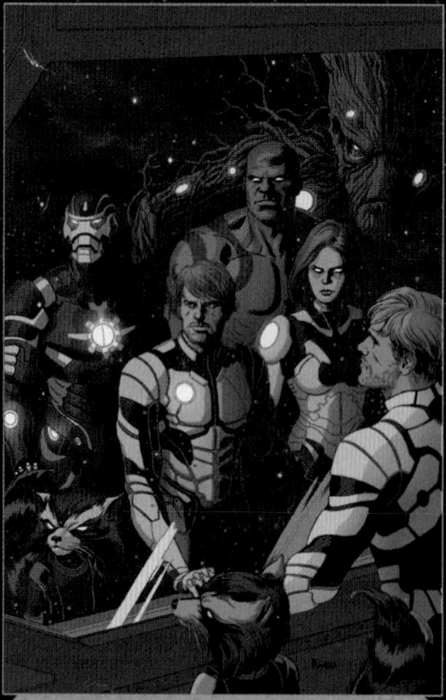

Guardians of the Galaxy #2
Variant by Paolo Rivera

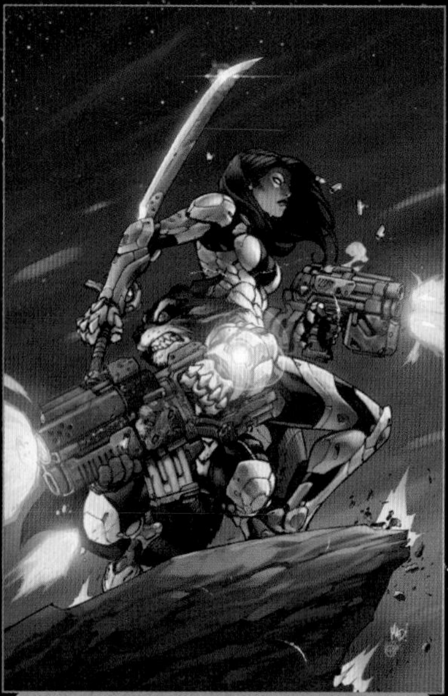

Guardians of the Galaxy #2
Variant by Joe Madureira

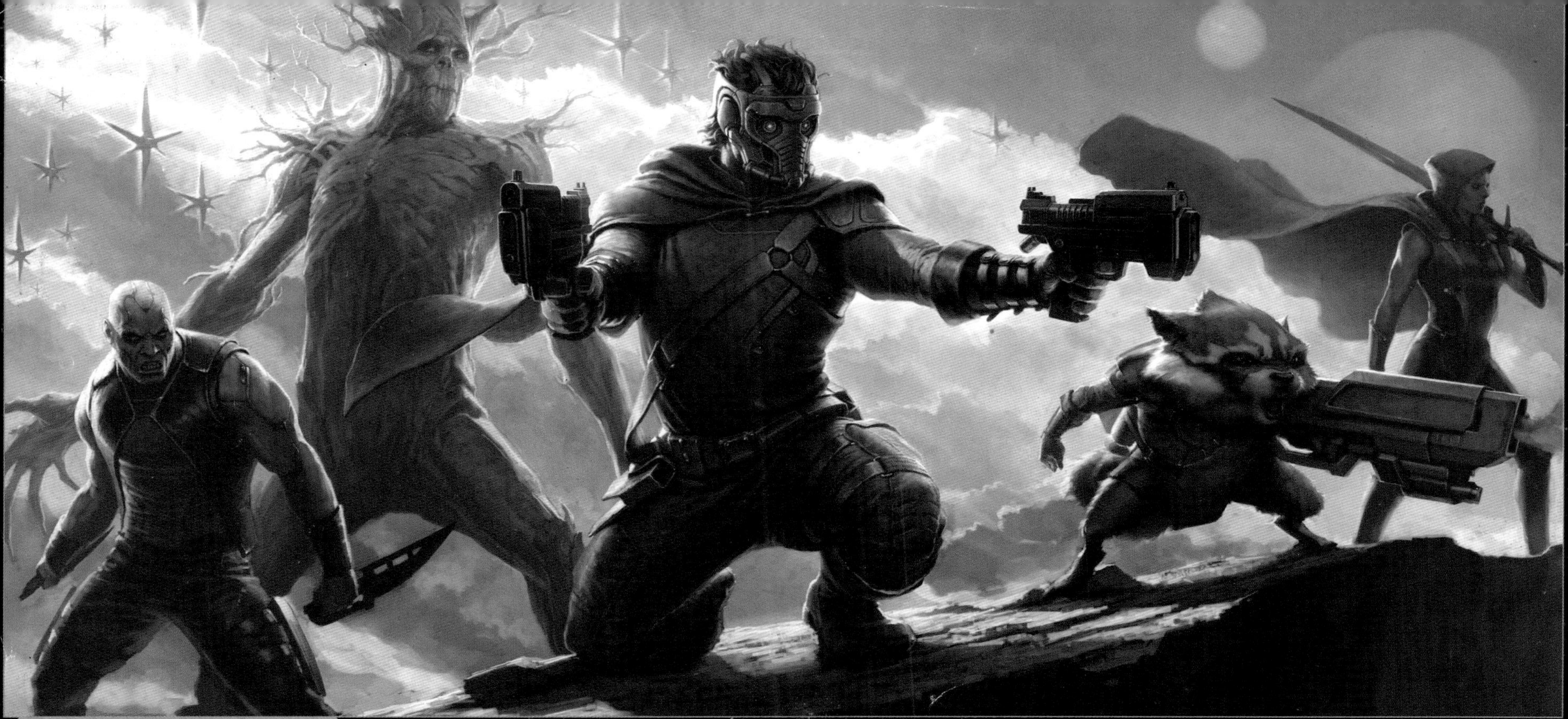

Guardians of the Galaxy #2, 3 & 4
Movie Variant

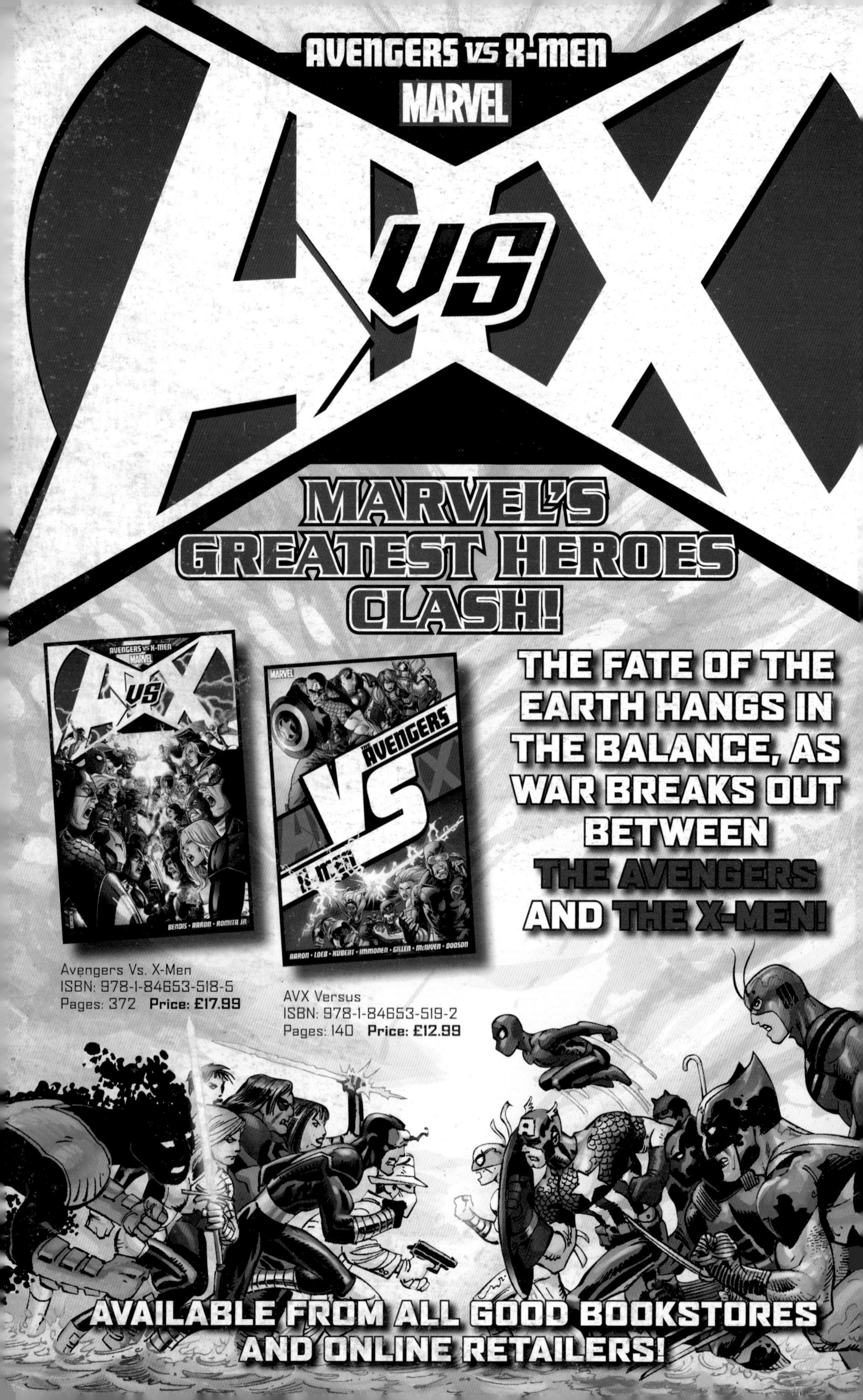
AVENGERS VS X-MEN
MARVEL
A VS X
MARVEL'S GREATEST HEROES CLASH!
AVENGERS VS X-MEN
MARVEL
BENDIS • AARON • ROMITA JR.
MARVEL
THE AVENGERS VS X-MEN
AARON • LOEB • KUBERT • IMMONEN • GILLEN • McNIVEN • DODSON
Avengers Vs. X-Men
ISBN: 978-1-84653-518-5
Pages: 372 Price: £17.99
AVX Versus
ISBN: 978-1-84653-519-2
Pages: 140 Price: £12.99
THE FATE OF THE EARTH HANGS IN THE BALANCE, AS WAR BREAKS OUT BETWEEN THE AVENGERS AND THE X-MEN!
AVAILABLE FROM ALL GOOD BOOKSTORES AND ONLINE RETAILERS!